*Charlotte Perkins Gilman
and Her Contemporaries*

Charlotte Perkins Gilman and Her Contemporaries

Literary and Intellectual Contexts

Edited by
Cynthia J. Davis and Denise D. Knight

THE UNIVERSITY OF ALABAMA PRESS
Tuscaloosa

Typeface: ACaslon

∞

The paper on which this book is printed meets the minimum requirements of
American National Standard for Information Science–Permanence of Paper for
Printed Library Materials, ANSI Z39.48–1984.

Library of Congress Cataloging-in-Publication Data

Charlotte Perkins Gilman and her contemporaries : literary and intellectual contexts /
edited by Cynthia J. Davis and Denise D. Knight.

    p. cm. — (Studies in American literary realism and naturalism) Includes biblio-
graphical references and index.
    ISBN 0-8173-1386-9 (cloth : alk. paper) — ISBN 0-8173-5072-1 (pbk. : alk. paper)
1. Gilman, Charlotte Perkins, 1860–1935—Criticism and interpretation. 2. Women and
literature—United States—History—19th century. 3. Women and literature—United
States—History—20th century. 4. Gilman, Charlotte Perkins, 1860–1935—Friends and
associates. 5. American literature—19th century—History and criticism. 6. American
literature—20th century—History and criticism. 7. Gilman, Charlotte Perkins, 1860–
1935—Contemporaries. 8. United States—Intellectual life. 9. Sex role in literature.
I. Davis, Cynthia J., 1964– II. Knight, Denise D., 1954– III. Series.
    PS1744.G57Z6 2004 818'.409—dc22

                                                                    2003022014

The authors gratefully acknowledge Permission to reprint material from the following sources: Letter from Charlotte Perkins Stetson to Brander Matthews, October 19,
1892, Brander Matthews Papers, Rare Book and Manuscript Library, Columbia University. Various letters from the Charlotte Perkins Gilman Collection, the Arthur
and Elizabeth Schlesinger Library on the History of Women in America, Radcliffe
Institute for Advanced Study, Harvard University; used by permission. Letter from
Charlotte Perkins Gilman to Frank Ward, Ward Papers, Brown University. Letter from
Katharine Beecher Stetson Chamberlin to Lyman Beecher Stowe, August 30, 1935,
and letter from Katharine Beecher Stetson Chamberlin to Willis Kingsley Wing,
August 30, 1935, from Beecher-Stowe Collection, the Beecher Stowe Family Papers,
Schlesinger Library, Radcliffe Institute, Harvard University. From letter to Lummis
from Charlotte Perkins Gilman, April 1, 1898, Manon Parks Collection courtesy of the
Southwest Museum, Los Angeles, CA. Letters from Martha Luther Lane, Charlotte
Perkins Gilman Letters, Manuscripts Division, Rhode Island Historical Society,
Providence.

Contents

Acknowledgments

We wish to thank everyone who has supported this project through its various phases. To the anonymous readers who reviewed the initial manuscript, we extend our sincere gratitude. We are indebted to Gary Scharnhorst for proposing the University of Alabama Press as publisher for our edition. The staff at the press deserves our appreciation for their guidance and expertise. Their thoughtful suggestions resulted in a stronger volume.

We also would like to express our gratitude to those institutions, presses, and journals that granted permission to reprint essays or to quote from unpublished sources: Rutgers University Press, *Journal of the West, Jack London Journal, American Journalism* (Columbia University), the Huntington Library, Brown University, the Rhode Island Historical Society, Smith College, the Southwest Museum, and especially the Schlesinger Library of the Radcliffe Institute.

Finally, we want to acknowledge our husbands, John M. Reagle and Michael K. Barylski, for their ongoing encouragement of our work.

Introduction

"Emerson's remark, 'Misunderstood! It is a right fool's word!' pleased me much."

Charlotte Perkins Gilman, The Living 74

Misunderstood in her own day, Charlotte Perkins Gilman is also misunderstood in ours. This would not have surprised her. Musing upon her own "absolute consecration to coming service," she wrote, "Regarding consequences I had no illusions. No one who sets out to make the world better should expect people to enjoy it, all history shows what happens to would-be improvers. . . . What I had to expect was mostly misunderstanding" (*Living* 73–74). In citing Emerson's quip, she aimed for a devil-may-care attitude, though her private writings suggest how often and how deeply being misunderstood wounded her.

By placing Gilman in the company of her contemporaries, this essay collection seeks to correct misunderstandings of not just her "consecration" but also its "consequences." An examination of the individual life can only clarify so much, for as Gilman believed and preached, no life is ever led in isolation; indeed, the cornerstone of her philosophy was the idea that "humanity is a relation" (*Home* 189). Situating Gilman in relation to others is the only way to understand fully how she thought and lived. As a methodology, it honors her own belief system even while interrogating its potential exclusions and generalities.

Among the consequences of her avowed devotion to world service and others' misinterpretations of this devotion, Gilman lists persecution and ostracism. Is it fair to say that she was ever the victim of either? If she was, it was not so much for public obligations as for a particular personal choice, although for her this choice was deeply informed by professional commitments. In 1894, struggling to support herself and launch a magazine as well as develop a career as a lecturer and writer, she decided to transfer the care of her nine-year-old daughter, Katharine, to her ex-husband, Charles Walter Stetson, and his fiancée, Grace Ellery Channing, who was also Gilman's "lifelong friend" (*Living* 334). When the news broke, a public outcry ensued. Gilman was shunned (and on one occasion even slapped) by friends she had previously counted on, until the sting of the backlash eventually drove her from her beloved California. Struggle as she might throughout the remainder of her life to define her decision as purely self-wounding—as having been made for Katharine's and the world's greater good—the label of "unnatural mother" would cling to her tenaciously. Her public stances, outlandish in some cases especially when misconstrued, never created a comparable stir.

Gilman may not be persecuted or ostracized today, but it is true that she remains misunderstood. For instance, one current critical trend is to chastise Gilman for her xenophobia and racism. The point here is not that her positions weren't objectionable—they were, and indeed they were objected to even in her own day. But we should also object to attempts to judge Gilman from our own present-day and more enlightened vantage point without fully situating her views in the context of her times and of her own larger systemic philosophy, as well as vis-à-vis the views of others within and outside the various reform communities in which she participated. The essays collected here aim to complicate any such reductive judgments by engaging in precisely this sort of historical positioning. Though attempts to historicize are occasionally informed by a desire to defend or excuse, the overall intent of this volume is not to paint Gilman as an object of pity or a victim of circumstances, especially as these too would be underhistoricized conclusions. She was a complex person, and explorations of her life must themselves be complex. Neither outright victim nor outright victimizer, Gilman helped to write the script of her life but was never its sole author and neither master of its outcome nor certain of its interpretation.

Gilman repeatedly lamented misunderstandings of her views. She was especially outraged by those who felt she wanted to destroy the home and family through her kitchenless houses and her baby gardens, whereas she proclaimed herself through these selfsame reforms the savior of both home and child. Still, as an active participant in and student of her times, she would have been perplexed by the misunderstandings that have resulted from taking her views out of context. For example, she has received a fair amount of deserved criticism of late for her proposed 1908

"A Suggestion on the Negro Problem," in which she envisions enlisting blacks in a civic army that would offer needed employment and discipline to the race she depicts as less capable of keeping up with the swift pace of evolution. No such plan was ever implemented, fortunately, and it ranks among the rankest of her ideas for racial improvement. All the same, to read this flawed solution as springing solely from Gilman's brain is to overlook the extent to which she was borrowing her martial ideal from the "Industrial Army" modeled in Edward Bellamy's utopian novel, *Looking Backward* (as her contemporary audience would have doubtless recognized, given the book's enormous popularity). It is also to isolate Gilman's plan from potentially ameliorative contrast with contemporaneous but far more extreme solutions to the selfsame "problem" proposed by the likes of Thomas Dixon or D. W. Griffith. When we tune out these other voices, we fail to hear Gilman correctly. Hers were never solo performances.

The blame is not solely ours, however. In certain instances, Gilman appears to have deliberately facilitated misunderstanding, nowhere more so than in her *The Living of Charlotte Perkins Gilman*. All autobiography is selective, of course, but Gilman's narrative omissions are telling. Joanne B. Karpinski has elsewhere noted the upbeat optimism that pervades *The Living*, stressing the harm done to women looking for models of economic sustenance therein, given Gilman's tendency to underestimate the obstacles and overestimate the profits of her own struggles for financial independence. Other autobiographical omissions might also be attributed to this optimistic strain, this eagerness to present herself in the best possible light. For instance, no mention is made of two provocative public defeats. The first occurred at a 1903 National Woman Suffrage Association convention held in Washington, D.C., at which Gilman was "alone in objecting" to a proposal establishing "Educated Suffrage" (Harper 5: 78). Suggesting that a clause restricting voting to the educated would harm "the laboring classes," she argued that the suffrage would educate and improve the "illiterate masses" far more than would "exclusion from the suffrage" (78). The proposal carried despite her objections.

Another and more bruising public defeat came early in 1909, at the hands of the president of the National American Woman Suffrage Association (NAWSA), the formidable Rev. Anna Howard Shaw. Both women took opposing sides in a debate held at the Carnegie Lyceum in New York City over the question of whether wives are supported by their husbands. Gilman took the affirmative point of view, arguing that a woman's housework does not make her self-supporting but husband-supporting, and that she was as currently constituted a nongainful, economic dependent —or, as she more colorfully put it, "man's horse." Shaw countered that although the husbands may bring home the money, their wives then transform it into goods to feed and clothe the family in addition to providing other essential services, and that, in fact, wives often manage to save the incomes their husbands earn and would otherwise waste. The debate ended with the audience voting resoundingly in favor of Shaw's position, repudiating the reasoning Gilman first expounded in book-length form in *Women and Economics* and thus essentially rejecting the arguments upon which she had staked her entire career (see Greeley-Smith).

Gilman's failure to mention these defeats in her autobiography may be attributed to a general tendency therein to gloss over the last thirty-five years of her life. All the same, these experiences must have smarted, especially the last one. Indeed, the Shaw debacle may provide a covert rationale behind the explanation Gilman openly offers in *The Living* for her decision later that same year to start her own one-woman magazine, *The Forerunner.* In her autobiography, Gilman suggests that it was after Theodore Dreiser, then editor of *The Delineator,* advised her to "consider more what the editors want" that she decided to take his advice and become her own editor and publisher (304). Yet the defeat at the Lyceum undoubtedly added considerable emphasis to her decision to start a magazine wherein her views would always be accepted without revision or debate. Indeed, within the pages of this self-protective forum, she would later essentially restage her debate with Shaw, albeit in cloaked form. In the September 1911 issue of *The Forerunner,* she ran a piece entitled "Does a Man Support His Wife?" The article is couched as a response to a British suffragist who recently raised the issue. She makes no mention of her prior encounter with Shaw or her defeat at her hands, and she does not in this controlled restaging allow room for rebuttal or audience vote; in fact, she doesn't even offer via reprint the opposing side (240–46).

Yet another omission that has facilitated misunderstanding might be considered an absent presence, informing the very tenor and tone of Gilman's autobiography for all the silence surrounding it. The majority of *The Living,* after all, was written in 1925, just six years after the red scare started and only one year after the infamous "spider web" chart began its circulation. Playing to Bolshevik hysteria, various conservative and patriotic groups denounced activists in the peace, women's, and temperance movements and disparaged organizations such as the Young Women's Christian Association, the League of Women Voters, and the American Association of University Women.

One particularly pernicious document in this smear campaign was generated by the government's Chemical Warfare Department, which compiled a chart identifying fifteen suspicious organizations and twenty-nine radicals including Jane Addams, Florence Kelley, Inez Haynes Irwin, and Zona Gale. The chart circulated fairly widely, thanks in part to its publication in Henry Ford's reactionary *Dearborn Independent* as well as in the National Association Opposed to Woman Suffrage's *Woman Patriot* (see Cott 248–50; Lemons 209–25). Gilman was a card-carrying member of many of the organizations named on the chart and an intimate of many of the reformers it indicted. Nancy Cott notes that "One Spider-Web spawned another (perhaps many others)" (250), and Gilman's name eventually appeared on one of these spawns. Her sustained activism in the wake of these charts and in the midst of the decade-long red scare suggests that Gilman boldly opted against the self-suppression that was the recourse of other and perhaps wiser activists. Nevertheless, her reticent representation of her socialist views and activism in the autobiography deserves to be read through the lens of the ongoing "scare." In *The Living*, she repeatedly denounces Marx and Marxism, moderates her socialist activities, and insists on her status as an evolutionary rather than revolutionary reformer. Though she understates rather than misstates her views and activism in this self-portrait, restoring the context of the decade of slander and suppression in which it was drawn helps us to understand her need to tint it in hues closer to pink than "red."

Omissions thus inform Gilman's own rendering of her life story, just as they inform the misunderstandings of her life and work that linger even today. One oversight we hope to redress in this volume is the minimal attention paid in the existing scholarship to Gilman's relationships with other contemporaries. We say "minimal" because there have been some notable exceptions to this rule, four examples of which we are pleased to reprint here in revised form. The volume's essays are arranged according to a rough chronological order, as this has the added benefit of placing many of the essays within loose thematic groupings. We begin with the most biographical of the essays collected here. In it, Cynthia J. Davis grapples with the complex triangle formed between Charlotte, her first husband, Walter Stetson, and her best friend and his second wife, Grace Channing. By zooming in on the summer of 1888, when the first Stetson marriage was on the brink of breakup, Davis seeks to untangle the complicated skein that bound these three figures together throughout their respective lifetimes and that informed their subsequent decisions and writings, whether public, collaborative, or private.

A key if underacknowledged figure behind the scenes of Gilman's own emergence on the public stage was William Dean Howells; he generously praised her celebrated satire, "Similar Cases" (1890), and remained throughout her lengthy career a supportive correspondent and surreptitious facilitator. Yet as Joanne B. Karpinski's reprinted essay discusses, Gilman was reluctant to credit Howells fully for his mentoring role (thus further proving Gilman's tendency to foster misunderstanding where it served her purposes). Her reluctance stemmed from a need to appear more accomplished and independent than any such acknowledgment would indicate. She was not alone in receiving Howells's aid, of course, as he assisted many aspiring authors through his influential editorships of leading periodicals and his position as leading literary lion. Nor was she alone in biting the hand that helped to feed her, though hers seems a harmless if thoughtless nibble when compared with the way Howells was chomped on by some of the other writers he had nurtured.

Gilman knew what it was to be treated unkindly. Of all her opponents, none was more caustic than Ambrose Bierce. As Lawrence J. Oliver and Gary Scharnhorst demonstrate, Bierce proved a thorn in Gilman's side during the early 1890s—the years during which she struggled to establish herself in California—poking fun in his columns at her activist work as well as her relationships and aesthetics. Reeling from these jabs, Gilman tried various lines of defense, including seeking an ally in literary critic Brander Matthews. Since the publication of an earlier version of their article in 1993, Oliver and Scharnhorst have discovered that Matthews actually responded to Gilman's beseeching letter, though not in any way that could be construed as heartening. Oliver and Scharnhorst incorporate their findings in the essay published in this volume.

Yet another of Gilman's California adversaries in the early 1890s was William Randolph Hearst, Bierce's employer at the *San Francisco Examiner*. Scandalmongering coverage by the Hearst newspapers of Charlotte and Walter's eventual divorce induced Gilman's lifelong antipathy to Hearst and his media empire, as Denise D. Knight documents in a revision of an essay reprinted here. Gilman's critique of salacious news reporting—variously expressed in poetry, fiction, lectures, and essays—rings true today, though in fact it appears that the mainstream press had even greater freedoms in her day than in ours. Gilman's boycott had its costs: not only did she deny herself access to a number of remunerative venues in Hearst's vast, ever-expanding conglomerate, but in addition many potential interviews were lost because of the gossip-filled newspaper coverage of her divorce, after which she refused, except on rare occasions, to talk to reporters.

While Gilman considered Bierce and Hearst to be her nemeses, most critics have considered Lester Frank Ward to be her staunch friend and ally. While conceding Ward's importance to Gilman's theories, Judith A. Allen revisits their interchange from the time the two began to praise each other in the mid-1890s and draws a more complicated picture of both the man and his influence on Gilman. By exploring Ward's private life and letters, Allen brings to light Ward's caution and conservatism despite the potentially radical implications of his sociological theories, implications that Gilman seized upon and ran with.

Gilman and Ward first met at a women's suffrage campaign in Washington, D.C., in January 1896. In June later that year, Gilman traveled to London as a delegate to the International Socialist and Labor Congress. There she met and was embraced by the Fabian socialists, including George Bernard Shaw. Janice J. Kirkland's essay explores Gilman's relationship with the British Fabians, which was cemented one weekend at Sidney and Beatrice Webb's country home, where Gilman engaged in a battle of wits with the imposing "GBS." Juxtaposing Gilman and Shaw affords us a more careful accounting of what passed as feminism and socialism in these days, since both figures counted themselves as members of these movements while defining them quite differently; it also helps us to explore what each gained and lost through their particular and again divergent understanding of what counted as "art."

Upon returning to the States, Gilman also began to return to her roots in search of a theory to explain women's confining, dependent roles as wives and mothers. Monika Elbert compares Gilman's preoccupations with motherhood and health in her turn-of-the-century treatises and later short stories with those of Gilman's great-aunt, Catharine Beecher.

She locates similarities—and some telling differences—between each woman's thematic concerns and rhetorical styles. Elbert's comparison of Gilman to an antecedent rather than a contemporary suggests that influence runs in many directions; Elbert's essay helps to expand this volume's focus from the synchronic to the diachronic and adds a literal punch to our emphasis on Gilman-in-relation.

From 1895 to 1900 Gilman had no permanent address, locating herself if pressed as "at large." One region she came to know intimately during these itinerant years was the American West, and one novel she consumed avidly after its publication in 1902 was that seminal western, Owen Wister's *The Virginian*. Jennifer S. Tuttle explores the influence of the West and the Western on Gilman's oeuvre. Tuttle focuses specifically on Gilman's novel *The Crux*, which she suggests directly responds to while revising Wister's *The Virginian*. Shifting the perspective and allowing the typically mute Eastern woman to narrate her own story, Gilman changes the Western formula, merges it with its supposed antithesis, the domestic novel, and redefines both in the process.

While Gilman may have experimented with literary formulas, her friends and critics alike in New York—where she took up residency after 1900—bemoaned her reluctance to be more experimental when it came to literary form. Indeed, Gilman seemed at times serenely deaf to the intended influence of her contemporaries, as the case of Mary Austin proves. In her revised essay, Melody Graulich updates her analysis of the similarities and sympathy between the two literary iconoclasts who first met in California in the 1890s and renewed their acquaintance in New York City in the early 1900s. Both women lived and wrote in the Pasadena area in the late nineteenth century, both "lost" daughters through different means, and both praised each other's works and decisions, though this support would be tempered over time. Austin's criticism of Gilman's consistently didactic style is echoed by many modern critics, but her contemporary testimony supports Gilman's own claim that it wasn't artistic talent she lacked but rather any sustained interest in aesthetics, given the fact that she consistently prioritized message over medium.

Among the other New York contemporaries who influenced and were influenced by Gilman were "a small band of women" who called their club Heterodoxy and themselves Heterodites. Charlotte Rich examines an again unacknowledged, direct influence upon Gilman by tracing her relatively friendly relationship with fellow New Yorker and Heterodoxy member Inez Haynes Irwin Gillmore. Rich suggests that Gillmore's 1914 utopian novel might have significantly influenced not only Gilman's *Herland* but her decision to write such a novel at such a time in the first place. Lisa A. Long also addresses the influence of Gilman's membership in the Heterodoxy Club in the process of examining Gilman's sustained, radical feminist work in a culture increasingly indifferent or even hostile to her aims. Long argues that this persistence in the face of indifference or hostility provides a context for *With Her in Ourland* (1916), Gilman's underexplored sequel to *Herland.* Like her mouthpiece, Ellador, Gilman remained both an interested and an aloof student of "Ourland"; like Ellador, she at first identifies with other feminists and activists, including Margaret Sanger, sharing for a while their goals and enthusiasms but ultimately finding herself a disappointed outsider. Unlike Ellador, though, Gilman had no recourse in the end but to remain in our land, for good or ill.

Mary M. Moynihan brings our volume to a close by looking toward the next generation and a figure we might want to call a "daughter" of Gilman, Karen Horney. Moynihan simultaneously explores Gilman's antipathy for her nemesis Sigmund Freud. Indeed, like Davis in the essay we begin with, Moynihan in this concluding piece focuses on a triangulated relationship, connecting the dots between Freud, Horney, and Gilman by exploring and comparing both women's modifications of and resistance to the psychoanalyst's theories, a resistance that has often, in Gilman's case at least, been misconstrued as prudery.

While during her lifetime it may have been easy—and for some of her most severe critics, even enjoyable—to misunderstand Gilman, the purpose of this volume is to make such misinterpretation harder from now on. Anticipating misunderstanding, Gilman also anticipated no "reward" from her "steady lifetime of social study and service . . . , on the theory that one should face life giving all and asking nothing" (*Living* 74). It is true that Gilman gave us much, though many of these gifts contained hidden costs. But it is not true that she asked nothing. This volume of essays aims to illuminate both the questions and the expectations she raised, and by providing them with a rich context, offer interpretations that we hope are neither facile nor, bearing in mind Emerson's scoff, foolish.

*Charlotte Perkins Gilman
and Her Contemporaries*

1

The Two Mrs. Stetsons
and the "Romantic Summer"

Cynthia J. Davis

Charlotte Perkins Stetson Gilman's biographers have yet fully to unravel the nature of the entangled relationship among Charlotte, her first husband, Charles Walter Stetson, and his second wife, Grace Ellery Channing. The two women were the first to become intimate: their friendship began around 1878, soon after Mary, Grace's elder sister, and Charlotte met while both were enrolled at the Rhode Island School of Design. In Grace, Gilman found a "lifelong friend" who came to seem "closer than a sister" (*Living* 334, 49).[1]

Charlotte's relationship with Walter Stetson was both more tumultuous and more short-lived. Their marriage was ambivalently launched in 1888 and finally dissolved in 1894, concomitant with the news that Walter would marry Grace with the former Mrs. Stetson's full approval. If anyone, Charlotte envied Walter more than she did Grace, complaining to the latter, "It is awful to be a man inside and not able to marry the woman you love! . . . I think of you with a great horrible selfish heartache—*I* want you—*I* love you—*I* need you *myself*!" (December 3, 1890). This consensual triangle combined with Charlotte's apparent willingness to "abandon" her child to the soon-to-be newlyweds' care made for a scandal sensationalized by newspapers on both ends of the nation. Despite rough patches, the two women remained close until the very end; indeed, Grace was informed and nearby when Charlotte took her own life in 1935. Walter, who died after complications from surgery in 1911, loved both women, though with varying intensity, and it is difficult to pinpoint precisely when he transferred his affections from the

first to the second Mrs. Stetson, if indeed he ever wholly did. His sur-
viving letters suggest that he retained a passion for Charlotte he was
willing to confide to her only a month before marrying Grace. In the
early years of the triangle's formation, Grace managed both to sympathize with and chuckle over Charlotte and Walter's histrionic relationship; she was to lose this sense of humor over the years.

These are choppy waters to navigate, but the seaside summer of 1888,
during which the relationship first became three-cornered, offers a safe
point of entry, a relatively quiet pool wherein the currents that would
come to govern this love triangle first began their whorl. Letters sent by
Grace to her mother, Mary J. T. Channing, back home provide daily
coverage of the events of this pivotal period, their disclosures all the
more revealing because Charlotte kept no diary for those months and
Walter's diary entries at this time were sporadic and not reproduced in
Mary Armfield Hill's edition of the diaries. Though perspectival, Grace's
epistolary account is detailed and informative; without these letters, we
would have little insight into what Grace even while living through it
considered "quite a romantic summer" (Channing to Mary Channing,
June 26, 1888).

Romance might be one way to frame the summer's unfolding events
—especially given the main players' preoccupation with both playwriting
and lovemaking (and unmaking). But we could also think of these Bristol months as an informal summer school, a liminal, learning period
during which Charlotte Perkins Stetson began to calculate her emerging theories of life, literature, love, and work, crafting essential formu-
lae for both health and happiness and eradicating the obstacles strewn
across her path by subtracting them, at times quite cavalierly, from the
equation.

Notwithstanding Weir Mitchell's best efforts the preceding year, by June
1888 Charlotte and Walter Stetson's marriage was disintegrating. On
June 6, Grace Channing arrived in Rhode Island from Pasadena to lend
a hand, both literally and figuratively. Over the course of Grace's nearly
four-month visit, Charlotte took giant strides toward ending a marriage
she had entered with grave reservations. She also continued testing the
waters of a writing career before taking the final headlong plunge. She
needed Grace that summer as both an emotional prop and a professional
collaborator. Driven to frequent "attack[s] of hysterics" by her husband's

melancholy presence, Charlotte was desperately seeking an escape route, and the two friends had latched on to playwriting as the key to financial and existential freedom (Channing to Mary Channing, July 9, 1888).

Given the importance of playwriting to Charlotte's future prospects, it is surprising that so little attention has been paid to her plays, numbering at least seven, quite a few of these collaborative. She apparently thrived on this sort of "collaborative work—it cheers and stimulates me" (Gilman to Houghton Gilman, November 3, 1898). Her first collaborative venture commenced during a postpartum visit to Grace in Pasadena over the winter of 1885–86, where the two friends not only wrote but also acted in the play they would revisit during the summer of 1888.

On June 7, 1888, the day after Grace's arrival on the East Coast, the two friends decamped for the "fine old-fashioned" house they had rented through September 1 in nearby Bristol, Rhode Island (Channing to William Channing, June 7, 1888). There, ensconced every morning in a "delightful nook" by the shore, Charlotte and Grace set out to revise and rewrite what they hoped would prove to be "the only great Comedy of the age" (Channing to Mary Channing, June 12 and 21, 1888). Their literary pretensions were immodest: Grace declared their ambition to "make the Anglo-American Studies of Howells and James pale before this [play] and those great luminaries shake in their shoes" (June 12, 1888).

Regrettably, no known copy has surfaced of *Noblesse Oblige,* the play upon which these pretensions rested, though a copyright was recorded for it in 1889. Charlotte did write a poem by that title which first appeared in the *American Fabian* in 1898 and which may suggest the thematic thrust of the eponymous play. The poem is a lengthy one, but the potential insight it sheds on the absent script warrants citing significant lines:

I.

I was well born. . . .
A wise, free maiden grew to womanhood,
Guiding and training her young life for me;
With splendid body, vigorous and strong;
A heart well used; a brain of fluent power.
She gloried in the crown of motherhood,
And chose a father fit to share her reign; . . .

II.

I was well trained.
. . . Life came to me translated to the tongue
That I could understand and profit by.
. . . They taught me—all who ever lived before—
Taught me free use of body, use of brain,
And sent me forth a full developed man,
With easy mastery of his powers.

III.

And I am rich.
I revel in immeasurable wealth;
. . . So rich, so rich beyond all fear or doubt
That no desire for my own private need
Can ever enter my untroubled mind.
. . . And there remains but this: To Act! To Do!

IV.

Shall I not work?
I, who am wholly free and have no care;
I, with such press of power at my command;
. . . Shall it be said, "He took, from all the world,
Of the accumulated countless wealth,
As much as he could hold, and never gave!
Spiritless Beggar! Pauper! Parasite!"

Life is not long enough to let me work
As I desire. But all the years will hold
Shall I put forth. Perhaps it may be mine
To do some deed was never done before
And ease my obligation to the world!

(*Woman's Journal* 302)

After first establishing the speaker's excellent birth and training, rich-
ness in talents and intangible yet "immeasurable wealth," the poem suggests that such a person ought to feel obligated to contribute to the
world's progress. This take on duty is quintessential Gilman: considering
herself blessed in both genes and genius—having been bequeathed what
the poem elsewhere refers to as an "entailed heritage"—how could she

not give back, or as she would have it, give forward, to future generations?

Grace shared Charlotte's feelings of noble entitlement and obligation.
Both aspiring playwrights were from illustrious lineages—Grace the
granddaughter of William Ellery Channing, father of Unitarianism, and
Charlotte the granddaughter of Lyman Beecher, "the father of more
brains than any other man in America" (Theodore Parker qtd. in Stowe)
and no slouch himself. Each of these scions had imbibed since birth a
need for the limelight: where better to seek it but the stage? Their dramatic models were as illustrious as their ancestors and ambitions. The
play the two cowrote is particularly indebted to Henry James, whose "Art
of Fiction" they were anxious to read and whose international theme
held strong attractions. As Grace explained to her mother, the central
idea of *Noblesse Oblige* is "a study of strong devotion and magnanimity
between English and American types" (June 12, 1888). Had they but
known it, the aspiring dramatists could hardly have chosen a more in-
auspicious role model, given that James's own pretensions to the stage
were to be punctured by boos and catcalls.[2]

At the same time, James is an oddly chosen model because Charlotte
and Grace's heavily plotted, highly coincidental and ultimately moralistic
script (which even Grace's kind-hearted father criticized for having "*too
much* incidence and story" [Grace Channing to Mary Channing, July 4,
1888]) would never have measured up to James's formalist aesthetic standards. Though Grace became a dedicated aesthete in her mature years,
Charlotte consistently belittled art for art's sake and believed instead in
its necessary utility, in its role as a tool for world uplift and human
growth.

In this early effort, the coauthors seemed content to relegate both
mimeticism and didacticism to the wings, leaving on center stage enough
melodrama, romance, and comedy to appeal to popular tastes. This may
have been a wise decision, as their finished draft managed to interest the
"great Gillette" in the play. The celebrated actor eventually took *Noblesse
Oblige* outright, and were it not for the untimely death of his wife, his
waning if intermittently waxing interest, and the two women's difficulty
securing financial backing, the living of Charlotte Perkins Gilman might
have taken a very different course.

What is most intriguing about this dramatic summer is not the play in and of itself (happily, as it is not extant) but the context in which it was written and what that play and that context disclose about Charlotte's living. For starters, Grace's letters home help clarify the dynamics of the Charlotte-Walter-Grace triangle and reveal much about both the dwindling and the kindling romances. In fact, not two weeks into her Bristol stay, Charlotte would tell Walter, "You are very dear to me my love; but there is no disguising the fact that my health and work lie not with you but away from you" (*Endure* 364). The problem was that Walter believed the reverse: at the time he felt that he could sustain neither work nor health without Charlotte by his side. Through all Charlotte's ups and downs, his love appears to have endured. As he would inform Grace's mother soon after he and Grace had decided to marry, "I am afraid that when I love I love tenaciously—probably forever"—and here, in this letter to his future mother-in-law, he was referring to his love not for her daughter but for Charlotte (May 10, 1892). Walter's tenaciousness is apparent in the frequent, often uninvited and unwelcome visits the achingly lonely artist made to the seashore that Bristol summer, moping and mooning about until he drove his estranged wife to the brink of madness.

Grace's intimacy with both Stetsons prompts us to listen when she places a sizeable portion of the blame for the break-up on Charlotte's doorstep. For all Walter's obstinacies—chief among them his conventional, idealized view of Woman with a capital *W*—for his day he was more or less consistently a caring partner and an involved parent, whereas it is hard to conclude the same of Charlotte during those years, especially given her mental state. As Grace told her mother with only veiled reference to Charlotte, "Things are hard to us chiefly because we dwell upon them until they lose their due proportion and seem bigger than anything else in the sunrise. . . . If you have other interests to distract and soothe you, the worse part of trouble seems to drop away" (June 21, 1888). Charlotte's melancholia was aggravated by her obsession with the "mistake" she had made in choosing marriage over career; her belief that this mistake was irreparable became her idée fixe and fueled her despair.

By the summer of 1888, however, Charlotte was beginning to find her escape in work and what Grace deemed "other interests," a methodology that would become the cornerstone of Charlotte's philosophy and preaching in years to come and that may owe its origins to Grace's concerned counsel. Indeed, Charlotte situates Grace as midwife to her own emergent work ethic, crediting her Bristol confidante with saving "what there is of me. Grace Channing pulled me out of living death, set me on my staggering feet, helped me to get to work again" (Gilman to Martha Luther Lane, January 20, 1890).

Even though witnessing the mad, sad dance between the two Stetsons led Grace to realize that Walter "is a terrible drain upon Gilman and I begin to understand *why* and *how* he is so" (Grace Channing to Mary Channing, June 22, 1888), her loyalties ineluctably began to shift toward the husband. Despite assurances that she "can't say too much in praise of C.," she also told her mother she found the "delightful and exasperating" Walter "more to be pitied than" Charlotte—a sentiment she would come to harp on as the years passed—and that she also found him "very love-able" (July 7 and 9, 1888). Being found lovable was precisely what Walter was seeking that lonely summer, and the fact that it was Grace and not Charlotte who found him so provided no small consolation. He had known Grace for five years by the time the Bristol summer arrived and from the first considered her "sensible . . . graceful . . . refined . . . and kind . . . and very earnest: a good companion for my darling" (*Endure* 196). Still, it was as a "companion to his darling" and at least for a while as a surrogate for her that he continued to think of Grace for many years to come. Which is not to say that the eventual Grace-Walter marriage was unhappy. As dedicated to art as they were to each other, they also were loving and concerned parents to Katharine, who ultimately came to feel more at home with them than with the Gilmans. The second Mr. and Mrs. Stetson shared above all what Charlotte would ruefully describe as an aesthetic temperament that allowed them increasingly to disdain those like Charlotte herself who found joy in more mundane pleasures and to don a shabby gentility through which the couple sought to convey their lonely superiority and their sacrifices for art's sake.

During that formative summer of 1888, however, Grace's sympathies were not divided so much as all-encompassing, and she readily volunteered herself as intermediary between the hapless pair, keeping Walter from Charlotte and trying to convince the heartsick husband that the cure lay in separation. As she wrote her mother about the wretched Stetsons, "They just *prey* upon one another. He makes Charlotte absolutely sick—she gets so exhausted and depressed.—before night yesterday there were great circles under her eyes and she was white as a ghost, purely from the mental fatigue. . . . And he grows as bitter and cynical in five minutes with her. But they are both charming, lovable, gifted people!" (June 18, 1888). Grace repeatedly reassured her mother that she was standing up under the strain of the Stetsons' marital debacle and the onslaught of each one's charged confidences, yet by the end of July she began confessing that she longed for the ordeal—hers as well as theirs—to be over. Her time with the Stetsons convinced her that happy marriages often meant suppressing one's individual personality but that a misfortunate marriage like Charlotte's might ultimately involve less suffering since it involved less suppression—a lesson Grace seems to have forgotten after embarking upon her own "happy" marriage (July 28, 1888).

Although by August Grace had apparently confided to Walter that she loved him, it would seem that both he and she took this to indicate a warm fellow-feeling rather than a heartfelt passion. Though she may have insisted on Walter's lovableness, Grace was not at this point in love with him; indeed, throughout the summer Grace had her hopes raised by another suitor, a young rector, only to have them dashed when he chose another. It was later, during Walter's final attempt at reconciliation with Charlotte in 1889, that his relationship with Grace began to turn romantic. During this ultimately frustrating visit to Pasadena, the artist began painting a sensual portrait of Grace that was tellingly bedecked with passion vines and flowers; upon its completion Walter asserted that the portrait represented "what she is to me" (qtd. in Eldredge 59). By the end of 1890 the two had pledged their love and were looking forward to a future together as man and wife.

Charlotte regarded Grace and Walter's growing intimacy with a combination of fondness and relief. Her once passionate feelings for Walter had grown decidedly cooler over the years. Walter and Charlotte shared much in common when courting in the early 1880s: most of all they shared a talent for art, a sense of their own as yet unappreciated genius, and a profound loneliness. Yet the two grew apart, so much so that in the post-divorce period Charlotte would eventually revel in her ability to continue to "grow and grow and have him see it" (to Houghton, March 2, 1899)—a comment that implies her sense that Walter's aim had always been to stunt that growth. She came increasingly to feel that her decision to end the marriage to Walter—though reached at a time of mental instability—represented wisdom incarnate. "Dear me! What a disagreeable looking man he is!" she was to confide to her cousin and future husband Houghton Gilman. "Isn't it funny how one can go through things and come out *absolutely*—as if never in!" (December 25, 1899). The locks of Walter's curly blond hair she retained until her death and which reside among her papers at the Schlesinger Library may thus indicate not so much a suppressed but abiding passion as a confirmed and indiscriminate tendency to horde memorabilia.

What Charlotte relinquished gladly, Grace came to cling to with a passion tinged with worship. A year after Walter's death, Grace told one of his oldest friends that she pitied Gilman more than anyone for having "actually *had* in her very hands, heaven on earth, and threw it away" (qtd. in *Endure* xli). It is not clear whether Walter ever developed a love of reciprocal intensity for Grace; he did write her appreciative and occasionally lusty notes throughout their protracted courtship and marriage, and the couple let passion and need take precedence over public and parental approval when they decided by the spring of 1893 to begin living together (Stetson to Mary Channing, March 10, 1893). Still, only a month before his delayed wedding to Grace, Walter was confessing his love to Gilman and discussing Grace's flaws, a letter Grace seems to have eventually discovered, read, and tried to conceal. Since the last seven pages of this letter were considered missing or destroyed until I discovered them recently among the unprocessed Channing papers at the Schlesinger Library, I want to reprint them here to give readers a sense of the nature of the triangle from Walter's perspective circa July 1894.

To set the stage: Accompanied by Frederic Perkins, Gilman's erstwhile father, and at Gilman's behest, Katharine had recently traveled cross-country to live with her father and his soon-to-be-wife, Grace. The rediscovered letter fragment, dated July 9 (and its first pages reprinted as incomplete in the appendix to Denise D. Knight's edition of Gilman's diaries) was written shortly after the father-daughter reunion and prior to Stetson's second marriage. Part of the letter is excerpted below, at the point where Knight breaks it off (see Appendix, p. 15, for full text of the first pages of this letter):

[We have spent a half a hundred trying to find] a boarding place for the summer, and only at noon today did we get one. Mrs. Rudd, at last, and to Katharine's delight, says there are rooms in Norwich Town for us, ready Thursday. So they will go Thursday!

Perhaps I have done wrong, dear, to treat Kate's arrival as I have, but I simply couldn't find the heart to be a stern parent. I have actually devoted myself to her. She has done practically what she desired to do every day. She has "fed" very extremely, and been perfectly lovely always. Down the river, out to the Park—*any*thing. Of course it can't be kept up forever, because it costs astonishingly considering the small fortunes[?] the items come to, and principally because I *can't* work. Grace, truly dear, is in no way fitted to care for her. Grace is ill constantly, and she can't do her work & take care of Kate too—neither can she neglect her comfortably. Grace has certain habits Kate must not contract, & though Grace does most nobly & beautifully, I can see very well that Kate must have other care eventually.

I'm not going to make a long letter. I want to tell you that Katharine insists—Oh, very, very gently—upon having my portrait of you displayed, & it is on the easel now, decorated with a dozen little American Flags & a blue scarf: & under it is a Pasadena landscape in which you & she are in the foreground. She is charmingly & unobtrusively loyal to you, dear; she *loves* that portrait, & finds in it the "Mama" you desired as being in it. God bless her! She is fond of Grace, but I am very sure that in her secret heart she thinks her a very inefficient person, she is politeness itself & would not intimate that Grace was inefficient, but she smiles at me once in a while in a most unmistakeable way.

Sometimes her comprehension is perfectly uncanny.

She has prepared lots of pictures to go with this, mostly of Park affairs. Her transcript of the portrait of you seems especially good to me. The dear, she holds you in such perfect remembrance; and she shares our eagerness for news of the [railroad] strike & wonders which side you are taking in the Oakland v. S. Francisco affair. It is all very sad—and very promising.

There is no knowing when this will reach you. We have had no letters from the west in two weeks. Only a telegram from Harold [Grace's brother]. I wish you could see Katharine. She's cleaning her new water colour box,—on the floor, in her pretty gown of blue & red & white. Do you know—it *hurts* me intensely that you could not have bought her pretty things to delight *your own* eye. It was *my* fortune, not yours, dear. If I could have sent you more————!

Well, my turn will come.—And really I have spent already on this dear child as much as I was supposed to send [spend?] for a year. Meanwhile she is unmistakeably *yours* in every movement of her body.

We still love you deeply, she & I—and may all good be yours. As ever, Walter

Letters such as these, presumably discovered after Walter's death, would likely have accelerated Grace's descent into bitterness and pettiness.[3] It had long been Grace's belief that she paled beside Charlotte; during their summer in Bristol she rather blithely compared Charlotte's "exceptionally beautiful" person with her "own insignificant phiz" (July 24, 1888). Her later temperamental drift toward crankiness was doubtless hastened by miscarriage and failed ambitions during her marriage to Walter and by penury and deafness in her widowhood.

Though she was to complain vocally about her friend's lack of tact and surreptitiously about her dubious skills as wife and mother, Grace doubtless also resented Charlotte's international fame, especially as she felt it to have been earned at her own expense. After all, the years she served as Katharine's "other mother" and Walter's second wife were years she put her own career on virtual hold. Her resentment of Charlotte permeates a short story Grace published in *Harper's Monthly* in March 1907. The revealingly titled "The Children of the Barren" indicts a married couple—particularly the unflatteringly portrayed wife—who on the excuse of travel leave their two eldest children with an unmarried relative for six years (precisely the length of time Charlotte initially transferred primary care of Katharine to Walter and Grace). While Grace's protagonist and surrogate, Anne, is only an aunt, she comes to care for the children as a real mother would and, it is suggested, far better than their real mother does. The story vindicates the surrogate mother when the children turn to her in their adulthood for solace and credit her for their successes in life; in the end, she is recognized—though not by the thoughtless and brittle "real mother"—as having "saved the children" (518).

In this same story, Grace refers to her heroine's "sunny perspective" and "healthy sense" as having allowed her to see "the comedy in the tragedy of the young lives about her," and at least initially this appears to have been true of the author herself. In Bristol in 1888, Grace was more inclined to smile than to whine. Indeed, Grace was not just writing a play; she was watching one as well, and she managed to find the unfolding Stetson melodrama, for all its sorrows, occasionally side-splittingly funny. For instance, after one "absurdly unfortunate" visit from a "ghost-like" Walter, wearing his broken heart on his sleeve, Grace took one glance at the look on Charlotte's face and had to run away "to laugh to [my] heart's content!" (to Mary Channing, July 7, 1888).

Grace's ability to see comedy in the midst of tragedy may help to explain the friends' collaborative decision to write a farcical comedy in the midst of the serious drama of marital breakdown—in the midst, we might say, of the very stuff of "The Yellow Wall-Paper." Should we read their turn to comedy as a form of denial or as a means of escape or of release? Could it be that Charlotte found something stimulating, even enjoyable in Walter's depression, if only in that turnabout can feel like fair play? While these possibilities may help to explain this lighthearted choice in a summer of heavyheartedness, the most pressing reason for both authors was money. Grace and Charlotte were financially strapped, Charlotte especially so: when she set off for California that September, she had only ten dollars in her pocket. And, as Charlotte had written to Grace in 1887 while laying short- and long-term plans for her escape: "My dear girl, a good play is a paying thing . . . " (November 21, 1887).

Both Charlotte and Grace wanted the thing to pay, and to pay hand-somely, rewarding them with fame and fortune. And yet, as Charlotte would later ruefully concede, to write for money was not the surest recipe for success: "Necessity is no incentive to me," she wrote Ho, "—at least a very poor one . . . " (July 6, 1898). During this romantic summer, Grace's ambitions are the most naked as they are the most faithfully recorded; they also are the most startling as the received image of her reflected by other biographers is as a self-sacrificing, modest, true woman. These let-ters reveal a more complex portrait, and Grace's repeatedly expressed desire for literary greatness further explains her sniping at Charlotte in later years, given Charlotte's lingering renown and her own relative ob-scurity.

That summer it was difficult to predict which of the collaborators would attain fame first. As late as 1890 Charlotte would note that "Grace is rapidly sailing into public recognition. . . . I hope to follow soon in her wake" (to Martha Luther Lane, March 15, 1890). Even at her most de-spondent, Charlotte shared Grace's sense of ambition. Indeed, Charlotte was the first to boast of writing a play that would take "the world by storm." In a letter to Grace written the preceding winter, she proclaimed that "we will be the leading dramatists of the age! We will create a new school! We will combine the most literal realism with the highest art, and cover both with the loftiest morality!!!" (November 21, 1887). By the time summer came around, Grace had repeatedly informed her mother that "it was a matter of life and death with Charlotte" to have the play succeed (June 20, 1888), suggesting that it may have been during these stress-filled months that Charlotte sealed what for her would remain an essential equation between "human work," health, and salvation. Even though she wrote for money, it is important to remember that she saw wealth not as an end but as a means. Specifically, she considered playwriting, as she considered all work, to be not only a way to wealth but also a way to health. As she signed off on her aggrandizing letter to Grace: "Our names shall be long in the land. Dr. Mitchell be—!" (November 21, 1887). In a number of her subsequent stories and essays, Charlotte would prescribe work as the best medicine for curing personal and social ills, and her prodigious output suggests the extent of her self-medication.

Still, as she would confide to her friend Martha Luther Lane, even Charlotte thought playwriting—especially "a comedy"—an odd choice for launching her public career (March 13, 1886). Indeed, the choice raises several provocative questions, among them: does her avid interest that summer in both profit and popularity put the lie to her later outspoken disdain for both potboilers and moneygrubbers? In *Human Work,* for instance, she dismissively concludes that "a man should no more prostitute his 'trade' than his 'art.' It is as base to make a 'pot-boiler' of your day's work as of a book or a picture" (253). Yet her contempt for both money and moneymakers was likely more assumed than heartfelt, derived in part from her failure to produce either and belied by her lifelong obsession with accounting and her delight in mysteries and other page-turners.

At the start of her career, Charlotte had faith in her abilities to earn her living by her pen, and she willingly dipped into the well of her own life story for inspiration. Indeed, during this romantic summer, it would have been impossible to keep the written and lived romances from impinging on each other. In one of her letters home, Grace confided a central theme of *Noblesse Oblige,* besides the one implied by the title: "It is a sin to keep an engagement if you find you've made a mistake!"—a lesson Charlotte had learned the hard way and that must have been a bitter pill for Walter to swallow, as he had pressed his suit despite Charlotte's strong misgivings, and as he was among the first to read and critique the

play. He may have found a basis for his criticisms in the play's simultaneous assertion of "the divine right of true lovers" (to Mary, July 13, 1888).
These two imperatives certainly were in conflict in the Stetson marriage,
with Walter asserting his divine rights and Charlotte conceding her mistake. The fact that the play remains stubbornly in a comedic vein despite
such potential conflict suggests that the demands of the purse and audience took precedence over claims to strict verisimilitude. For all her
avowed idealism, in playwriting as in her other ventures Charlotte remained a confirmed pragmatist, with no apparent internal contradiction.
An impecunious childhood had taught her the power of the purse, and
she was to clutch hers to her side for all the years to come.

A Pretty Idiot, cowritten on the heels of *Noblesse Oblige,* would seem
to share enough thematic and formal similarities with *Noblesse Oblige*
that we might consider it the next best thing, allowing us to get a glimpse
of what the two friends were capable of producing when they put their
heads together.[4] In *A Pretty Idiot,* the heroine, a gifted author, decides
to hide her talents and instead to play the true woman—read, "pretty
idiot"—in order to teach a wealthy and arrogant suitor a hard lesson
about feminine ideals. Yet her best laid plans go astray, and she finds that
dishonesty does not pay and that revenge is bittersweet. After revealing
the "true woman" behind the "pretty idiot"—that is, after revealing her
brains and abilities as an author and actor—the heroine rights her own
and others' wrongs and falls willingly into the arms of her cousin Jack,
who had always accepted her as the talented career woman *and* womanly
woman she was born to be. The fact that this scenario replicates scenes
not only in the Stetson marriage but also in the author's second, happy
marriage to her first cousin a decade later suggests that from 1888 on,
Charlotte was not just writing but actively directing the script of her life.
This latter play contains within it the repressive script of her first marriage, taken to the brink of tragedy before it relapses into comedy, into a
happy ending that would, in fact, bear out in her own life the second
time around. Though Walter still clung to hopes that his marriage would
survive well into 1889, it is clear, if only from this script, that his wife had
other scenarios in mind. Noblesse oblige: nobility had its obligations,
and for Charlotte Stetson these were not to one man but to all mankind.

It was a romantic summer, all right, but for Charlotte, at least, the
romance was impersonal. Her romance was with humanity, with a career,
with a place in the public arena as a world servant. Though a romantic

comedy may seem an idiosyncratic venue for achieving such goals, venue was never her chief concern. Throughout her life she was at least formally no puritan, willing to experiment with a wide array of genres. It was the work that mattered, and so long as she felt she was getting her message out, she was living, she was working, she was happy. Indeed, from a certain perspective a play would have provided the perfect springboard for her public career, since what Charlotte Perkins Stetson most desired was for all the world to become her stage.

APPENDIX

The following is Denise D. Knight's transcription of the first half of Walter's letter to Charlotte. It was written in Walter's hand just weeks after Katharine left Charlotte to live with him and Grace.

9th July 1894—

Late Afternoon.

My dear Charlotte—
We would like to see you—and we send you our love—Kate and I. She sits at arm's length from me—oh so beautiful! It makes tears fill my eyes—drawing for you. We have been to the Park again, she & I. No two persons could be more companionable than we are. I know what she wants before she says it. I can *feel* her completely. And I think she knows it; and she's becoming fonder & fonder of me; and truly, dear, I do not see how I can ever let her leave me again. I wish I need not—rather I wish we could have her *together*. You see, dear Charlotte, I have been with her now most intimately. Grace has no care of her when she is with me, and I have had a chance to

(she interrupted me there to tell me about an "Infant Camel who went to walk with a baby-carriage—"of course it isn't true" she adds. She is drawing you the Park camel "Rachel"—an aged camel verily, so *droll*!—she has drawn Baby Roger, the elephant"). It is now the 10th, dear. I was interrupted by the return of Grace from Bristol where she had been to try to find board & lodging for the dinner—and unsuccessfully. She boldly went to Wm Trotter & found him with his 7th month's old baby—and "another coming" Grace says. Which shall be the 3d since his marriage!! She feels she escaped some thing. Yes, I think she did. We were in a heavy quandary last night as to what we should do. It is impossible for me to work with them in the studio. They have been here now since Friday morning. Saturday we all went to Sakonnet in the search of rooms fruitlessly—and were held up by a highwayman. It was a pleasant trip which cost about $15.00!—We have spent a half a hundred trying to find . . . [The remainder of this letter is missing]. (Knight, *Diaries* 2:900–02)

NOTES

1. Though throughout this volume we have sought to standardize all references to Charlotte Perkins Stetson Gilman as "Gilman," in this particular essay, given its predominant focus on the summer of 1888, any reference to her as Gilman while she was Walter Stetson's wife would violate chronology and sense. We have therefore opted for first names for her and others. Whenever the reference is to her life and work after her 1900 marriage to Houghton Gilman, "Gilman" is used.

2. James's 1895 debut of his play *Guy Domville* was poorly received and more or less rang down the curtain on his dramatic career.

3. Walter's letters have been edited with a severe pair of scissors wielded most likely by Grace, though Katharine is also a candidate.

4. Accompanying a copy of *A Pretty Idiot* in the Schlesinger Library's Gilman archives is a synopsis that mentions two characters, Sophronia and Amelia, who do not surface in the final draft of *A Pretty Idiot* (though Sophronia makes an appearance in a later play, *Changing Hands*). It may be that these names were imported from the hapless *Noblesse Oblige*. They would continue to mean a good deal to the coauthors, who would refer to each other as "Amelia" (Grace) and "Sophronia" (Charlotte) sporadically throughout their correspondence for the remainder of their lives.

2
When the Marriage of True Minds Admits Impediments

Charlotte Perkins Gilman and William Dean Howells

Joanne B. Karpinski

At first glance, the intellectual minuet between Charlotte Perkins Gilman and William Dean Howells seems vulnerable to Gertrude Stein's complaint about Gilman's onetime home of Oakland, California: "There is no there, there" (Stein 298). Unlike the Lucy Larcom–John Greenleaf Whittier relationship, for example, this one lacks an elaborate prior myth to deconstruct.[1] Nor is there a complex text of correspondence to (mis)-read, as in the case of Emily Dickinson and Thomas Wentworth Higginson. But postmodern criticism alerts us to the heuristic value of absence, allowing us to focus on Howells's cautious fulfillment of the mentorial role he had initiated with such rhetorical fervor. Sincere but correct, Howells was not suited by temperament or conviction to become the passionate champion that Gilman had hoped for.

Gilman's first major poem, "Similar Cases," was published in the April 1890 issue of the socialist periodical the *Nationalist*, where it attracted the appreciative attention of William Dean Howells. Gilman recorded his "unforgettable letter" and her reaction to it in her autobiography:

DEAR MADAM,

I have been wishing ever since I first read it—and I've read it many times with unfailing joy—to thank you for your poem in the April *Nationalist*. We have had nothing since the Biglow Papers half so good for a good cause as "Similar Cases."

And just now I've read in *The Woman's Journal* your "Women of To-day." It is as good almost as the other, and dreadfully true.

> Yours sincerely,
> WM. DEAN HOWELLS.
> That was a joy indeed. . . . There was no man in the country whose
> good opinion I would rather have had. I felt like a real "author" at
> last. (Gilman, *Living* 113)

Gilman's enthusiastic response to Howells's letter may seem overdone to twentieth-century readers for whom Howells's reputation has been eclipsed, but in 1890 Howells was a name to conjure with. As editor of the prestigious *Atlantic Monthly*, as a contributor of fiction and reviews to such significant periodicals as the *Century* and *Scribner's*, and as writer of "The Editor's Easy Chair" column for *Harper's Monthly*, he was "in a position of greater prestige and authority than any other reformer of his time" (Hough 4). Thus, Gilman had good reason to be pleased. As fellow socialist Edward Bellamy wrote to Howells in thanks for his praise of *Dr. Heidenhoff's Process,* notice from such an august quarter was "as refreshing to me as you may suppose a note from Hawthorne in recommendation of one of your earlier efforts would have been to you."[2]

The esteem in which Howells held Gilman's writing receives forceful expression in his 1899 article, "The New Poetry," published in the *North American Review:*

> Her civic satire is of a form which she herself invented; it recalls the
> work of no one else; you can say of it (and I have said this before),
> that since the Biglow Papers there has been no satire approaching
> it in the wit flashing from profound conviction . . . but the time has
> not yet come when we desire to have the Original Socialists for our
> ancestors, and I am afraid that the acceptance of Mrs. Stetson's
> [Gilman's first married name] satire is mostly confined to fanatics,
> philanthropists and other Dangerous Persons. But that need not
> keep us from owning its brilliancy. (Howells, "The New Poetry"
> 589–90)

As Gloria Martin points out in her dissertation on women in Howells's criticism and fiction, the irony of Howells's assessment might seem at first to be directed against Gilman but is in fact directed at his audience, "implying that only when the country has accepted the humane theories of socialism will Stetson's work become as respectable as Lowell's famous satire has now become." Martin characterizes this passage as "a rare acceptance of another author by Howells into the privacy of the editorial tone" (Martin 170).

Personal similarities and political sympathies disposed Howells to be appreciative of Gilman and her work. Both writers experienced financially insecure childhoods, with their mothers marshaling the family struggle for economic security. Each fought with recurring depression from adolescence until late in life. Gilman's affiliation with socialism came early and enthusiastically, while Howells embraced the same social philosophy later in life and more gradually. Never the ardent feminist that Gilman was, Howells nevertheless supported the cause of women's equality with a vigor unusual for a man of his time.

With so much in common, it would seem inevitable for the dean of American letters to foster the professional fortunes of the young woman whose work he praised so highly. Instead, Howells temporized, using his influence to get her work from publishers other than those with which he was directly associated. Why did the budding mentorial relationship not flourish? Apparently, it suffered from a residual timorousness on his part about the bitterness of her social indictment, even at its most humorous. Moreover, Howells's relationship with his oldest daughter and with the female writers whose work he did promote suggests a patriarchal temperament poorly suited both to Gilman's emotional needs and to her style of writing.

Gilman's father, Frederic Beecher Perkins, held a variety of editorial and library jobs while trying unsuccessfully to establish himself as a fiction writer. He left the family when Charlotte was nine years old, and after his departure any contributions from him were both meager and irregular. Charlotte's mother supported the household by taking in boarders or by acting as companion to invalid relations. Periodically, Gilman would attempt to reestablish contact with her absent father, but she found him emotionally as well as physically distant (Hill 38–41 and passim).

Howells's praise of her poetry and political opinions thus satisfied a deep thirst for something like paternal approval. However, Gilman could no more rephrase her polemics to please Howells's sense of decorum than she could retract the impolitic kiss she once offered her father in the Boston Public Library.

Like Gilman, Howells had spent his childhood wandering nomadically on the frontiers of respectable poverty. His father, William Cooper Howells, began married life as an itinerant printer. He moved rapidly into the editorial office, but his radical opinions in both religion and politics cost him this promotion. The senior Howells had "the heroic superiority to mere events and shifts of fortune which was in keeping with his religion and his temperament as an idealist" (Cady 28–29), but the loss of income and alienation from community life were more difficult for his wife and family to bear.

Staunchly loyal to her husband, Mary Dean Howells undertook the financial management of their affairs to protect the family from the consequences of his principled indifference to money. Like Mary Perkins, she took in boarders. When Howells again found editorial work in a more congenial political climate, she had title to the business and the property placed in her name and that of her oldest son.

These mothers, forced into roles of unusual self-reliance, were deeply influential on Gilman and Howells. Neither woman particularly liked the autonomy that was thrust upon her: Gilman's mother cast herself as the victim of fate, while Howells's steeled herself to endure what she could not cure. The frictions produced between their dislike of their new roles and their competence in pursuing them greatly affected their children.

Gilman's physical and emotional makeup might have disturbed Howells by its likeness to himself refracted through the lens of gender. For both, adult life alternated between periods of exultant productivity and paralyzing depression.

Paradoxically, these depressions spurred Gilman's literary career. Her poem "The Answer," an outcry against the "work that brainless slaves might do" that ultimately kills an optimistic bride, won first prize for the year from the *Woman's Journal:* more important, it strengthened her affiliation with the American Woman Suffrage Association, which sponsored the journal ("The Answer," qtd. in Hill 136). Also, Gilman's struggle with the misdirected therapy prescribed for her depression formed the anecdote for "The Yellow Wall-Paper," the story for which she is best known today.

Unable to endure the tension between growing public success and the domestic misery she experienced after the birth of her only child, Gilman sought professional help. Dr. S. Weir Mitchell, who had treated several of Gilman's Beecher relatives for "nervous ailments," prescribed his six-week rest cure: bed rest, massage, lots of food, and complete avoidance of mental stimulation. Gilman followed the regimen under Mitchell's supervision, but once she returned home, his admonition— "live as domestic a life as possible. Have your child with you all the time. Have but two hours intellectual life a day. And never touch pen, brush or pencil as long as you live" (Gilman, *Living* 182)—drove her to the brink of mental collapse. Ironically, Howells successfully recovered from bouts of an acute but obscure malaise that left him unable to work or study by periodically resorting to the type of rest cure imposed on Gilman with such disastrous results.

Gilman wrote that "Mr. Howells told me that I was the only optimist reformer he ever met" (Gilman, "Mr. Howells' Socialism" 2), but for much of his life this evaluation was also true of Howells himself. Brought up in the golden age of American rural egalitarianism, Howells increasingly saw the values of that era sacrificed to the rampant acquisitiveness of the industrial Gilded Age. Howells was one of the few opinion leaders of the era to defend the Haymarket anarchists in print, and he was pilloried in the press for it. Although Howells vacillated for weeks after writing to the anarchists' defense attorney that he believed the defendants to be innocent, he ultimately acted courageously on the attorney's advice that Howells initiate a press campaign on their behalf. Thus it appears that fear of controversy alone cannot account for Howells's holding back in his mentorial relationship with Gilman.

At various times, Howells published his admiration for Gilman's writing. A summary statement late in his career praised her work as "witty and courageous," adding, "the best things that have been said about woman suffrage in our time have been said by Charlotte Perkins Gilman" (Kilmer, December 16, 1914). His correspondence with Gilman, however, offers a more ambiguous assessment over the years.

When Gilman received Howells's compliments on "Similar Cases," she sent a copy of his letter to her friend Martha Lane, with the following comments: "I'm glad you thought my poem funny. I herein boastfully enclose a copy of a letter showing it was thought rather more of by some! . . . isn't that a delightful letter? I am so pleased too to find the man thinks well of Nationalism in spite of its 'flabby apostle'" (qtd. in Hill 176). The "apostle" was Edward Bellamy, whose novel *Looking Backward* was helped to prominence by Howells's favorable review.

Gilman was prepared by nature and education to embrace the Nationalist creed, which expounded the necessity of the government's taking complete control of the means of production in order to eradicate the panoply of evils generated by laissez-faire economics. Nationalism and feminism worked together, in Gilman's view. She believed nationalism to be "the most practical form of human development," but equality of the sexes was "the most essential condition of that development" (qtd. in Hill 182).

Like Howells, Gilman had grown up in a family atmosphere suffused with belief in progress. As Howells had also done, Gilman rejected sectarian Christianity in favor of a God-ordered universe in which Christian ethics assisted the laws of evolution to pursue the perfection intended by the Creator. Both authors linked social responsibility to religious tenets rather than political ideology.

For both Gilman and Howells, the political rights of women were founded on their equality with men. Howells was frequently misunderstood on this topic, because his fiction treats women evenhandedly rather than idealistically. In his "Editor's Easy Chair" column, Howells argued that women had the duties of citizens and therefore should have the rights of citizens as well. Since women lived within the state, they ought to be able to vote on its practices, and since they had to pay taxes, the principle of no taxation without representation ought to entitle women to suffrage (*Harper's Monthly* October 1905: 796, May 1909: 967). Howells wrote on women's issues as part of a general commitment to social reform. Gilman did the reverse: she committed herself to a general reform of "masculinist" social order as a precondition to the achievement of equality for women.

Gilman's utopian novel, *Herland,* produces a humorous and satirical indictment of sex-specific divisions in human activity. Howells, too, used the utopian genre to envision a society based on gender equality. His Altrurian romances assume that an enlightened proletariat would avail themselves of the democratic process to ensure that men and women have not only equal opportunities but equal obligations in the economic, political, and domestic spheres as well. Curiously, the American woman who travels to Altruria and marries there follows a career path not unlike Gilman's; she becomes a traveling lecturer, combining intellectual work and domestic chores through a communal housekeeping arrangement.

More important to the cause of gender equality than Howells's fiction, however, was his editorial support of women writers. In "Recollections of an Atlantic Editorship," Howells lists nineteen women whose work appeared during his tenure and adds that he does not know whether he published more men or women, "but if any one were to prove that there were more women than men I should not be surprised. . . . For in our beloved republic of letters the citizenship is not reserved solely to males of twenty-one and over" (qtd. in Martin 186).

Howells held up for special praise several representatives of the local-color school, finding their "directness and simplicity" to be of a piece with "the best modern work everywhere" (Howells, *Criticism and Fiction* 134, 168–69). While the high quality of the local colorists' literary achievement and the sincerity of Howells's support for them are incontestable, these women's motives and methods were so different from Gilman's that it is easy to see why Howells, admiring the former, would be disconcerted by the latter.

The qualities of style that Howells praised in the work of the local colorists were on the whole foreign to Gilman's. While they wrote in the realistic mode, Gilman's fiction and poetry were unabashedly romantic in the intensity and extravagance of her expression. In general, Howells disparaged the romance genre for presenting women with unwholesomely exaggerated role models and for making it possible for them to take refuge from their real problems in a world of fictional triumphs. Gilman's utopian novels and serial fiction could be seen as vulnerable to such a critique, but oddly enough in this context, the Gilman short story that Howells elected to anthologize belongs to the Gothic tradition. Even when Howells writes about Gilman's poems, which do not exhibit the presumed defects of the romance genre, a consistent motif of his letters to Gilman is enthusiasm for her convictions tempered by genteel consternation over her verbal deportment.

The restraint that differentiated the local colorists' literary style from Gilman's extended to their professional styles as well. Contrasting them to the assertively professional women of the earlier sentimentalist school, Ann Douglas Wood notes that the local colorists tended to be reclusive "pure artists," neither subscribing to the cult of domesticity nor competing in the male-dominated marketplace (Wood 4).

In several respects, Gilman's career differed from those of the local colorists whom Howells deservedly placed on a critical pedestal. Gilman made her living by writing, while of that group "only Freeman and Stuart supported themselves by their pens" (Wood 15). In addition, she earned money from public speaking, still a daring occupation for a woman at the turn of the century. She wrote and spoke explicitly about the invidious way "in which the sexuo-economic relation has operated in our species" (Gilman, *Women and Economics* 75), while the local colorists' frequent focus on female protagonists living independently from men only implicitly addressed the material price paid for this autonomy. Neither in their person nor in their work did the local colorists challenge conventionally imposed standards of feminine virtue, while Gilman did both.

These differences are significant because Howells indulged in the unfortunate habit of impugning the femininity of women writers with whom he disagreed. He once wrote to Henry James about his unpleasant meeting with "a certain celebrated lady novelist, who once turned to criticism long enough to devote me to execration" that "I find I don't take these things Pickwickianly; but she avenged me by the way she dressed and the way she talked. I wish I could present you with the whole scene, but I mustn't" (Howells, *Selected Letters* 4: 305).

It should be noted that Howells's admiration for Gilman's writing evidently did not extend to appreciation for her unconventional domestic arrangements: her divorce from Walter Stetson and relinquishment of their daughter's custody to him and his new wife, who happened to be Gilman's best friend and her housemate during her year of separation. Mary Armfield Hill asserts that Gilman encouraged Stetson to court her friend (158).

Howells attached this acidulous biographical account to a letter from Gilman recommending some stories written by her "friend and co-mother," Grace Ellery Channing: "Mrs. Stetson's 'co-mother' is married to Mrs. Stetson's divorced husband. Mrs. S. attended the wedding and gave her young daughter to her 'co-mother' as a wedding present" (Gilman to Howells, March 8, 1898). Nevertheless, Howells's privately expressed opinion did not prevent him, or his wife and daughter, from socializing with Gilman. He attended her lectures—indeed, on one occasion she substituted for him on the lecture platform when he was unable to keep a speaking engagement—and she visited Howells's family at home. Gilman regarded this friendship as a "special pleasure" (Gilman, *Living* 222).

Howells could offer unqualified enthusiasm for Gilman's "Similar Cases" because it satirized resistance to social change without going into embarrassing particulars. In his letter congratulating Gilman on the appearance of "Similar Cases," Howells also complimented her poem "Women of To-day." That Howells read it in the *Woman's Journal,* sponsored by the American Woman Suffrage Association, testifies to his sympathetic interest in this issue. He somewhat overstated the case when he told Gilman that this poem "is as good almost as the other—it lacks the lash of wit to give it energy, and tries to supply the missing verve with exclamation points"—but he was no doubt correct in calling it "dreadfully true." However, as will be seen more strongly in his response to "The Yellow Wall-Paper," the word *dreadfully* and its synonyms apparently cut two ways in Howells's lexicon: the production of dread in the reader may be a worthy aesthetic goal yet not be worthwhile as a publisher's risk.

Six months after his first paean, Howells again wrote to Gilman, this time on letterhead from the *Cosmopolitan Magazine* editorial department: "Do you think you could send me for this magazine something as good and wicked as Similar Cases, and of the like destructive tendency? And could you send it 'in liking'?" (Howells to Gilman, December 10, 1891). Gilman sent him "The Amoeboid Cell." Howells's letter of response to this offering giveth with one hand and taketh away with the other, as do many of his assessments of Gilman's writing: "The Amoeboid Cell is so good that I think it deserves working over more carefully, and condensing a good deal. I don't like any part of the joke that's in the spelling, like 'individualitee' and 'anybodee,' and I think your moral is a little too sharply pointed. Couldn't it be incidental, somehow? Perhaps I am over-particular, but then I always think I am worth pleasing, as an admirer of your gifts" (Howells to Gilman, January 31, 1892). The available correspondence does not indicate whether Gilman made the effort to please the "admirer of her gifts," but "The Amoeboid Cell" never appeared in the *Cosmopolitan Magazine.*

Gilman's and Howells's estimates vary about his role in the publication of "The Yellow Wall-Paper." By Gilman's description, Howells was an ineffective advocate for the story:

This ["The Yellow Wall-Paper"] I sent to Mr. Howells, and he tried to have the Atlantic Monthly print it, but Mr. Scudder, then the editor, sent it back with this brief card:

Dear Madam: Mr. Howells has handed me this story. I could not forgive myself if I made others as miserable as I have made myself! (Gilman, *Living* 119)

After lamenting Scudder's lapse of perception—"I suppose he would have sent back one of Poe's on the same ground" (*Living* 119)—Gilman notes that she then put the story in the hands of a commercial agent, who placed it with the *New England Journal.* The agent never transmitted the journal's stipend to the author.

In "A Reminiscent Introduction" to the anthology in which Howells finally reprinted "The Yellow Wall-Paper," however, he credits himself with assuring the story's first appearance in print:

It wanted at least two generations [after Poe] to freeze our young blood with Mrs. Perkins Gilman's story of *The Yellow Wallpaper,* which Horace Scudder (then of *The Atlantic*) said in refusing it that it was so terribly good that it ought never to be printed. But terrible and too wholly dire as it was, I could not rest until I had corrupted the editor of *The New England Magazine* into publishing it. Now that I have got it into my collection here, I shiver over it as much as I did when I first read it in manuscript, though I agree with the editor of *The Atlantic* of the time that it was too terribly good to be printed. (Howells, *The Great Modern American Stories* vii)

While Gilman could scarcely blame Howells for Scudder's refusal to print "The Yellow Wall-Paper" in the *Atlantic Monthly,* she either did not know about Howells's efforts to "corrupt" the editor of the *New England Journal* or did not appreciate them sufficiently to take note of them in her memoir, where she records only the activities of the tightfisted commercial agent.

In addition to accounting himself more active in the publication of "The Yellow Wall-Paper" than Gilman acknowledged, Howells's introductory assessment of the piece in his anthology suggests—by its repetition of the adjective *terrible*—the grounds for his reluctance to press Scudder more assertively for the story's publication. During his own tenure as editor of the *Atlantic Monthly,* Howells had a sampling of the consequences that could attend the publication of material "too wholly dire" for the public taste.

In September 1869, Howells published "The True Story of Lady Byron's Life" by Gilman's great-aunt, Harriet Beecher Stowe, which included Lady Byron's accusation that her husband had committed incest with his half sister. The context of the charge was moral indignation about the things a married woman must endure with patience, but public indignation at the *Atlantic Monthly*'s putting such shocking material in print cost the magazine 15,000 subscribers. Since Stowe was absolutely determined to publish her exposé somewhere, and since Howells wanted to keep her contributing to the *Atlantic Monthly* despite his reservations about any particular article, he could hardly have refused to print it. This episode, however—the third publication scandal to plague the magazine during Howells's association with it (although the only one for which he was accountable)—made Howells somewhat more chary of offending the subscribers' sense of decency (Cady 136). This hard-earned editorial caution would have led Howells to respect Scudder's decision not to "make others miserable" by publishing "The Yellow Wall-Paper."

Gilman was not unaware of Howells's aesthetically if not politically conservative tastes. Although she valued his praise, his writing was "never a favorite of mine you know. His work is exquisite, painfully exquisite, but save for that Chinese delicacy of workmanship it seems to me of small artistic value. And its truth is that of the elaborate medical chart, the scientific photograph" (qtd. in Hill 176). However, she apparently was not aware of the painful personal connection that Howells had had with the rest-cure regimen lambasted by "The Yellow Wall-Paper."

S. Weir Mitchell, who had supervised Gilman's disastrous rest cure, was a personal friend and artistic discovery of Howells, who published some of the doctor's fiction in the *Atlantic Monthly*. Mitchell had also prescribed this treatment for Howells's daughter Winifred, who gained physical strength but died of "a sudden failure of the heart" while under his care (Howells, *Letters* 3: 247). Even after Winifred's death and despite his own successful experience with Mitchell's rest cure, Howells continued to associate his daughter's symptoms with a level of intellectual activity deemed excessive for a woman (Howells to S. Weir Mitchell, March 7, 1889). Gilman's personality may have disturbed Howells by its similarity to Winifred's as he understood it.

It is unclear whether Howells realized that Mitchell's methods were the particular target of Gilman's wrath in "The Yellow Wall-Paper" at the time that she sent it to him for the *Atlantic Monthly*. Not until her letter to Howells accepting his invitation to anthologize the story in 1919 does Gilman make this explicit:

> Did you know that one piece of "literature" of mine was pure propaganda? I was under Dr. Weir Mitchell's treatment, at 27. . . . I tried it one summer, and went as near lunacy as one can, and come back. So I wrote this, and sent him a copy. He made no response, but years after some one told me that he had told a friend "I have completely altered my treatment of neurasthenia since reading 'The Yellow Wallpaper.'" Triumph! (Gilman to Howells, October 17, 1919)

Gilman's failure to credit Howells with facilitating the initial appearance of "The Yellow Wall-Paper" in print follows a pattern of denying the actual contributions of those who, in Gilman's opinion, ought to have done more. Her correspondence with Theodore Dreiser and Lester Ward shows a similar reaction.[3]

In 1893, the year following the publication of "The Yellow Wall-Paper," Gilman brought out a volume of her collected poetry, entitled *In This Our World.* Again, Howells sent Gilman a letter praising the poems and their author in the warmest terms: "I am ashamed not to have said long ago how much pleasure we have all taken in your book of poems. They are the wittiest and wisest things that have been written this many a long day and year. You are not only the prophetess of the new religion (in the new conception of religion) but you speak with a tongue like a two-edged sword." Once again, however, Howells's reservations begin to appear even as he praises: "I rejoice in your gift *fearfully* [emphasis added], and wonder how much more you will do with it. I can see how far and deep you have thought about the things at hand, and I have my bourgeois moments when I could have wished you for success's sake to have been less frank. But of course you know that you stand in your own way!" (Howells to Gilman, July 11, 1894).

Thus it comes as no surprise that Howells graciously declined the opportunity to escort any more of Gilman's poems into print: "I like your Immortality, but I can understand why magazines would not. As to the volume of poetry, I suggest your sending it by Ripley Hitchcock, the literary man of Appletons, who have just brought out Bellamy's book. He will give it intelligent attention, and I beg you to quote me as cordially in its favor as your self respect will allow. I will tell him you are going to send it" (Howells to Gilman, June 25, 1897).

Since Gilman published only the one collection of poetry, it is not clear whether Howells's letter refers to a projected second volume or to the 1898 reprint of *In This Our World*. In either case, Gilman's self-respect apparently would not allow her to quote Howells cordially enough to "the literary man at Appletons"; no second volume ever appeared, and the copyright to the 1898 reprint was entered by Small, Maynard and Company of Boston.

Except for including "The Yellow Wall-Paper" in *The Great Modern American Stories*, Howells's mentorial efforts for Gilman did not operate on the practical level. However, he never ceased to offer her sweeping moral support on the order of "when the gods really wake up and begin to behave justly you will have no cause to complain" (Howells to Gilman, May 8, 1911). Why did Howells prefer to leave Gilman's career in the lap of the gods when he took other women writers under his own wing? The evidence suggests that while Howells held in high esteem Gilman's passionate defense of principles he, too, held sacred, he could not espouse her rhetorical and personal flamboyance. From childhood on, the ideal of the gracious lady exercised a powerful attraction over him.

Even on the issue of women's suffrage, about which Howells believed Gilman to have been the best and wisest exponent, his approach is genteel where Gilman's is wryly impatient. Howells believed that suffrage would come to women (in some unspecified, spontaneous manner) when women themselves sufficiently wanted this right. Gilman gleefully satirized this point of view in a poem entitled "Women Do Not Want It":

What women want has never been a strongly acting cause
When woman has been wronged by man in churches, customs, laws:
Why should he find this preference so largely in his way
When he himself admits the right of what we ask to-day?
(Gilman, *In This Our World* 156–57)

Perhaps, too, Gilman sought a mentorial relationship with Howells at a level of emotional intensity to which he was not prepared to respond. Her letters of compliment to him are couched in no more exaggerated terms than his to her, but women of that period were expected to express themselves to men more circumspectly; apparently even Walter Stetson felt that his wife's demonstrations of emotional need were a little too frank (Hill 123). Their correspondence indicates that Gilman initiated all the meetings that took place between them, with Howells occasionally, though graciously, demurring on the grounds of his own or his family's ill health.

Certainly her need for his assistance was great, since she published almost all of her works at her own expense, but the directness of her appeal may have put off a man accustomed to being the patriarch in such situations—he wrote to Lucy Larcom, for example, "You take rejection so sweetly that I have scarcely the heart to accept anything of yours" (qtd. in Cady 242).

In the letter that thanks Howells for wishing to include "The Yellow Wall-Paper" in his anthology, Gilman anxiously seeks his approval of her magazine: "Please—did you ever receive either one of the bound volumes of the first year of my precious *Forerunner*? . . . I did want you to notice *my baby,* and tried twice, letter and book" (Gilman to Howells, October 17, 1919, emphasis added).

Howells's one-line reply simply regrets that he never received her book, ignoring her plea for reassurance. Summing up the successes and failures of her efforts to place work in magazines other than *The Forerunner,* Gilman made a list of those who were "good friends among editors." Howells's name is not among them, although she claims to have had so many that she can "by no means remember them all" (Gilman, *Living* 302–03).

Taking into account its defensively self-congratulatory tone, this explanation seems essentially valid with respect to Howells's unwillingness to publish Gilman's work himself or to strongly advocate its publication by his powerful friends. It was undoubtedly easier for Howells to praise Gilman's opinions than to take responsibility for them. Nevertheless, Howells's public votes of confidence in Gilman's writing enhanced its credibility and gave it a broader forum than it had achieved on its own. Despite his reservations, Howells kept faith with Gilman—in his fashion.

NOTES

A longer version of this essay originally appeared in *Patrons and Protegees: Gender, Friendship, and Writing in Nineteenth-Century America,* edited by Shirley

Marchalonis (New Brunswick, NJ: Rutgers University Press, 1988), 212–34. Reprinted by permission.

1. The Howells biographies I consulted simply do not mention the Gilman connection, probably because the major ones were written before interest in her work was revived in the early 1960s. Hill's biography of Gilman merely refers to Howells's enthusiasm for Gilman's "Similar Cases" and *In This Our World* and notes his socialist sympathies. Hill goes up only to 1896 in this volume. In her introduction to Gilman's *Herland* vii, Ann J. Lane says that Howells "did much to sustain her career," but she does not go into detail. So far as I know, the present study is the first treatment of the Gilman-Howells relationship.

2. Cady, *The Road to Realism* 173. Bellamy probably did not know how close to the mark his compliment came. When Howells first arrived in New England, he managed to secure an audience with Nathaniel Hawthorne. Upon learning that Howells intended next to visit Ralph Waldo Emerson, Hawthorne gave Howells one of his visiting cards to take to Emerson. It bore the message: "I find this young man worthy" (Hough, *Quiet Rebel* 1).

3. Gilman was very impressed with Ward's gynaecocentric theory of evolution, which held that in most species the female controlled both selection of the mate and reproduction, making her rather than the male the dominant partner. She did much to popularize it in her own writing. When Ward complained that his theory had not received the attention it deserved, Gilman wrote several letters reminding him of her appreciative efforts on its behalf. When no acknowledgment of her reminders appeared, she sent him a copy of her book *Human Work* and expressed the hope that she would someday have the time to read more of his writing: "So far—except for the Phylogenic forces in Pure Sociology; and some of the shorter papers— . . . I have not really read you at all." Thus prodded, Ward finally produced the desired tribute: "I have read your book. I could hear my own voice all the time. But of course, it was not an echo. It is pitched much higher than I can strike and differs also entirely in timbre" (qtd. in Hill, *Gilman* 266–67).

Recalling Theodore Dreiser's gloomy advice to "consider more what the editors want," Gilman explains the reason she ignored his counsel: "There are those who write as artists, real ones; they often find it difficult to consider what the editor wants. There are those who write to earn a living, who if they succeed, must please his purchasers, the public, so we have this great trade of literary catering. But if one writes to express important truths, needed yet unpopular, the market is necessarily limited" (Gilman, *Living* 304).

3
Charlotte Perkins Gilman versus Ambrose Bierce

The Literary Politics of Gender in Fin-de-Siècle California

Lawrence J. Oliver and Gary Scharnhorst

"With rare exceptions," Ambrose Bierce asserted in his October 4, 1891, "Prattle" column in the *San Francisco Examiner,* "women who write are ... moral idiots." A woman, he continued, may be a "bright, pleasing, conscientious and companionable creature" until she starts writing for newspapers, at which time she invariably becomes a "sore trial to the spirit of every one who loves her, offensive to every taste that she formerly gratified, and breaking in succession all the moral laws that can be broken with a pen and ink" (6).[1]

Most of the female "moral idiots" who were writing for California newspapers at the time Bierce's essay appeared belonged to the Pacific Coast Women's Press Association (PCWPA), founded in San Francisco in 1890. The war of words Bierce provoked with the PCWPA may fairly illustrate, if only in the extreme, a pattern of gender conflict among western writers at the turn of the century.

The "creasy dames and tendinous virgins" of the PCWPA, Bierce sneered, could not distinguish between poetry and pottery; their fate and function were merely to amuse, and what amused him most was their aggressive campaign against "wicked critics who [did] not accept the Women's Press Association view of California's opulence in female intellect." The members of the "Hen Press Association" tended to "lie and cheat with as little concern, and apparently as little consciousness of wrong as a pig with a mouthful of young larks"; they were as deficient in literary ability and sense of humor as they were in moral sense, and they were ever ready to defile their art in the service of "any fad engaging [their] favor, from religion to spatter-work." In response to a PCWPA member who insisted that there "is no sex in the brain," Bierce begged to disagree. "In no respect," he rejoined, "do men and women differ so widely, so conspicuously, so essentially as in mind," adding that to any "competent and comprehensive observer," the female mind is clearly inferior to the male's (*SFE*, October 4 and 27, November 1 and 15, 1891).[2]

Bierce's remarks outraged many women, of course, especially those who belonged to the PCWPA. Virtually all of the members whom Bierce lambasted in the pages of the *Examiner* week after week are forgotten, with one notable exception: Charlotte Perkins Stetson Gilman.

There is no doubt that Bierce counted Gilman among the PCWPA "moral idiots," for she was a prime target of his taunts. In his September 20, 1891, column, Bierce—who begs his readers' forgiveness for being so preoccupied with the PCWPA, because its members' literary pretensions so amuse him—sneers that the verse of "those sweetsingers of Pickerville, Mesdames Stetson and Lillian Plunkett," will be "something to remember on one's deathbed—something to remember and forgive." In his October 4 essay he makes an equally unkind remark about Gilman. Complaining that the "three most active members" of the PCWPA have received inordinate and undeserving attention in the newspapers, he states, "I may as well explain that I refer to Mesdames Stetson, [Emily] Parkhurst, and [Eliza] Keith. Of the first I know nothing discreditable except that she is a show and permits herself to be feted—lunched, for example, by the fashionable women of Oakland, who have a national reputation for lunching imposters and being lunched upon by them. It does not follow that Mrs. Stetson is an imposter. I do not say that she is not a worthy and clever woman: I only say that her claque is working the oracle in her service with more diligence than discretion" (*SFE*, October 4, 1891). Obviously, Bierce scorned Gilman's effort to earn a reputation if not a living by her pen. One can only imagine how he would react to the fact that she had succeeded in rifting the veil of obscurity and had secured a space in the canon, with "The Yellow Wall-Paper" now only a few pages from "Chicamauga" or "An Occurrence at Owl Creek Bridge" in the major anthologies of American literature.

On her part, Gilman tried to respond to Bierce's attacks, albeit from a position of disadvantage on the fringe of the literary establishment. On October 7, 1891, three days after she was skewered in "Prattle," she wrote a satirical poem titled "'The War-Skunk,' apropos of Ambrose Bierce of the Examiner" (*Diaries* 477). From all indications, however, it was never published. She also enlisted the help of her friend Alice Stone Blackwell, coeditor of the Boston *Woman's Journal,* the leading suffragist paper in America. Blackwell branded Bierce's October 4 column "one of the most extraordinary criticisms upon newspaper women ever perpetrated" and excoriated him especially for his "savage and personal onslaught, by name, upon three members of the Pacific Coast Women's Press Association," two of them (including Gilman) "valued contributors" to her paper.[3] Unfortunately, Blackwell's defense of the PCWPA from the other side of the continent seems to have made no difference to Bierce, if indeed the news of it even reached him. At length, Gilman wrote Brander Matthews, professor of dramatic literature at Columbia College and one of the most influential and well-connected men of letters on the New York literary scene, to urge him to find some way to censure Bierce for these verbal attacks on women writers. Excerpted below, this hitherto unpublished letter reveals not only the extent to which Gilman was stung by Bierce's contemptuous remarks but, more important, the extent to which she was entrapped by the patriarchal culture of her day.[4]

1258 Webster St., Oakland, Cal.
Wed. Oct. 19th 1892
Mr. Brander Matthews:

Will you excuse a very earnest woman for appealing to you as a *critic* of high standing, and a gentleman, to know if there is not some literary tribunal before which a writer of peculiarly scurrilous and evil habits may be brought, exposed, and punished?

The faults I allude to are not those of a personal character, but of a professional character; and the more blamable that the writer is a powerful one.

As a soldier may be a good fighter, and yet conduct himself in a manner "unworthy of an officer and a gentleman," so may a man be a good writer and yet commit insufferable offense with his pen.

The person against whom I make this charge is Mr. Ambrose Bierce of San Francisco.

I have recently read your notice of his book in "More American Stories" in a recent magazine; and while I would like to take issue with you on the artistic merits of that mechanical chamber of horrors I will let it stand merely as a proof that the man is a writer of ability.[5]

Being such, and so presumably able to maintain himself by honest productive work, he consents to write for the S.F. Examiner at a high salary, and to write for it such unmanly gossip and slander as no city *but* San Francisco would tolerate I think.

I speak generally, but am willing to produce evidence in plenty if it will be really of use.

Mr. Bierce has an outspoken contempt for women. "Lovely woman" he says "has no thinker." The domestic woman he treats gently, but let her touch the pen and he uses his to flay her.

Do you chance to know my father—Fred. B. Perkins, formerly of New York?

You have mentioned one of his stories "The Devil Puzzler" as one of the ten best short stories—in your Pen & Ink Sketches. I wrote and asked him if any good thing could be said of Ambrose Bierce?—I had heard naught but evil.

He answered that nothing good could be said of him—that he was the meanest hound that wrote—that "he thinks nothing of blackguarding women publicly, by name;" and more of as strong a nature.

He never strikes at large game—well known writers or women with lively and pugilistic "protectors," only at the weak women, the defenseless, the easily discouraged; women who are struggling and climbing, generally for the very lack of the husband or brother whose presence would close the sneering mouth.

What he dare not say directly he insinuates; as for instance he once spoke of me as "allowing herself to be lunched and fêted by the ladies of Oakland, who delight to so honor any impostor who comes along." Then hastily adding "Not that this lady is an impostor. For aught I know she is a most estimable woman and writer"— etc. etc. I enclose the most recent specimen I have of his delicate touch.

Miss Coolbrith is a poet of real merit—, a "lone woman" not well to do, and liable to real injury from such usage.[7]

The point is that an able writer constantly attacks and insults defenseless women; regarding neither truth, honor, nor common decency; this all our reading public know.

The Examiner stands here as an example of the corrupt and does not stand at all elsewhere! Sensational and venal press, and Mr. Bierce's "Prattle" is a most juicy column in the Sunday edition.

It is difficult to reach a man of such nature in any sensitive place;

but surely there must be *some* way of getting at him, some tribunal whose judgement he would feel.

It's not an indictable offense to ridicule and covertly slander the weaker works in one's own line; but it is an offense against common decency; and a crying shame on the noble art of letters.

I wish I could claim perfect immunity for myself, and so perfect disinterestedness; but there are few women writers of this coast who could—he scorns us all.

But I can honestly say that my personal offense never moved me to action—is more than a year old; and that this laborious and far-sent effort is due to purely impersonal resentment based on a widening knowledge of his immeasurable, ingenious, baseness.

Somebody ought to do something—can you advise any possible measures? Attacks from the local press are meat and drink to him—he has plenty, and minds them not a whit.

Is there no way by which his literary conscience could be reached?

> Sincerely—somewhat apologetically,
> Charlotte Perkins Stetson (Matthews Papers)

Bierce presumably never read Gilman's letter, though he was familiar enough with the indictments it contains, for he received many such letters from irate women (and men). He steadfastly denied the charge that he held women writers in contempt. Women writers who believed that he was biased against their sex, he stated, were unduly sensitive to what he rather disingenuously called "good natured raillery"; moreover, they could not tolerate being subjected to the same literary standards that he applied to male writers. "Imposture," he bristled in another "Prattle" piece, "is of no sex and is entitled to no immunity when it wears a petticoat. Women who are ambitious to get out of that garment to have an 'equal chance with men' are quick to get back into it when threatened with an equal switching for the same misdeeds" (qtd. in Pope 151). A chauvinist rather than a misogynist, Bierce adored properly conventional "True Women" (especially those who were young and attractive); but he ridiculed, for whatever reason, all women who dared to challenge patriarchal power and agitate for social and political equality. In such essays as "Emancipated Woman" and "The Opposing Sex," in fact, he declared that granting women the right to vote would be "one of the most momentous and mischievous events of modern history" and that the women's movement overall had benefited a few individuals but "distinctly damaged the race" (Bierce, *Collected Works* 291).

That Bierce verbally "switched" male as well as female authors in his "Prattle" columns is amply supported by the evidence. His attack on the young San Francisco poet David Lezinsky was so severe and relentless that many people held Bierce responsible for the fellow's death. And contrary to Gilman's charge, Bierce was not hesitant to turn his invective on prominent writers who were capable of retaliating. Though he never took on Mark Twain, he did belittle Henry James, Joel Chandler Harris, Walt Whitman, and the dean of American letters, W. D. Howells. Bierce routinely blasted "Miss Mary William Dean Howells" and the "detestable" school of literary realism; like H. L. Mencken and Sinclair Lewis later, Bierce portrayed "the dean" as a genteel and feminine writer, ambling among the "trim hedges of Philistia" with the other literary "old maids."[8] Years later, Bierce would even complain that Brander Matthews had degraded "the art of criticism by practicing it for comfort in the shadow of a personal bereavement" in writing an essay eulogizing a friend (*SFE,* September 6, 1896). Bierce, of course, did not restrict his acid pen to literary figures. He pilloried politicians, union bosses, religious leaders, plutocrats—any person or organization that roused his hatred for "hypocrisy, cant, and all other shams" (Fatout 94).

Bierce was not implacably hostile toward all women writers, his reputation notwithstanding. Responding in 1891 to the accusation that he scorned California authors, male as well as female, Bierce recalled the praise of, among others, Ina Coolbrith, whom Gilman would portray in her letter to Matthews as Bierce's victim. Though Bierce certainly denigrated some of Coolbrith's poems, he extolled others. In his "Prattle" essay of December 6, 1891, for instance, he praised Coolbrith's sonnet "Beside the Dead," which, after quoting the full text, he honors as "excellent work." Coolbrith's verse, he wrote, is not flawless (no writer's is, he adds), but her best poetry is "sweet and true and tender" (*SFE,* May 1, 1892). Coolbrith once wrote their mutual friend Charles Warren Stoddard that Bierce had "been as kind as a brother . . . and I consider his friendship and interest a great honor. . . . In fact, if I were younger and he single I might be tempted to fall desperately in love with him" (qtd. in Rather 16).

Bierce's long relationship with Coolbrith was not, as Gilman implied to Matthews, one-dimensional; it was complex and fluid. Moreover, Coolbrith was by no means the weak and vulnerable woman Gilman makes her out to be in her letter. She was a well-known and influential poet who had secured a place in the inner circle of San Francisco literary culture and who would become poet laureate of California in 1915; Jack London was one of several young writers whom she mentored. Though Bierce skewered many women writers, especially those affiliated with the PCWPA, Gilman's charge that he invariably employed his considerable power to damage the literary careers of every woman writer he encountered was simply not true.

In portraying Coolbrith as the hapless/helpless victim of Bierce's verbal assaults, Gilman was projecting her own feelings; for it was she, not Coolbrith, who was struggling at the time to establish her literary credentials and who was vulnerable to his sarcastic jibes. She had moved to California in 1888 hoping to recover from the "hysteria" for which S. Weir Mitchell had treated her, but her early years in the Bay Area were extremely difficult. In her autobiography, Gilman regarded the early 1890s as the hardest period of her life and 1892—the year in which she sought Matthews's assistance—as the nadir. On December 31, 1892, she wrote in her diary: "It has been a year of great and constantly increasing trouble. Poverty, illness, heartache, household irritation amounting to agony, Care, anxiety, grief and shame for many, many failures" (*Diaries* 507). Her mother's terminal illness and her divorce from the artist Charles Walter Stetson had combined to cause her extreme anguish. In her diary entry for New Year's Day, 1893, she prayed for "a little less pain if you please! I can do more work if I suffer less" (*Diaries* 509). To make matters worse, the *Examiner* sensationalized its treatment of her divorce (her name, she recalled, became a "football for all the papers on the coast"), providing her with another reason to detest William Randolph Hearst's "yellow" paper (*Living* 144). Looking back on this period of her life, Gilman reflected that, though she had been remarkably prolific ("The Yellow Wall-Paper" had been written in 1890 and published in 1892), she often felt "like a drowned thing, drifting along under water and sometimes bobbing to the surface" (*Living* 143).

She had hardly bobbed to the surface in Oakland when Bierce attempted to push her down again. Contrary to her claim that her letter to Matthews had sprung from a "purely impersonal resentment" of Bierce's verbal attacks on other women, it seems clear that Gilman's enmity toward Bierce was deeply personal—as personal as her implicit condemnation of Mitchell in "The Yellow Wall-Paper." As Joanne Karpinski has argued, Gilman—whose father had abandoned the family when she was a child and who had remained emotionally distant from her in her adult life when she tried to reestablish a relationship with him—craved paternal approval.[9]

Gilman was buoyed during these years by the support of Coolbrith, who lived across the street from her in Oakland, and other PCWPA friends; but it was not until she received the approval of Howells that she "felt like a real 'author'" (*Living* 113). If Howells played the role of the kindly father figure, Bierce was, like Mitchell, a bête noire, a tyrannical male determined to silence women's voices. Or perhaps it is more accurate to say that, in Gilman's mind, he was the figure of her brother Thomas, whose constant tormenting of her during her childhood, as she confided in an unpublished autobiography, was "just unbearable," and she "rebell[ed] at the injustice of it, steadily resenting what [she] could not escape" (Lane, *To Herland* 42). Steadily resenting the injustice, Gilman appealed to such Eastern arbiters of culture as Alice Blackwell and Matthews. But Blackwell's stern words in the *Woman's Journal* had been ineffectual. In a patriarchal society, only other men were able to punish someone like Bierce in a "sensitive place." (Gilman may have said more than she knew with that phrase.) Thus, from this perspective, Gilman sought the help of a male authority figure for entirely pragmatic reasons.

Yet, if Gilman's attempt to have Bierce tried by a male tribunal does not necessarily diminish her reputation as the embodiment of fin-desiècle America's Independent Woman, the language of the letter betrays her complicity with the very patriarchal values that she was bent on deconstructing. She presents herself as a "very earnest woman" who is "somewhat apologetically" appealing to a "gentleman" for protection. She indicts Bierce for his "unmanly gossip" about "defenseless" women who lack male protectors, for "blackguarding women publicly, by name," and for engaging in other actions that were "unworthy of an officer and a gentleman." Gilman thus projects not the image of the New Woman who challenges patriarchal culture, but of the True Woman who demands that men behave as gentlemen and have proper respect for the "weaker" sex. That such an implied subscription to the Victorian code of manners should have come from the same pen as "The Yellow Wall-Paper" may be less surprising than it might seem at first, however. For as Susan Lanser contends in her provocative rereading of "The Yellow Wall-Paper," Gilman was, like the narrator of her famous story, unable to escape the "patriarchal prisonhouse"; that is, she remained convinced that "progressive" White Anglo-Saxon Protestants of both genders were natural allies, and she shared her patriarchal culture's race and class prejudices—prejudices that, as Lanser demonstrates, are inscribed in "The Yellow Wall-Paper." We must see Gilman, Lanser argues, not as an "essential" feminist but as a subject "constituted in and by the contradictions of ideology." Referring to "The Yellow Wall-Paper," Lanser asserts that the "patriarchal text and the woman's text are in some sense one. . . . The narrator's text is also the text of her culture" (Lanser 235). The same argument obtains for Gilman's letter to Matthews.

In any case, Gilman was correct in believing that Matthews might be a powerful ally in her cause. Her reference to his review of Bierce's book and to his praise of her father's story suggest that she read and respected his criticism. Certainly Gilman would have responded enthusiastically to his essay "Of Women's Novels," which appeared in September 1892, shortly before she wrote him. In that essay Matthews asserted that women writers such as Jane Austen, Charlotte Brontë, George Eliot, and Harriet Beecher Stowe were on equal footing with the best male novelists, and he urged critics to give more attention to lesser-known women writers such as Margaret Oliphant, Margaret Deland, Susanna Rowson, and Catharine Maria Sedgwick.[10] Whether or not she read the piece, Gilman apparently assumed that Matthews would share her disgust at Bierce's ridicule of women writers.

Ironically, however, Matthews's views on the "woman question" were in line with Bierce's. Gilman might have had second thoughts about entreating Matthews for help had she known that in years to come he would stubbornly resist efforts by his Columbia colleagues to allow women to enroll in his literature classes; that he would fight to prevent members of the "unfair sex" (as he once quipped) from being admitted to the National Institute and National Academy of Arts and Letters; and that he would publish in 1900 a novel, *The Action and the Word*, which portrayed the New Woman as selfish, flighty, and prone to fits of hysteria.[11] Intended, it seems, as a rebuttal to Henrik Ibsen's *A Doll House* (and perhaps to Kate Chopin's *The Awakening*), *The Action and the Word* ends with the heroine's "awakening" to the fact that she prefers the nursery to a room of her own. Ibsen, she now realizes, was an "old bore" who knew nothing about the American girl, and "a wife's duty is to wait on her husband."

Predictably, Matthews refused to be drawn into the controversy. As he replied to Gilman on October 28, 1892, "I do not see that any one as far removed from the seat of war as I am can express any opinion or make any suggestion likely to be of service to those better acquainted with the circumstances" (Matthews to Gilman, October 28, 1892). In effect, that is, the author of *The Action and the Word,* though he may have considered Bierce something less than a gentleman, dismissed out of hand Gilman's earnest request that he intervene on her behalf, and thus he became yet another male figure in whom she had misplaced her trust.

There is no evidence that Bierce was tried or punished by a literary tribunal, and his attacks on the PCWPA and female "impostors" did not abate during the years that followed. In the winter of 1892–93, in fact, he flung several darts at Adeline Knapp, a salaried writer for the *San Francisco Call,* a prominent member of the PCWPA, and perhaps more to the point, Gilman's companion at the time.

Friends since the spring of 1891, Gilman and Knapp would finally part in the summer of 1893. Deliberately or not, Bierce ridiculed them both in the throes of their breakup. In his column for December 25, 1892, for example, he described Knapp as a "horse-reporter for the *Call,* . . . the distinguished penlady from Squedunk," and added that "every woman who writes does so with one eye on her paper and the other on some man. In the case of Miss Knapp of Squedunk I have an ambition to be the man" (*SFE,* December 25, 1892).

In the same "Prattle," Bierce also made cutting reference to Gilman's pending divorce: "If Mr. Charlotte Perkins Stetson [Charles Walter Stetson] had sincerely desired not to cast reproach upon his wife," he should "have based his suit for separation upon the quality of her writing." There is no judge on the bench, he averred, who would hold one of her poems "an insufficient ground for divorce. Apart from her work in literature, she is said to be a very good man" (*SFE,* December 25, 1892).

In March 1893, he coupled the names of "Colonel Charlotte Perkins Stetson" and "Miss Adeline Knapp of Podunk" with an image of sexual perversion: they were two "battering lambs habitually engaged in breaching the foundation walls of nature" (*SFE,* March 17, 1893).[12] A few months later, Bierce abandoned all pretense at subtlety in the gender war by referring derisively to "Col. Charlie Perkins-Stetson" (*SFE,* November 12, 1893). She had been "resexed" by her literary ambitions, it seems, not merely "unsexed" by them.

In the fall of 1893, when she became editor of the Bulletin of the PCWPA, Gilman again became an inviting target for Bierce's barbs. When she complained that she was "chained to the editorial desk," he rejoined that "she is supplying the other members with a profitable example of what it is like to be connected with a newspaper" (*SFE,* October 1, 1893). After her prize-winning essay, "The Labor Movement," was published, he printed a parodic "Song of the Workman" which he claimed was "from the Colonel's pen" (*SFE,* November 12, 1893). Gilman's retorts in her magazine over the months seem pallid and bland by comparison. She again tried to respond, but to little avail: a critical review of Bierce's "revolting" stories in April 1894, a passing reference to his "foolishness" three months later.[13] "That man ought not to go unwhipped," she noted in her diary, and she submitted "things about Bierce" to the San Francisco *Star,* the *Call,* and the *Woman's Journal.*[14] Yet the first paper, a weekly, had so modest a circulation that no copy survives of the issue that contained her essay, "A Reproach to San Francisco," and the editors of the *Call* and *Woman's Journal* chose not to print her contributions. *The Impress* "corruscates in its every column, like iron under the hammer of the smith," Bierce averred shortly before the magazine suspended publication early in 1895 (*SFE,* March 3, 1895). When the suspension was formally announced, he celebrated with a sarcastic eight-line ditty:

> There is weeping in the office, there is wailing in the ways,
> In the market and the workshop is unutterable woe;
> For the woman-paper, *Impress,* hasn't lived out half its days,
> And the Colonels all are sad to see it go.
> The Stetson sits disconsolate upon the dusty press,
> While the Gaden packs the editress's incapacious trunk.
> Ah, indeed, there's some dejection and exceeding dire distress
> In Utopia. There's rapture in Podunk!
> (*SFE,* April 28, 1895)

The Sunday *Examiner* had a circulation in the tens of thousands, the *Impress* no more than a few hundred.

Only once, in February 1894, did Bierce praise Gilman, albeit by paying her a backhanded compliment. In his "Prattle" column, he described "Similar Cases"—which he claims to have stumbled upon while searching Gilman's *In This Our World* for "something to poke fun at"—as "admirable," a "delightful satire" of hidebound conservatives, adding that despite its faults, it is full of wit and spirit and is as fine a poem as some of the most admired pieces of Bret Harte. If the poet had written nothing else, he concluded, "the pleasure of reading 'Similar Cases' would lack the element of surprise" (*SFE*, February 4, 1894). Bierce "couldn't apologize gracefully," the *Stockton Mail* editorialized two days later. The "very wording" of his column betrayed the fact "that the Prattler knew little or nothing" about "the woman whom he nevertheless hooted and jeered and pelted" with mud over the months ("Bierce and Stetson" 3). Not that Bierce had changed his overall opinion of Gilman. Shortly after he praised her poem, he made a disparaging remark about her in private correspondence. Facetiously chiding his friend Blanche Partington for having the audacity to criticize him, he exclaims that she will soon "challenge Man to mortal combat in true Stetsonian style. Know thy place, thou atom!" (Pope 38). He also printed in "Prattle" a savage parody of "Similar Cases" in which "Emancipated Woman," the product of evolution, searches in vain for "Expurgated Man" (*SFE*, June 10, 1894).

Still, Gilman had the last word. In 1915, the year after Bierce disappeared in Mexico, she modeled the male villain in her utopian romance *Herland* on him, or so it seems. While on expedition, the male-supremacist rages repeatedly against the "old Colonels" he encounters in the utopia, toys with the notion of reporting its existence to "Mr. Yellow Press" (Hearst), and is finally expelled for attempted spousal rape (*Herland* 7, 20, passim).

In 1929, Bierce's first biographer wrote Gilman, who by that time had retired, to ask her impressions of him. "He was," she replied, "the Public Executioner and Tormentor, daily exhibiting his skill in grilling helpless victims for the entertainment of the public—for wages. He was an early master in the art of blackening long-established reputations of the great dead, of such living persons as were unable to hit back effectively, and at his best in scurrilous abuse of hard-working women writers. He never lost an opportunity to refer to cotton-stuffed bosoms of the women writers" (McWilliams 156).[15]

Though nearly four decades had passed since Bierce had derided her and the PCWPA in his "Prattle" columns, Gilman's animosity toward him had not softened. She remained steadfast in her view that Bierce employed his enormous power to keep struggling women writers in their place and was paid handsomely by the unscrupulous Hearst for doing so. He personified, to her mind, the most pernicious aspects of patriarchal and capitalist culture and of the "yellow" journalism that served that culture.

NOTES

An earlier version of this essay appeared in *Journal of the West* (July 1993), 52–60. Reprinted by permission.

1. Each of Bierce's "Prattle" essays in the *San Francisco Examiner* (hereafter abbreviated as *SFE*) appeared on page 6.

2. In addition to the "Prattle" columns cited elsewhere, see also "Prattle" for November 22, 1891; January 24, May 29, June 12, July 24, August 28, September 18, 1892; March 26, July 23, August 6, August 20, September 10, 1893; June 24, September 9, November 4, 1894; and May 26, December 8, 1895.

3. See Blackwell, "Gems from the Pacific Coast."

4. The letter is in the Brander Matthews Papers, Rare Book and Manuscript Library, Columbia University, New York. Permission to publish granted by Columbia and by the Arthur and Elizabeth Schlesinger Library, Radcliffe College, which holds the copyright to Gilman's unpublished papers.

5. See Brander Matthews, "More American Stories," *Cosmopolitan* 626–30. The essay reviews Bierce's *Tales of Soldiers and Civilians* along with collections of short stories by several other authors, including Henry James, Mark Twain, and Joel Chandler Harris. Though Matthews faults Bierce's tales for their "unredeemed monotony of insistent horror," his critique is very favorable overall. Bierce overcame his oft-voiced disdain for Eastern "smugwumps" and wrote Matthews a polite note of appreciation for his review (Bierce to Matthews, November 28, 1892, Brander Matthews Papers).

6. Frederic Perkins's story, the title piece of his *The Devil-Puzzlers,* is praised by Matthews in "The Philosophy of the Short-Story" 70, 93.

7. In his "Prattle" essay of October 16, 1892, Bierce ridiculed poet Ina Coolbrith, claiming that she had been fed full of local adulation and had, as a result, formed much too high an opinion of her literary abilities. Published three days before Gilman wrote Matthews, this essay was no doubt the "most recent specimen" of Bierce's "delicate touch" that she enclosed with her letter. Bierce's attack on this occasion, Coolbrith believed, had less to do with aesthetics than with her

attempts to protect her niece from his clutches (Coolbrith to Charles Warren Stoddard, October 15, 1892, in Rather, *Bittersweet* 67).

8. See Carey McWilliams, *Ambrose Bierce: A Biography* 129; Paul Fatout, *Ambrose Bierce: The Devil's Lexicographer* 188–89; and Bierce, *SFE,* May 22, 1892, and September 6, 1896. Lewis's famous attack on Howells in his Nobel Prize address echoes Bierce's "old maid" sneer.

9. See Joanne B. Karpinski, "When the Marriage of True Minds Admits Impediments: Charlotte Perkins Gilman and William Dean Howells," reprinted in this volume.

10. See Brander Matthews, *Americanisms and Briticisms with Other Essays,* 169–77.

11. See letter from Brander Matthews to Robert Underwood Johnson, January 6, 1918, American Academy and Institute of Arts and Letters; Oscar James Campbell, "The Department of English and Comparative Literature" 80; Blanche Colton Williams, "Brander Matthews—A Reminiscence" 1, 19; Brander Matthews, *The Action and the Word.*

12. See also Bierce's review of Adeline Knapp's book *One Thousand Dollars a Day* in *SFE,* March 31, 1893. Gilman's affair with Knapp is detailed in Mary A. Hill, *Charlotte Perkins Gilman* 188–93, 201–07, passim; and in Lane, *To Herland* 165–81.

13. See Gilman, *The Impress* April 1894: 5; July 1894: 3; September 1894: 1.

14. See Gilman's diaries for June 29, July 1, 3, 4, 1894.

15. See also Richard O'Connor, *Ambrose Bierce: A Biography* 138.

4
Charlotte Perkins Gilman, William Randolph Hearst, and the Practice of Ethical Journalism

Denise D. Knight

> They today of the Yellow Press
> Grow rich in hardened wantonness
> By the "nose for news" and the "enterprise"
> Of insolent shameless hireling spies....
>
> On sin and sorrow the ferret thrives;
> They finger their fellows' private lives,
> And noisily publish far and wide
> What things their fellows most fair would hide....
>
> Under the Press Power great and wide
> Their unsigned slanders cower and hide
> From outraged Justice they slink behind
> Shadowy Companies false and blind....
>
> Charlotte Perkins Gilman, "The Yellow Reporter"

In a diary entry dated February 23, 1893, American feminist author Charlotte Perkins Stetson [Gilman] (1860–1935), who was embroiled at the time in a highly publicized and controversial divorce proceeding, noted an encounter that would mark a turning point in her career: "The Examiner sends me a man, Mr. Tod [*sic*], to interview me on my views on the Marriage Question—the decrease of marriage [in society]. I refuse on the ground of the Examiner's reputation—will not write for the paper. He begs, he tries to fool me into conversation, he argues, he offers to pay me, he threatens covertly—I succeed in getting rid of him. Am exhausted by the contest, however" (*Diaries* 518).

The *San Francisco Examiner,* a William Randolph Hearst publication, did, however, print a highly inflammatory full-page news story on the subject. That article, along with another on her marital separation published by the *Examiner* the year before, so infuriated Gilman that she vowed never to write for a Hearst publication as long as she lived. In spite of being frequently courted by editors of various Hearst-owned magazines—*Cosmopolitan, Bazaar, Good Housekeeping*, and several large newspapers—and even after being assured that she would never have to see Hearst in person, Gilman remained steadfast in her refusal to be associated in any way with the vast and monopolistic Hearst empire. "When they asked for contributions," she would later write, "I always explained that nothing would induce me to appear in anything of his" (*Living* 303).

In Gilman's opinion, the newspapers and magazines published by William Randolph Hearst (1863–1951) epitomized the practice of yellow journalism in the United States. That view was echoed by numerous critics, including Oswald Garrison Villard (1872–1949), president of the *New York Evening Post*, who charged that Hearst had lowered the whole tone of American journalism "by the example and competition of one whose newspapers were not only unprincipled, but frequently dishonest" (qtd. in Debbel 129). Indeed, as Gilman argued, in its "endeavor to reach the largest number of readers," Hearst's vicious and sensationalistic stories preyed upon "the lowest average mind" ("Newspapers" 315). An eloquent champion of ethical journalism, Gilman proffered a reason for the enduring popularity of the yellow press:

> [It] frankly plays on the lowest, commonest of its traits; tickling it with salacious detail, harping on those themes which unlettered peasants find attractive, and for which most people retain an unadmitted weakness.
>
> This is the secret of our "yellow press"; and of the strange prominence given to unimportant stories of vice even in the mildly creamcolored variety. ("Newspapers" 315)

Among those "unimportant stories" trumpeted by Hearst was Gilman's impending divorce from her first husband, Charles Walter Stetson. Her earliest encounter with a Hearst-owned publication occurred in the fall of 1892, when a reporter from the *San Francisco Examiner* requested information about the divorce suit filed by Stetson on the grounds of desertion. Possessing little experience in interviews and trusting that reporters were "men and women like the rest of us, governed by similar instincts of decency and kindness," Gilman revealed to the reporter the details of her separation but naively asked that he "please not spread it about," since she wished to keep it from her dying mother, to spare her any worry (*Living* 142–43). Ignoring Gilman's request, however, the *Examiner* published a full-page story. As a result, not only were her mother's last days "further saddened by anxiety" about Gilman's future, but Gilman's "name became a football for all the papers on the coast" (143). From that moment on, Gilman refused to cooperate with any Hearst publication, either in terms of submitting to interviews or by contributing articles. Years later, when she attempted to place some of her writing with American author Theodore Dreiser, then editor of the *Delineator*, he "gloomily" suggested that she "should consider more what the editors want" (304). Gilman, however, rejected his advice. Rather than compromising both her journalistic integrity and her agenda for social change by considering "more what the editors want," Gilman instead formulated a bold new plan—to single-handedly write, edit, and publish her own monthly magazine, *The Forerunner*, in circulation from 1909 to 1916. Although she could never rival William Randolph Hearst (though that was not her aim), so determined was Gilman "to express important truths" (304), to uphold an ethical ideal in journalism, and to try to educate the news-hungry public about the corruption inherent in the yellow press, that she risked financial ruin to undertake the new venture. *The Forerunner* would become the most ambitious project of Gilman's long career as a social reformer.

A direct descendent of the celebrated Beecher family of New England, Charlotte Perkins cultivated an ethical foundation in her youth by "establishing a habit of absolute truthfulness" that she "meant to practise [with] the most meticulous accuracy" (*Living* 59). She spent much of the summer of 1882 reading Herbert Spencer's *The Data of Ethics*, and ten years later, at the age of thirty-one, became a founding member of the Oakland Ethical Society. Those early-formed values fueled Gilman's contempt for yellow journalism, particularly in cases where, from either "honest incompetence or malicious intent, the subject is 'misrepresented'" ("Interviewing" 36). "The main business of the newspaper is to furnish news—not gossip," Gilman insisted. "It may properly add advice, information, instruction, entertainment, and legitimate advertising, but when in any department it perverts its own real purposes in order to 'sell goods,' it is in the same position with the grocer who adulterates his food supplies and displays painted candy to attract children," she charged (35).

Although she was not the first writer to comment on the journalistic ethics (W. S. Lilly had published an article titled "The Ethics of Journalism" in the July 1889 *Forum* [Dicken-Garcia 8]), Gilman was certainly one of the most vociferous. Among those she denounced for perverting journalistic integrity was writer Ambrose Bierce, a columnist for the *San Francisco Examiner*.[1] A few months after helping to organize the Oakland Ethical Society, Gilman blasted Bierce for his "scurrilous and evil habits" in attacking struggling women writers with his "unmanly gossip and slander" (Oliver and Scharnhorst 53). As an active participant in the Pacific Coast Women's Press Association (PCWPA), founded in San Francisco in 1890, Gilman was particularly incensed by Bierce's relentless assaults on its members. "The point is that an able writer constantly attacks and insults defenseless women; regarding neither truth, honor, nor common decency; this all our reading public know. The Examiner stands here as an example of the corrupt and does not stand at all elsewhere! Sensational and venal press, and Mr. Bierce's Prattle is a most juicy column in the Sunday edition" (54). Despite her plea that Bierce stop committing "insufferable offense[s] with his pen" (53), his attacks on Gilman and other members of the PCWPA continued.[2]

Bierce and other reporters justified their journalistic tactics by virtue of the public's desire to know. "What if it does [desire to know]?" Gilman retorted. "A newspaper reporter has no more right to intrude upon a private family and demand information as to their private affairs than has the ice-man," she declared ("Newspapers" 316). "That a number of people have the instincts of Peeping Tom does not give them the right to intrude upon personal privacy, nor does it give that right to those papers which pander to a depraved taste, and seek continually to deprave further the taste to which it panders," she argued (316). Particularly insidious, she believed, were reporters who would stop at nothing to get a story. In March 1894, for example, the *Examiner* published yet another article on Gilman's impending divorce and also on Walter Stetson's growing relationship with Gilman's lifelong friend, Grace Ellery Channing.[3] When a reporter from the *San Francisco Call* contacted Gilman at home and asked her to respond to the *Examiner* story, she refused comment. The following day, however, Gilman called upon an unlikely sympathizer—Mrs. Phebe Elizabeth Hearst, William Randoph Hearst's mother—to vent her anger over the story. Although Mrs. Hearst did not know which reporter had written the "outrage," she was "much moved" by Gilman's visit and promised to look into it (*Diaries* 575).

In their biography, *The Hearsts,* Lindsay Chaney and Michael Cieply corroborate Gilman's version of the *Examiner's* methods of obtaining headline stories:

> *The Examiner* stopped at nothing in its zeal to create a sensation. At the behest of its frantic young publisher, the paper sent train-loads of artists and writers flying through the night to scoop its rivals on a story as routine as a hotel fire; it dispatched its report-ers to traipse through the hills in quest of grizzly bears and gun-slinging fugitives; it escorted Sarah Bernhardt on a tour of the city's opium dens . . . all for the sake of a few column inches. (32)

Gilman's autobiography offers yet another example of the *Examiner's* unprincipled conduct. After an Oakland woman, a victim of domestic violence, shot her abusive husband as he was about to attack her with an ax, the *Examiner* sent a reporter, Winifred Black, to interview the woman in jail. The woman's lawyer had warned her not to comment on the case, but Black allegedly posed as a sympathetic ally and "told the poor, frightened, remorseful little woman that she was not a reporter, that she had come because her sister had once been in prison for the same offense" (*Living* 145). Having won the woman's trust through de-ception, Black managed to get her scoop, and the story with all of its grisly details was published. In another incident involving the brutal murder of a casual acquaintance, the decedent's husband asked Gilman to speak at the funeral. When she arrived at the funeral parlor, "there stood like a row of vultures, reporters, ready to make the most of every detail and to make it all as hideous as they could—to keep up the story" (176). Gilman was infuriated when newspaper accounts of the service accused her of thrusting herself into the limelight "for the sake of noto-riety" (176).

Despite her repeated failure to cooperate with the press, or perhaps because of it, Gilman continued to find herself the subject of news stories in the *Examiner*. In June 1894, the *San Francisco Call* again sent a reporter to her home. After handing her a clipping of an *Examiner* story detailing Walter Stetson's remarriage to Grace Channing, the reporter waited for a reaction. Having already learned of the wedding in a letter from Walter and Grace, however, Gilman offered no response. The reporter persisted. "The *Call* sent me to see if you had anything to say on the subject," he said. "Do you think a self-respecting woman would have anything to say to a newspaper on such a subject?" she responded (*Living* 167–68). The reporter left without his story, and the *Call*, "at the time a decent newspaper," simply reprinted the *Examiner* story without additional commentary (168).

Gilman's battle with Hearst continued even after her death by suicide in 1935, as her daughter, Katharine Stetson Chamberlin, assumed her mother's cause. When Gilman's literary agent, Willis Kingsley Wing, attempted to serialize her posthumously published autobiography, *The Living of Charlotte Perkins Gilman*, in the Hearst-owned *Cosmopolitan* magazine, Chamberlin was incensed. To Wing she wrote that "no Hearst publications were eligible" for serialization. "Perhaps my mother failed to tell you her lifelong stand against all Hearst publications," she remarked. "Ther [*sic*] is quite a little in her book about it all," she continued (Chamberlin to Wing, August 30, 1935). And to Gilman's cousin and literary executor, Lyman Beecher Stowe, Chamberlin complained, "Of course if [Mr. Wing] had had an offer from a monthly other than a Hearst publication, I would have gladly accepted," she wrote (Chamberlin to Stowe, August 30, 1935). "And I really don't see how he could have known Mama without knowing her feeling for Hearst," she continued, implicitly questioning Wing's integrity. Although the serialization could have been potentially lucrative, Chamberlin respected her mother's wishes.

After Gilman's experiences with Hearst-owned publications in the early 1890s, she resolved to uphold ethical standards in her own forays into newspaper writing. In the summer of 1894, she assumed the management of the *Impress*, a California literary weekly, which had previously been published by the PCWPA as the *Bulletin*. Gilman hoped to make the *Impress* into a "good family weekly" which would be "varied and interesting" (*Living* 171, 177), but the publication lasted for only twenty weeks. A "clean and handsome paper," judged by "a competent critic as the best ever published on the [west] coast" (173), the *Impress* became a casualty of the public reaction against Gilman's unconventional lifestyle.

According to her account in *The Living*, the paper's demise was a result of the bias expressed by "the San Francisco mind" that found her reputation intolerable (173). Not only was Gilman a divorcée, but she was also branded an unnatural mother after relinquishing custody of her then-nine-year-old daughter to Walter Stetson. Adding to the public condemnation was Gilman's decision to publish in the *Impress* a poem, "a beautiful poem, of a nobly religious tendency" (173) by Grace Channing Stetson—Walter Stetson's new bride. Embittered by the public outcry condemning her choices, Gilman left California a few months later and spent much of the next five years on the lecture circuit.

During that period, Gilman published *Women and Economics* (1898), the magnum opus of her long career. Winning international acclaim from the publication's instant popularity, Gilman received numerous solicitations for journalistic contributions at the turn of the century. It was only a matter of time, however, before Gilman found herself rejecting requests, as William Randolph Hearst acquired ownership of an ever-growing collection of popular publications. Initially, "there were ever so many who asked for my work," Gilman reported in her autobiography (302). For instance, "James Brisbane Walker of the *Cosmopolitan*, before it became Hearst's *Cosmopolitan*, was more than cordial; Margaret Sangster of the *Bazaar*, before it became Hearst's *Bazaar*, was very kind; Mr. Towers of *Good Housekeeping*, before it became Hearst's *Good Housekeeping*, was very interested in my stuff," Gilman lamented (302–03). She remained adamant, however, in her refusal to write for any Hearst publications. At one point, she was approached by "a very nice young man" about writing for *Cosmopolitan*. She had some difficulty convincing him that her rejection of his offer, for which she would have been well compensated, was not merely the result of "some personal dislike" toward Hearst but rather that it was his unscrupulous methods, both in obtaining stories and in reporting them, that she found intolerable (303). "My refusal was not based on my own experience alone," she insisted, "but on the well-known character of the Hearst papers and methods" (*Living* 145).

When she launched the publication of *The Forerunner* in 1909, therefore, Gilman strove to educate her readers not only on social issues but on matters of ethical import as well—not the least of which was her condemnation of the practice of yellow journalism. In numerous essays and commentaries published during *The Forerunner*'s seven-year run, Gilman frequently took swipes at the very visible William Randolph Hearst, whose muckraking tactics helped to sell newspapers.

In a two-part essay titled "Newspapers and Democracy," published in the November and December 1916 issues of *The Forerunner*, Gilman affirmed the value of the press, writing that "no social function today [is] more important than The Press" (300). But "every social function," she continued, "is liable to its own excesses, perversions, and diseases," the popular press being no exception. Gilman featured several examples of the gross misuse of the press, which made it subject to "tyranny," "corruption," and "falsehood." Likening the potential abuses of a newspaper editor to those of a "despotic monarch," Gilman recounted her own experience with Harry Todd of the *San Francisco Examiner* and maintained that, although "the tremendous power of the press is essential to its function and [needs] to be preserved, . . . it should be safeguarded at every point so that it might never be used by private malice or private greed" (303). But perhaps the greatest evil, she suggested, was in "the suppression, misstatement, falsification, and fabrication of 'the news.'" "The majority of our papers," she wrote, "are 'special pleaders.' . . . Instead of faithfully setting before the public facts in the case, that the public may be fairly informed and use its own judgment . . . [they] too often . . . [present] their own views, buttressed by selected facts, as seem most useful" (303).

In part two of the essay, Gilman entertained the question, "What makes an item newsworthy?" and charged that not only did many contemporary editors have difficulty in discriminating "between fact and fiction" but that most "endeavor to furnish as an attraction [a] glowing list of accidents and crimes" (314). She wrote:

These pages and pictures and floods of words about some murder, unsavory divorce case, or the like, are furnished as entertainment, to please the reader, to secure subscribers. The news involved is merely "At 12:30 last night, at 41 M[ain] Street, John Smith fatally shot his wife Mary." The "particulars" belong to the police gazette, to special study by criminologists. What the people need to know about Murder is how much of it there is among us, does it increase or decrease, how can it be prevented.

There is no reason whatever why they should be given detailed information as to "where the body lay"—that is not news. "It interests them" say the papers, and so admit that they are misrepresenting the news in order to sell papers. News is not necessarily amusing; its value is quite aside from that quality. (316)

As the press grew, Gilman reasoned, it "succumbed to the abuses of power, as does the crown, the church, the army—any social function. It has never been safe to give any person or group of persons too much power," she concluded (315). Again, some twenty-five years after first being subjected to his "abuse," the main target of Gilman's wrath was still William Randolph Hearst. "For one man to own and dominate a great paper or group of papers is more insidiously dangerous," she contended, "than to have him dominate railroads, churches, or armed men. Private ownership of public utilities is mischievous enough, as we are rapidly learning; but the press is in no true sense 'a business,' it is an educational function, like the school or college" (315).

In a short article appearing in the September 1914 issue of *The Fore-runner,* Gilman was even more direct in her contempt for Hearst. Citing some of the apparent inconsistencies in Hearst's publicly stated position on the politically sensitive issue of war and peace, Gilman's commentary, titled "From a Hearst Paper," was riddled with sarcasm:

I have received a telegram—a long night letter—full of windy words about the advancement of humanity, asking me to enroll my name as one of an International Committee to be gathered together in the interests of Universal Peace—reply by wire, paid by them.

And who do you imagine is getting up this great Committee? What noble-spirited citizen, what power making for righteousness, what beneficent engine of civilization?

The proposition comes from *The Chicago Examiner*—one of the chain of papers owned and managed by Mr. William R. Hearst!

This man, whose papers have always flamed with frantic jingoism, who has used his enormous power to do all that was possible to promote the Spanish war, who has in every way fomented all our difficulties with Japan; who, but a few weeks since, openly tried to force on the war with Mexico, now takes the present opportunity to pose as a promoter of peace!

Everyone is shocked at the Pan-European war. Everyone would like it stopped. Appeal then to the popular feeling and make credit for the beneficent Hearst newspapers as champions of human progress!

I have not replied. It would be hardly fair to expect a Hearst paper to pay for my opinion of it. (251)

An outspoken proponent of free speech, the place for it, Gilman maintained, was exclusively on the editorial page of a newspaper or magazine. "In the news columns there should be no 'freedom' other than that required to furnish the news," and the presentation of that news should be consistent in all of the various papers. Particularly important to Gilman was the right to personal privacy. "The importance to the public of a free press," she wrote, is "first, that the press may set forth facts necessary to be known; and second, that the press may be free to express opinion on the facts. But it is not in the least necessary, not in any way important or useful, for the public to be provided with the information as to how many buttons there may be on a great man's pajamas" ("Newspapers" 316).

Contributing to the proliferation of yellow journalism, Gilman insisted, was the attendant desensitization of the reading public, which had grown accustomed to "an ever lower standard of journalistic decency." While she conceded "that even the worst of [the newspapers] do some good," that good could never balance "the evil they do." Only when the reading public acknowledged the damage done by the yellow press, and ceased to support it, could a "legitimate press" emerge. "We need to establish the evil results, to show that the good could be accomplished without the evil, and then to take strong measures to protect society against this depraving influence" (317–18).

Gilman's sentiments were echoed by American journalist Lincoln Steffens (1866–1936), managing editor of *McClure's Magazine,* in his article "Hearst, the Man of Mystery." "There isn't room even for a list of good things Mr. Hearst has done or tried to do," he wrote. Steffens added, "There isn't room either for a list of the bad, the small things he has done; the scandals he has published, the individuals he has made to suffer beyond their deserts. He has sent his reporters slumming among the rich; he has pandered to the curiosity about the vice and wickedness of wealth. His papers 'appealed to the people'; yes, to the 'best interest,' and to their worst."

With the introduction of *The Forerunner*, Gilman intended to demonstrate that news and commentary could be reported in an informative and objective manner. Even though there were already a number of magazines in print that addressed themselves to issues of concern to women, such as Alice Stone Blackwell's suffrage publication, the *Woman's Journal*, or the narrowly conceived and gender-specific monthlies such as the *Ladies' Home Journal* and Hearst's *Good Housekeeping*, *The Forerunner* broke new ground. While the majority of the 1,500 subscribers were women, Gilman insisted that the magazine was about "people. . . . It treat[s] all three phases of our existence, male, female, and human" (*Forerunner*, November 1909, 32).

Not only did *The Forerunner* advocate human rights, but it also became a vehicle through which Gilman could call for social reform. On the pages of *The Forerunner*, she proselytized on topics ranging from venereal diseases and prostitution to the need for child labor laws and academic freedom. Every *Forerunner* was filled with candid discussions of topics affecting the quality of human life—the crucial need for economic and reproductive freedoms; pleas for safer and more affordable housing; calls for environmental awareness. The unique blend of feminism and socialism featured in *The Forerunner* was inextricably linked to Gilman's firm belief in the potential growth of humanity through productive thought and honest work.

In addition to essays on current social issues, *The Forerunner*, which sold for ten cents a copy or a dollar a year, also boasted annually one complete novel, one nonfiction book, several short articles, a dozen or more poems, twelve short sermons, commentary on various news items, numerous book reviews, and twelve short stories. In an attempt to champion various causes, including the practice of ethical journalism, Gilman often used *Forerunner* fiction to advance her arguments. In the April 1916 issue, for example, she included a short story, titled "His Excuse," to not only reflect her contempt for the disreputable reporters who distorted facts about her personal life on numerous occasions but also to censure the abuses of freedom of speech, which she found wholly reprehensible.[4]

The central character in "His Excuse" is Norman Parker, a talented young reporter who "set forth boldly to face the apprenticeship for his Life['s] Work." Parker proved so competent, Gilman tells us, "that he was offered better pay to do similar work on one of the Hearst papers." The narrative continues: "Parker was not in favor of this grade of journalism, but, he told himself, a man must not let his prejudices hinder his advancement. . . . Spurred by his editors, praised and well-paid for his successes, insensibly lowering his standards as his work required it, and convincing himself by easy arguments and the press of opinion all around him that what he did was essential to the profession—and so quite justifiable, he became a star reporter" (87–88). It was precisely this brand of star reporter that Gilman found contemptible, and she relished the fact that while living in California in the early 1890s, she had "thirteen times . . . the pleasure of refusing them, and many times since, in more than one of Mr. Hearst's enlarging list of publications" (*Living* 144–45).

While taking every opportunity to damn both the character of the Hearst empire and their reportorial methods, Gilman made certain that although freedom of expression was the mainspring of *The Forerunner,* the professionalism of the publication was never compromised and no single individual was defamed in any way. So critical was the issue of integrity, in fact, that despite the loss of revenue, Gilman refused to advertise products that she could not personally endorse (*Living* 305).

In her autobiography, Gilman recalled that the very mission of *The Forerunner* encountered considerable opposition because it departed so radically from conventional wisdom. "So general an attack," she wrote, "upon what we have long held incontrovertible must needs have met misunderstanding and opposition. If the world had been able to easily receive it then it would not have been necessary. The clear logic of the position, the reasoning which supported it, made small impression on the average mind" (*Living* 310). Yet the central "purpose" of the paper seemed innocuous enough; it strove to "stimulate thought; to arouse hope, courage and impatience; to offer practical suggestions and solutions, to voice strong assurance of better living, here [and] now" (*Forerunner,* November 1909, 32).

As the magazine drew to a close at the end of 1916, when Gilman finally conceded that the financial burden made it impossible to continue, she presented her readers with a retrospective synopsis of what she had set out to accomplish. Whether she was addressing dress reform, economic disparity between the genders, or the ongoing problem of yellow journalism, the common ideological denominator for Gilman was the power of each individual to effect change. "Our dawning social consciousness finds us bound, suffering, thwarted, crippled in many ways," she wrote in the November 1916 issue. "The more we see the possible joy of human living, the more painful become present conditions—if unchangeable. But they are changeable," she insisted (290).

And change, of course, was what Charlotte Perkins Gilman believed was necessary in the press. Undoubtedly, Gilman's boycott against Hearst was costly in terms of both some much-needed financial security and reaching a potentially enormous reading audience with her ideas. But Gilman's principles were inexorable. Moreover, in spite of the fact that the details of her personal life were frequently printed in various publications, her condemnation of the yellow press was not simply a personal or self-serving reaction to the invasion of privacy. Rather, she felt that the acceptance of the yellow press was an indignity against all of society that should not be tolerated by the reading public. Her plea for the practice of ethical journalism was intended, ultimately, to serve every human being. Locking horns with the very powerful William Randolph Hearst and developing her own magazine were just two of the means by which Charlotte Perkins Gilman hoped to transform American journalism. Unquestionably, she would be deeply saddened by the proliferation of tabloid journalism to which we are exposed today.

Notes

This essay was originally published in *American Journalism* 2.4 (fall 1994): 336–47. Reprinted by permission.

1. See Lawrence J. Oliver and Gary Scharnhorst's essay reprinted in this volume on the acrimonious relationship between Gilman and Bierce.

2. In his "Prattle" column in the June 24, 1894, edition of the *Examiner,* for example, Bierce made some disparaging remarks about Gilman's edition of verse, *In This Our World,* first published in 1893. Gilman noted in her diary entry for June 29, 1894, that she had "read Bierce's last Sunday abomination. That man ought not to go unwhipped," she remarked (*Diaries* 590).

3. See Cynthia J. Davis's essay in this volume on the triangular relationship among Charlotte Stetson, Grace Ellery Channing, and Charles Walter Stetson.

4. Another good example of Gilman's fictional treatment of the yellow press can be found in "An Unwilling Interview" in the April 1912 issue of *The Forerunner* 85–89. The story was later reprinted in the March 29, 1913, edition of the *Woman's Journal,* 98–99.

5
"The Overthrow" of Gynaecocentric Culture

Charlotte Perkins Gilman and Lester Frank Ward

Judith A. Allen

> I want to thank you so much for the *Man-Made World,* and especially for the Dedication, which I esteem a great honor, albeit couched in too extravagant terms. . . . No one is doing as much as you to propagate the truth about the sexes, as I have tried to set it forth. . . . How I would enjoy a good talk with you.
>
> Lester Frank Ward, letter to Charlotte Perkins Gilman, February 11, 1911

> The civilized world is a "man-made" world: for this statement we have the authority of the foremost American feminist [Charlotte Perkins Gilman] who ought to be on her guard lest women do not unmake it. . . . The idea suggested especially by the term "matriarchate" or "matriarchy," of mother rule, is unobjectionable if confined strictly to the rule of mothers over their children; but extended as it generally is, in parallelism with "patriarchy" to mean the rule of women over men (more definitely expressed by "gynaecocracy"), the implication is false; for there is no evidence, not even in Egypt, that women ever ruled over anything but children.
>
> Correa Moylan Walsh, *Feminism* 81–82

Charlotte Perkins Gilman, America's foremost Progressive Era feminist theorist, embraced reform Darwinism. Transcending the liberal individual-rights tradition of nineteenth-century Anglo-American feminism, she argued that women's subjection to men within the era's androcentric culture hijacked evolutionary progress (Palmeri 114–15). Scholarly consensus is that Gilman was a Wardian—a follower of reform Darwinist and Neo-Lamarckian sociologist Lester Frank Ward (1841–1913) (Egan 106).[1]

Ward's "gynaecocentric theory," explaining the rise of androcentric culture, engaged Progressive Era feminists such as Eliza Burt Gamble, Jane Johnstone Christie, Catherine Gasquoine Hartley, Otis Tufton Mason, Rosa Obermeyer Mayreder, Scott Nearing and Nellie Nearing, and Anna Garlin Spencer. Ward's hypothesis addressed an explanatory gap in Darwin's theories. Presenting male sex selection as a given of *human* evolution, Darwin had overlooked the need to explain female sex selection in other mammals, so colorfully depicted in his 1871 classic, *The Descent of Man and Evolution in Relation to Sex*. Ward held that women's original selection of stronger, larger, smarter, and more handsome mates led to human encephalization (brain development) and rationality. But then males, desiring constant rather than periodic coitus—in line with their function as fertilizers and motivated by belated discovery of paternity—subjugated women through rape and violence and installed male sex selection, with all its dire consequences.

Commentators provide a mixed portrayal of Gilman and Ward's relationship. Polly Wynn Allen claims that Ward gave Gilman "a sense of belonging to a vanguard of intellectuals" (P. Allen 43). Mary Armfield Hill depicts Ward as Gilman's lifelong mentor, their relationship one of mutual admiration, though she also cites more ambiguous evidence: "Ward only reluctantly acknowledged her support, and that after considerable prodding" (*Charlotte Perkins Gilman* 264–65, 266). Gilman considered herself his longtime (but by him unacknowledged) defender. With further prodding Ward offered her this acknowledgment using a sculptural analogy: he had merely blocked out the statue from the slab, telling his sociologist nephew by marriage, Edward Alsworth Ross (1866–1951), that he would have to "finish it up." Then "you come along and touch it up with a fine-pointed chisel" (Ward to Gilman, February 9, 1907).[2] This tribute was generous yet distinctly ambiguous.

Hill speculates that "Ward may have been pleased (or was he annoyed?) that at least through Gilman's work his ideas would reach a far wider audience than they otherwise would have," noting the seven printings and multiple language translations of her most famous work, *Women and Economics* (1898), compared with Ward's *Dynamic Sociology* (1883), which sold only 500 copies over ten years (267). For her part, though publicly deferring to Ward, Gilman wrote her fiancé, George Houghton Gilman (1866–1932), about Ward in terms Hill calls "casual," reporting that she had not read Ward's most important texts prior to beginning *Women and Economics* in 1897, asking Houghton if she should do so and insisting on the originality of those of her arguments likened to Ward's (Gilman to Houghton Gilman, September 18, 1897). She declared: "I wrote the brood Mare long before I met Ward. I've been thinking those things—and much more—for many years," as if to undercut the charge that she was a mere disciple (Gilman to Houghton Gilman, July 22, 1897).

Ann J. Lane judges Gilman's claim "that Ward's philosophy was hers first as an adolescent" as overblown—the debt to Ward being clear throughout her work, some texts such as *Human Work* (1904) "essentially paraphrasing" him (Lane 57, 277). Nonetheless, Lane insists that Gilman "went beyond Ward's theories to envision a fully structured, cooperative, socialized world" (231). Alternatively, Ann Palmeri attributes Gilman's unwarranted obscurity precisely to her borrowing "from Lester Ward many of the ideas that buttressed her claims about the female half of the species"—ideas subsequently discredited by scientific skepticism about evolutionary thought (Palmeri 98). Historian of sociology Mary Jo Deegan calls Gilman vastly influenced by Ward, yet "Ward generally failed to acknowledge Gilman's brilliant non-fiction works in his writings" (Deegan 16).

Such inconclusive commentary suggests that closer scrutiny of Gilman and Ward's complex relationship of identification, exchange, and disavowal is warranted. Issues here entailed include: influence and originality, recognition and respect, education and sex discrimination, gender and professional status, and competing trajectories in the history of science. An interrogation of the Gilman-Ward correspondence, in relation to their relevant writings, can illuminate more precisely the significance of Ward's theories in Gilman's theoretical corpus.

Despite her reputation as a Wardian, Gilman engaged more selectively and critically with his theories than scholars have realized, challenging his periodization, causality, and hypothesis of a violent androcentric overthrow of gynaecocentric culture. According more agency to women than does Ward, her alternative hypotheses featured economic causes in posing substantial objections to his theory of women's subjugation. Proposing original and subversive revisions, she exceeded the role of disciple, in particular by hypothesizing the emergence of voluntary matriarchal polygyny, from which the worst of androcentric male characteristics resulted as an unintended side effect. The differences between their theories, then, are the subject of this essay's second section.

Their exchanges are illuminated further when viewed alongside Ward's exchanges with other Progressive Era women with whom he pursued more than *theoretical* "sexuo-social relations," scandalizing his invalid second wife's family. Championing women, this "ladies' man" enjoyed the role of gallant rescuer and sentimental pedagogue, preferring women like Gilman (and others) in the roles of poet, muse, helpmeet, translator, or biographer. Conversely, he proved inhospitable to their expectations of his respect for their theoretical work.

Gilman began an admiring friendship with Ward, at his initiation, in 1895, describing herself, like him, as a sociologist (Scott 106). Her widely reprinted evolutionary poem, "Similar Cases," caught his attention. He wrote her in Chicago, where she and reformer Helen Campbell (1839–1918) were at the time part of Jane Addams's settlement movement.[3] Seeking further copies of her 1893 poetry book, *In This Our World*, he invited her to meet him at home during the upcoming 1896 Washington, D.C., woman suffrage convention (Ward to Gilman, December 28, 1895). She was "exceedingly proud" of his interest in her poetry. He had used her verses in an 1896 attack on the theories and arguments of Benjamin Kidd (1856–1916), both in a lecture "pitching into Kidd the obscure" and in an article he published in *The Nation*.[4] She anticipated a mutually amiable alliance gleefully: "I felt like the stone in David's sling—supposing said stone too had a grudge against the giant!—and chuckling as it sped" (Gilman to Ward, January 1, 1896). Urging her to come "unfettered by duties," he was "counting on a charming visit" with her "now that I learn that you are so near to Mrs. Helen Campbell whom I have long known and admired." Listing guests to be assembled in her honor, he wanted "a good talk with you myself," a great honor for "your appreciative admirer" (Ward to Gilman, December 28, 1895).

Thereafter, Ward forwarded her his pamphlets, article offprints, and reviews, educating her on debates in reform Darwinism and sociology (Gilman to Ward, January 16, 1896). She constantly requested more: "Can't you get Dr. Baker to send me the pamphlet you spoke of? 'The Ascent of Man'? I want so much to see it" (Gilman to Ward, February 10, 1896). She asked him to send her his review of Veblen's *Theory of the*

Leisure Class (1899) (Gilman to Ward, April 18, 1901). Mentioning her friendship with Ross, Ward's principal professional confidant, she thanked him for his review of Ross's books (Gilman to Ward, July 22, 1908). She spoke of her other social scientist friends in Jane Addams's circle, such as Prof. Earl Barnes (1861–1935) (Gilman to Ward, January 1, 1896). Appreciating Ward's sources on ethics and "somebody's Principles of Sociology," she reported on her trip to England, including a few days visiting naturalist Alfred Russell Wallace (1823–1913), who arranged and chaired a lecture for her: "I felt so small—to stand up and lecture before that great man! He spoke of you most warmly" (Gilman to Ward, December 10, 1896). In Ward's 1897 article "Collective Telesis," he cited her on people's irrational resistance to imagining reformed future societies, through her "remarkable poem . . . 'Similar Cases'" (815).

Who was Ward for Gilman to so admire him? Born in 1841, the tenth child of a poor Illinois farming family, after negligible schooling and working as an agricultural laborer Ward married a shoemaker's daughter, Lizzie Caroline Vought, in 1862 before enlisting in the Civil War and being wounded three times in 1863. Their son, Roy Fontaine, born in June 1865, died in May 1866 from pneumonia, ending Ward's experience of fatherhood. Doggedly seeking a veterans' civil service post in Washington, D.C., then provision of night-college education for veteran civil servants like himself at the Columbian College (forerunner of George Washington University), Ward pursued education, self-improvement, and his dream of becoming a wealthy respectable professional man (Scott 16).

Earning a bachelor of arts degree in 1869, at twenty-eight years of age, he secured a bachelor of law degree by 1871. Failing to establish a practice, he attained a master of arts degree in 1872 and then concentrated upon natural science. His beloved wife suddenly died of appendicitis in March 1872, plunging him into a deep depression. Within the year he remarried, a young New York City widow, Rose Simons Pierce, who thereafter devoted herself to advancing his career.[5] Under the patronage of Maj. John Wesley Powell, Ward eventually became head paleobotanist with the new United States Geological Survey, while also developing the new field of American sociology and publishing numerous articles and books during the 1880s. From the 1890s, he became a key consultant on *Webster's Dictionary*, president of the Institute International de Sociologie in 1903, and then of its counterpart the American Sociological Association in 1905 (Scott 34–35, 37). Finally, in 1907, at the age of 66, he became Brown University's first chair of sociology, remaining until his death in 1913.

Ward became a favorite of women's rights advocates in the 1880s.[6] In 1888 he published "Our Better Halves," which was based on his "Sex Equality" talk at the Six O'Clock Club in Washington, D.C., where the audience included Elizabeth Cady Stanton (1815–1902) and Susan B. Anthony (1820–1906). Human history, Ward argued, had been a "prolonged struggle on the part of man to escape the tyranny of woman." Males, originally puny fertilizers who evolved to provide reproductive diversity, were eaten by cruel wives, as with spiders, or as drones treated contemptuously by queen bees, or as mayflies allotted but one day of mating, only to die of starvation. Then female birds became "so capricious and fastidious that they would have nothing to do with men unless they had some peculiarity that they imagined to be pretty . . . a crest of feathers, some bright gaudy color, long handsome tail feathers . . . or strong beaks or spurs that they could fight with." Because females selected the biggest and strongest, males acquired "great strength, size and fighting power." Then women "got somewhat higher ideas," choosing mates for "sagacity." Theatrically, Ward declared: "Ah! What a mistake! Slavery is incompatible with intelligence, and cunning was soon used as a means of throwing off the yoke. . . . At some point in this history, woman was compelled to surrender her scepter into the hands of man" ("Six O'Clock Club Speech" 8–11).[7]

Ward later called "Our Better Halves" the first "authorized statement of the gynaecocentric theory" (*Pure Sociology* 297). He refuted misogynist scientific and popular denunciations of women's rights and of sex equality as unnaturally countering evolutionary progress. His retrospective suggestion that the 1888 article offered a full general theory of women's oppression, however, overstates its contribution, though it did offer a simple, compelling proposition: far from natural, women's present inferiority was the result of the ending of female sex selection and its replacement by male sex selection among humans, a state of sexual relations "widely abnormal, warped, and strained by a long line of curious influences, chiefly psychic." Males provided "variability and adaptability," but the attempt "to move the whole race forward by elevating only the sex that represents the principle of instability, has long enough been tried." Instead he insisted: "The female sex is primary in both point of origin and of importance in the history and economy of organic life. . . . Woman is the unchanging trunk of the great genealogic tree; while man, with all his vaunted superiority, is but a branch. . . . Woman is the race, and the race can only be raised up as she is raised up. . . . Nature has no intentions, and evolution has no limits. True science teaches that the elevation of woman is the only sure road to the evolution of man" ("Our Better Halves" 268, 274–75).

These arguments popularized twenty years of work on the woman question, the need for a fuller explanation of women's oppression preoccupying him. Criticizing evolutionary anthropologists' theories of matriarchy and patriarchy, Ward hypothesized an ancient history of mother-centered cultures with large, strong females and reproduction-oriented sexual periodicity governed by female sex selection. Judging the prevailing matriarchy/patriarchy literature presentist and lacking sufficiently ample and critical theories of human social and sexual development, his bold theory cast human society as originally "gynaecocentric," wherein female sex selection determined parenthood and heredity (*Dynamic Sociology* 614–19, 649–55). Outlining the rise of man-centered culture with male sex selection determining population attributes, he advocated ending women's subordination and the establishment of true monogamy based upon *mutual* sex selection.

More significant, Ward hypothesized more precisely than had his predecessors the establishment and consequences for women of male domination. As a Lamarckian, he held that humans inherited culturally and behaviorally acquired characteristics of their forebears. Human males wrested sex selection from women through encephalization and used rationality and imagination to change female sexual habits. With constant rather than periodic sexual desire, man overcame "the apathies and aversions which nature gives her as a protection to her sex," appealing to woman's imagination to sexually arouse her "at times when pure instinct forbade it" ("On Male Sex Selection" 75).

Sexual mismatch—one sex governed by sexual periodicity, the other by constant and indiscriminate desire—set "natural" conditions for prostitution. The male was "able to secure submission at such times in exchange for other favors which he could confer" even outside estrus periods.[8] True to Lamarck, he held that "the constant exercise of these influences upon woman from generation to generation has . . . resulted in the radical differences between human species and the lower animals, proportional to degree of social organization and material prosperity" (*Dynamic Sociology* 608).

Women's loss of the "scepter" of sex selection wrought consequences beyond modification of female corporeality. Women's enslavement unleashed an array of "sexuo-social" inequities in dress, duties, education, and rights. Their embellished dress was chosen not for utility but to gratify their sexual masters. Women performed the bulk of domestic labor *and* the lowest status of nondomestic labor refused by men. Denied equal education and career opportunities, women everywhere were "destitute of both intellectual energy and aspiration" (646). They lacked men's legal, suffrage, and citizenship rights, while imposed sex divisions of labor and resources fostered female dependence, heightened by rape and violence, installing male sexual selection. Polygamy, marriage, prostitution, and other forms of female degradation followed.

With *Pure Sociology* (1903), Ward extended his narrative of the overthrow of female sex-selection, his lengthy chapter 14 judged the most complete statement of his gynaecocentric theory. He attempted a more exact explanation of *how* female subjugation replaced the ancient natural order of female-sex selection and mother-centered cultures. He called this new regime "androcracy," its cultural formations, philosophy, and customs "androcentric." Enlarged brain mass—and with it the rational faculty—literally became a secondary sexual characteristic. Rationality permitted men to overcome instinct in pursuit of other desires, but "a disproportionate share of the increment acquired went to the male," permitting men "to violate the restraints of instinct and inaugurate a regime wholly different from that of the animal world" (*Pure Sociology* 335).

This ascendancy over the animal kingdom occurred prior to the evolution of sympathy, sentiment, or morality. Hence, man cruelly employed superior force, "in exacting from woman whatever satisfaction she could yield him." The timing and process of this change were striking. "The first blow that he struck in this direction wrought the whole transformation. The aegis and palladium of the female sex had been from the beginning her power of choice. This rational man set about wresting from woman . . . and for the mother of mankind all was lost" (335). Unlike his earlier descriptions of the change as gradual, Ward now posed it as sudden. Males being larger and stronger than females facilitated this transfer of power, essentially via violence and rape, followed by marriage, enshrining men's proprietorship in women, with the wife's unreciprocated vow of obedience. Indeed, marriage began as "an institution for the more complete subjugation and enslavement of women and children" (353).

The precipitation of men's use of rationality in a forceful uprising against women was early man's realization of the connection between coupling and reproduction. Discovering his own fatherhood, man became unwilling to permit woman to completely control offspring. He forcibly seized mothers and children, instituting marriage and families— "the patriarchate"—which by 1903 Ward held was established by violent sexual abuse of women. Of course, Ward could not demonstrate on what fine day some man or men made this realization, or exactly what caused it, beyond its general encephalization framework. Yet, the fact that "primitive" peoples existed in the Progressive Era, unable to make the causal connection between coitus and pregnancy, confirmed his faith that the discovery of paternity was both an evolutionary and epistemological matter (340).

As the foremost Progressive Era academic critic of women's subjection, Ward naturally interested Gilman who, though formally uneducated, authored the era's most acclaimed work on the woman question. That she should be eager to secure his support, friendship, and even respect cannot be surprising. She confided to Ward her history and vulnerabilities, especially the insecurities of her position as an autodidact. In 1900, she requested sociological sources to supplement a new Italian edition of *Women and Economics,* her publisher seeking her "authorities" list: "My principal authority is you—but I have read a number of works on sociological lines . . . —without definitely remembering them. You know my head has been weak for fifteen years or so. Could you, who know the field, and who have read my book give me a little list of reliable authorities [to] bear out my position" (Gilman to Ward, November 28, 1900). This appeal recalled her request for a list of authorities by which she could educate herself, made when she was eighteen years old of her librarian father, Frederic Beecher Perkins (1828–1899), who had deserted the family in her childhood. The 1878 list he sent—including "Rawlinson's Five Great Empires . . . Dawkin's Cave Hunting . . . Lubbock, Pre-Historic Times, Origin of Civilization . . . Tylor, Early Hist. Of Mankind, Primitive Culture . . . Grote's Greece and then Momsen's

Rome"—well prepared her for Ward's critique of early anthropological theories of matriarchy and patriarchy (Perkins to Gilman, October 15, 1878).[9]

At nineteen years her senior, the authoritative Ward could have approximated a father-figure to help legitimate her aspiration to theorize and challenge women's oppression. She offered herself as both petitioner and disciple: "I think I have advanced nothing that conflicts with your teaching—have I? So if you'll tell me some of the best authorities on sociological development . . . who do not disagree with you—they will serve the desired end." She did not wish to appear to have invented her facts "as well as propounded an especial theory" (Gilman to Ward, November 28, 1900).

Often she wrote Ward deferential or self-deprecating letters, a response he seems to have aroused in many women. Apparently, he had charged her with being unfamiliar with his books. Her response, however, would have been cold comfort to a scholar expecting a close, appreciative reading: "Did you really think I did not know your books? I own the *Dynamic Sociology* and mean to have the "Psychic Factors" some time. And you should hear me refer other people to them!!" (Gilman to Ward, January 15, 1901). Gilman repeatedly explained that her mental difficulties obstructed serious study, confining her reading to only the more journalistic and brief of his works. In response, he constantly asserted that work pressures prevented him from reading hers (Ward to Gilman, January 3, 1907).

In 1900, she pointedly announced that she was no longer "Mrs. Stetson." Ward asked about her new marriage at the age of thirty-nine to her cousin George Houghton Gilman (six years her junior), compared with her former marriage to the troubled and highly patriarchal Charles Walter Stetson (1858–1911):[10] "How do I like it this time? Very well indeed thank you. Circumstances alter cases. Strong-minded girls should be allowed to 'sow their wild oats'—have their work free and full and have it early—they'll be willing enough to marry later." Wishing to discuss many subjects with him, she self-deprecatingly referred to her own work: "I've been writing a scrap of a thing on 'Man as a Factor in Social Evolution' and another on 'The Persistence of Primitive Tendencies in the Domestic Relation'"—probably early drafts of her text, *The Home: Its Work and Influence* (1903). Had he seen her new book, *Concerning Chil-*

dren? "It is comparatively slight and uneven, a book of essays" (Gilman to Ward, January 15, 1901).

Her deference halted, however, with the 1903 publication of Ward's *Pure Sociology*, its 126-page chapter on sexual relations setting forth his "gynaecocentric theory": "We bought *Pure Sociology* at once—I already have the *Dynamic Sociology*—and I pitched into that Woman chapter first because you asked me to tell you what I thought of it. . . . Now I am trying to arrange with some big magazine to write an article on that tremendous theory of yours—it ought to be popularized at once. Will you tell me if anyone else is doing it anywhere? And what in your judgment would be the best place for such an article?" (Gilman to Ward, June 30, 1903). Here she jettisoned disciple for aspiring manager. By 1904, she had worked as editor of several journals and magazines, as well as regularly placed her own work out for publication in a wide array of periodicals.[11] Her hard-won negotiating skills, she believed, could assist in publicizing Ward's theories. Although lacking his academic credentials, she could master the commercial publishing world and thereby earn his admiration and respect. Her desire for his recognition, however, was not satisfied by this proposal alone. She demanded that he acknowledge that they were both on the same mission on "the woman question"— implicitly, that she was his peer.

Five years after her acclaimed and internationally translated *Women and Economics* (1898), her response to Ward's success with *Pure Sociology* —as a contribution to contemporary feminist theory—manifested anxiety: "I was a little grieved in reading your statement that no one had taken up your theory—for I had stoutly defended it in my book *Women and Economics*. But perhaps you didn't consider that book of sufficient importance to mention. Or perhaps you haven't read it. I instructed the publishers to send you advance sheets of it—so sure was I that you would be interested, but evidently I overrated your interest" (Gilman to Ward, June 30, 1903). He had indeed received a personal copy of *Women and Economics* from Gilman and thereafter he lay somewhat greater emphasis upon economic factors in his prescriptions for ending androcentrism. While he contended that the monogamic era of sexual relations based on mutual selection and romantic love taking root in the Progressive Era could abate androcentrism, it had not resolved "the almost complete economic dependence of woman upon man" ("The Past and Future of the Sexes" 547). From the gynaecocentric to the androcentric state, "man . . . began to learn the economic value of woman . . . exacting not only favors but service from her" (*Pure Sociology* 345). Economic motives even paralleled sexual access as motives in women's subjugation. Yet his extensively referenced texts failed to mention Gilman's bestseller, lending support to Gilman's 1903 charge that he had not yet read it.[12]

Ward saw Gilman as a poet, whose creativity provided grist to his mill, an admired creative artist. Indeed, he often confided to his female correspondents that he had no such creativity himself but greatly admired this gift, this genius, in others (Ward to Joanna Odenwald Unger, October 27, 1903). Though sending Gilman copies of his articles and reviews, he did not see her as a peer contributor to sociological theory reciprocating in kind.

Gilman expressed very different expectations of their relationship. Judging from his extensive correspondence with women, Ward's appetite for praise and support was immense. She met his every request for evaluations of his published work. He sought such feedback on *Pure Sociology* (1903), especially from feminists and female reformers. In early 1904, Gilman responded, at once praising, modest, vicariously appropriating, and self-promoting:

> I want to tell you what I think of your Gynaecocentric Theory. You asked me to let you know. I think it is the most important contribution to the "woman question" ever made—(not excepting my own beloved theory)—and therein of measureless importance to the world. Moreover I mean to make it the recognized basis of a new advance in the movement of women. . . . I am to make it the subject of my address . . . in the International Congress of Women held in Berlin in June. I am preparing a very impressive article on it which I hope to bring out in the *North American Review.* (Gilman to Ward, January 20, 1904)

Moreover, lest he rest on his laurels, she stressed reviewers' neglect of his theory, videlicet: "It is a continuing surprise to me to find so little recognition of this great theory of yours in the reviews of your book or any other place." Perhaps, she asked, the reviews had been better abroad? Maybe there were good reviews "in this country" which had somehow failed to reach her? She implied that her role could be crucial in securing his rightful recognition. "I want to make the people feel what a great work you have done in this one thing—to say nothing of all the rest of your work" (Gilman to Ward, January 20, 1904). In the same vein, she wrote him a few months later from Berlin: "I have made known your name and work . . . in the great international gathering at Berlin to thinking women of a score of nations" (Gilman to Ward, June 3, 1903).

Still seeking his recognition of her independent efforts, she kept sending him her nonfiction work, with an added lure her tireless promotion of his work. For instance, in the summer of 1904, after her return from Berlin, she lectured in Brooklyn on "The Mother's Duty" and "rested the argument on your gynaecocentric theory. . . . My publishers have sent you my new book—*Human Work*. It is the biggest thing I've undertaken—too big to be done properly by my weak head" (Gilman to Ward, August 5, 1904).

Her own growing reputation intensified her quest for Ward's recognition. By 1904, as America's most acclaimed feminist theoretician, she had published five books, countless articles, reviews, short stories, and poems and was a contributing editor of the venerable suffrage magazine, *The Woman's Journal.* In the New York women's rights circuit she was feeling her oats and increasingly a force to be reckoned with.[13]

Just as she had tried to attach herself to Ward's coattails, he associated his ideas with hers in more popularized versions of his theories of sexual relations. Thus, in his 1906 article "The Past and Future of the Sexes," he cited Gilman, though still confining his references to her poetry: "The only person who, to my knowledge has clearly brought out this cosmological perspective, not merely in things human, but in the vast reaches of organic evolution, is a woman." His footnote was her poem, "Similar Cases" (541).

This mention mollified Gilman somewhat: "I am grateful to you for the most complimentary reference in your Independent article; which I prize the more now that you have sent it to me." Reiterating her plan to publicize and popularize his work, she noted that "it is a great pleasure to me to have a brief resume of your theory in purchasable and distributable shape." Again she railed against his nonrecognition of her as a social theorist: "As you may know I have been preaching your doctrine, with specific reference to you and *Pure Sociology* ever since it was known to me. By the way, I was grieved to see in *Pure Sociology* [page 171] that you have not read my *Women and Economics* or if you have you did not notice my explicit reference to your *Forum* article of 1888, because you say that to your knowledge no one has ever advocated your theory; and I've done my humble best at it, in lecture, book, and article these many years" (Gilman to Ward, March 15, 1906).

She laced this complaint with assertions of her own loyalty against the army of detractors in their midst, citing others' criticisms: "All my biological friends scoff at you, and say you have not the facts to rest the theory on—that they know no instance of a creature with the tiny transient male—the first stage of detached existence." Gilman's unwelcome reference to his critics was perhaps softened by: "I hear that you have been called to the Chair of Sociology at Brown. Power to your elbow!" (Gilman to Ward, March 15, 1906).[14]

Ward's 1907 appointment to a long-sought academic post accelerated her demands. Moreover, aspects of his account of the sexes bothered her. Though she had already sent him the book she regarded as her most important, *Human Work* (1904), in 1907 she sent it again, this time with passages marked, evidently no more confident that he had yet read it than her earlier sent, nonfiction works. Asserting self-importantly that "I truly think it will interest you to see how largely I have followed the same lines of thought you have covered so much more fully; and that one or two points may have fresh suggestions perhaps," she again declared that improved health now permitted her at last to read his earlier books, since "except for the Phylogenetic Forces—in *Pure Sociology*—and some of the shorter papers you were so kind as to send me—I have not really read you at all." Reporting on her and her husband's reading of Ward's 1906 text, *Applied Sociology*, she noted that, unlike her, Mr. Gilman had "read all the others" (Gilman to Ward, February 1, 1907).

That a female intellectual denied higher education because of her sex might be competitive and resentful when the glittering prizes came to men like Ward is not surprising. Any such feeling would have been heightened when the institution honoring him was the one shadowing her Providence adolescence and young adulthood, supplying her first suitors and yet locking her out—Brown University. Viewing his good fortune, she could only reflect that, after all, she was a Beecher, one of the most famous public intellectual families in American history.[15] Hence her good wishes on Ward's Brown appointment have a discernable edge, full of caveats: "I hope you are enjoying as you ought the Himalayan heights you have won—the glorious view—the light—the clear stimulating air; and best of all, the sure knowledge that this big job is for us all and will be reached by all. That is the real happiness—it does not much matter if only a few of us know you are there" (Gilman to Ward, January 1, 1907).

It was ironic that Ward of all people should be the focus of such ambivalence or passive aggression. Hardly the entitled scion of academe or of other learned professions and hereditary wealth—the background of so many of the white male university faculty of the period—his poverty was formative, his education uneven and hard won, and professional success elusive and belated.[16] For much of his sociological knowledge he, too, was an autodidact. Invariably short of cash and often dependent on others, he was out of his class and status element among the Brown dons (Scott 38–39).[17]

Gilman's demand for his recognition evoked apologies and appeasing gestures. Ward explained that his teaching obligations confined his reading to materials illustrating social science for his "greedy young students," all else becoming vacation reading, a pile which he assured her that her book would top. As if to soften the message that he judged her work to be lighter summer reading, he rewarded her assertions of their common ground with: "Of course we think alike," reporting that he commended her book to his educational sociology class. Even so, her significance to him remained stubbornly poetic: "To show the similarity of your point of view and mine I read them your 'Flagstone Method,' much to their amusement. . . . Thank you very much for sending it to me" (Ward to Gilman, January 3, 1907).

Gilman jealously guarded her own reputation for originality. Ward's rigid art-versus-intellect dichotomy riled and insulted her, because he relegated her to the role of an artistic mouthpiece for his ideas, casting her as a shallow popularizer rather than theorist. Hence, her great admiration for Ward was fraught with ambivalence, fear that her own contribution might disappear, unacknowledged in the shadow of this famous contemporary. In 1895, her use of the metaphor "the stone in David's sling" had signified her delight at being judged useful to the Great Man. But as their relationship unfolded, alongside her growing fame, she increasingly resented being treated as *merely* his bullhorn. Ten years and many publications later, no longer a mere stone, to extend the metaphor, she regarded herself as David's peer with her own slingshot. Moreover, by citing his work and bringing him the attention of her huge audiences, Ward incurred a debt to Gilman, and perhaps he had become a stone in *her* slingshot. Ward could not countenance such a prospect.

In February 1907, Gilman received a letter from Ward in which he wrote: "I have read your book. I could hear my own voice all the time. But of course, it was not an echo. It is pitched much higher than I can strike and differs also entirely in timbre" (Ward to Gilman, February 9, 1907). The tension detectable in the Gilman-Ward relationship would have had no significance had their contributions on the "woman question" been identical. Her difficulties with his preeminence and her autodidactic dependence upon him as an authority became complicated further, however, by disagreement between them over theorizing the "overthrow" of gynaecocentric culture. Her increasing skepticism after she read and reread Ward's *Pure Sociology* casts doubt on any claim that she was an uncritical Wardian.[18]

Her criticisms of his ideas culminated in 1907–09. On his "Social and Biological Struggles": "I should like to take issue with you if I knew enough. I think we overestimate the value of war—that civilization has progressed in spite of it—not because of it." She contended that war always halted progress, especially in industry, decrying "the destructive ferocity" of androcentric culture (Gilman to Ward, January 26, 1908). Ward's response, if any, to her objections has not been found, nor to another 1907 Gilman missive insisting he acknowledge that the acquisition and distribution of property involved social rather than familial processes—the family being a primitive physiological unit of personal, sex, and reproductive relationships. Social injury, Gilman insisted, resulted from connecting social processes with these primitive relations (Gilman to Ward, September 20, 1907). Instead of commenting or engaging with her points, Ward sent her another of his own published works, pointedly titled "The Value of Error" (Gilman to Ward, November 6, 1908).

For Gilman, the cause of the women's hypothesized subjection was "sexuo-*economic*" (*Women and Economics* 39). Men, uselessly hunting uncertain prey, naturally lazy and parasitic, faced an economically uncertain world. Over time, they jealously realized that nonhunting woman—that is, woman the gatherer, agriculturalist, artisan, trader, and manufacturer —enjoyed prosperity and predictable sustenance. Men followed, emulated, participated, then took over women's industries, forcibly excluding them, then advancing these industries over thousands of years into their modern forms. Thereby previously parasitic men robbed women. Men chose smaller, less vigorous women who were easier to subdue, their qualities inherited by subsequent generations. The ill effects of male sex selection were at the center of *Women and Economics*—her case for women's independence and citizenship.

Despite Gilman's admiration for Ward, she considered his explanations of women's oppression inconclusive and offered a different interpretation of the ending of female supremacy and female sex selection. Notwithstanding their forcible monopoly of women's industries, males were inherently work-averse, choosing the path entailing the least effort wherever possible:

> There seems to have come a time when it occurred to the dawning intelligence of this amiable savage that it was cheaper and easier to fight a little female and have it done with than to fight a big male every time. So he instituted the custom of enslaving the female; and she, losing freedom, could no longer get her own food or that of her young. . . . The man, the father, found that slavery had its obligations: he must care for what he forbade to care for itself, else it died on his hands. So he slowly and reluctantly shouldered the duties of his new position. He began to feed her, and not only that, but to express in his own person the thwarted uses of maternity: he had to feed the children too. (*Women and Economics* 61–62)

Elsewhere she described the "subjection of women" as involving the "maternalizing of man" (*Women and Economics* 144). This was, she argued, the silver lining in the otherwise diseased, sinful, and evil-studded era of mightily overgrown sex-passion caused by male dominance. Secluded ownership of erotically accessible women forced men to provide and improve, men assuming "the instincts and habits of the female." Though this outcome was not men's motivation "because of sex-desire the male subjugates the female. Lest he lose her, he feeds her, and perforce her young" (134). This economic focus in analyzing the origins of women's subjection was Gilman's and not Ward's. For him, economic dependence for women was a consequence—not a cause—of androcentric culture.

Gilman recast woman's admittedly painful and "long years of oppression" as a merely "temporary subversion" of her initial superiority, leading to the positive outcome of man's slow rise to "full racial equality with her." Originally "merely a temporary agent in reproduction and of no further use," or "merely a fertilizing agent," males could contribute more to race improvement if they equaled the already highly developed parent, the female. Thus their enhancement to race equality required women's economic dependence to make man "the working mother of the world" (136). Briskly gliding over the consequences of patriarchal oppression, she declared: "Women can well afford their period of subjection for the sake of a conquered world, a civilized man." She described women's historical enslavement to announce its passing—"And now the long strain is over, now that the time has come when neither he nor the world is any longer benefitted by her subordination." Rhetorically, she challenged the assumed naturalism of male dominance, casting it as a phase leading to a present in which it was no longer constructive for "the race" (136).

Gilman's *The Man-Made World, or Our Androcentric Culture* (1911) explored adverse effects of male sex-selection, especially in altered female secondary sexual characteristics—the whim of male choice. The "proprietary family" flouted nature's intent that men compete to be chosen by women as mates. Instead: "The man, by violence or purchase, does the choosing—he selects the kind of woman that pleases him. Nature did not intend him to select; he is not good at it. Neither was the female intended to compete—she is not good at it." Thus, men were freed from the "stern but elevating" effect of sexual selection. All they needed was power to take by force or buy a woman. Meanwhile, natural selection, formerly elevating women, now required only that she should please prospective masters—merely the average intelligence, strength, skill, health, or beauty of the "houseservant" or "housekeeper" (42, 57).

Gilman's and Ward's critique of men as sex selectors centered on the character of male desire. The sexes' desires pointed in opposite directions, yet with a ghastly symmetry. Under their regime, females enlarged males into equality, from the status of a puny dependent parasite. By contrast, male sex selectors reduced females into inequality, toward puny, dependent parasitism. Females sought to make males more like themselves—to their cost—while males, once equal to females, sought to make the latter less like themselves—to their benefit.

Despite their convergence on sex selection, Gilman ignored Ward's paternity hypothesis, advancing instead an economic and maternity-centered version of the story. In resisting the causal status attributed to discovery of paternity, she also declined the comparable claims of those revered mid- to late-nineteenth-century founding fathers of anthropology so palpably wedded to it—including those authorities recommended by her father. Insofar as she asserted explanations centered upon the evolution of motherhood and economic activities descending from it, Gilman rejected man-centered accounts. In this connection, she became particularly troubled by the role of sexual violence in prevailing man-centered accounts of the overthrow of women.

Why? Ward's account posed women's esthetically motivated equalizing through sex selection of originally inferior males as the last piece of female agency. Thereafter, they become the passive victims of male dominance. Gilman simply did not believe that the larger group of humans, industrious women, would have helplessly stood by and submitted to the kind of violent transformation Ward described. In her 1915 novel *Herland* the women of the imagined Amazonian country, when confronted with such a threat from the men remaining after a deadly war, rose up and slaughtered their would-be oppressors (*Herland* 55). Moreover, in *His Religion and Hers* (1923) she rebuked feminists who assumed that ancient man "with a club . . . suddenly rose up against his female and subjugated her by . . . force." Ward's idea that ancient sexual patterns could have been "instantaneously changed and inverted by one man—or one generation of men" was absurd (204).

Gilman referred to the ending of gynaecocentric culture as "The Overthrow." But against Ward's assertion that this development was purposive, she wrote: "As to the Overthrow: Not telic. Not sudden. Not a conquest by man. Ward's suggestion unsatisfying." She ventured that "peace, plenty, beginnings of wealth, considerable industry" were the good conditions of the "matriarchate," resulting in an excess of women over men. This development led to what she called "human matriarchal polygamy," wherein a group of women, "able, industrious, productive," maintained one male. Thereby valued for scarcity, males "kept in comparative idleness by a group of industrious women, and overindulged sexually, became proud, sensual, lazy and cruel. All this slowly and gradually introduced and produced by cumulation. No literature" ("Notes on the Overthrow").

In other words, she offered a gradualist account, insisting that the change occurred between the earliest appearance of savage humans and the beginnings of recorded history. She contended that the change happened more or less simultaneously in all races and places on earth. The cause was not discovery of the fact of paternity but rather the extension of motherhood centered on service. With the prolongation of human infancy, the same mother served multiple children of different ages. More highly evolved motherhood accompanying extended pregnancy, lactation, and rearing of homo sapiens infants led women to develop industries ("Wash Tubs and Woman's Duty" 153–54). Beyond "natural," periodic coitus related to reproduction, cohabitation with mothers began to have added attractions for primitive men—economic attractions. Men might claim the care mothers dispensed to children: "In this new relationship, with motherhood extended to benefit the father as well as the child, begins the swiftest stage of human advance. . . . Mother-care, given to the adult-male, seemed as nutritive as mother's milk given to the child. But the new attraction of service, added to the old attraction of sex, made the women so desirable that they became necessary possessions, and as possessions they were unable to avoid the quite natural abuse of their original function" ("Sex and Race Progress" 109, 112). Women's capacity for human service lay "at the root of our great race tragedy, the subjugation of the female." Contrary to Ward's raping and battering savage man in the vanguard of androcentrism, however, subjugation eventuated "not by any act of cruelty on the part of man but the increasing desirability of woman's services." With brief life expectancy, the age gap between a woman's oldest child and her current lover might be narrow; thus, the extension of her "mother-service" to the latter happened easily and unconsciously, as he "slipped into more and more dependence on her services." It thus was more motherhood than sex of which androcentric man "first took advantage" (*His Religion and Hers* 206–07).

Motherhood originated women's industries, services, and usefulness and was itself synonymous with women's sexuality prior to "the overthrow." Gilman provided a woman-centered account, insisting that the shift to male-dominated culture arose through mutual economic negotiation. She neither endorsed nor repeated Ward's theory of female enslavement as the exercise of men's hyperdeveloped rational faculties, overcoming natural instincts, and the discovery, through such rationality, of paternity, unleashing father-right and thereby male sex-right. Women's subordination was not a purposive undertaking, based on a pitiless and rational assertion of paternal control; and androcentrism did not derive from men's hypothesized realization of fatherhood; nor did rape and force establish it. In her alternative theory of the rise of androcentric society then, Gilman rejected apocalyptic versions of its process or periodization.

In 1908, still attempting to have him engage with her "fresh ideas," Gilman acquainted Ward with her alternative theory of "the overthrow." Contending that overthrowing matriarchy led to "the complete extinction of those races most violently androcentric, as well as in the visible decadence of so many others," she asked him to imagine another explanatory scenario:

Assume a matriarchal settlement under exceptionally good conditions—good climate, abundant food, peace and plenty. Under good conditions females are produced. Assume an excess of females. . . . Having now good conditions and surplus females, the male becomes increasingly valuable. The dominant females, already the industrial power and used to tribal communism, now establish a voluntary polygyny agreeing to maintain one male to each small group of females. If this were done, the male being now supported by the group of females and held in high esteem, is in a position to develop naturally, the excessive indulgence, cruelty, pride, etc. which would so lead to the more injurious effects of unchecked masculine rule. This hypothesis seems to me simple and genetic—requires no telic process, no determined action. (Gilman to Ward, November 6, 1908)

She concluded her hypothesis cheerily with a shorthand version: "Good conditions—excess females; excess females—male at premium. Male at premium—females establish polygyny. Polygyny—over-development of maleness. Predominant maleness—androcracy. Androcracy—the world as we have it." With a flourish she asked him, "How's that?" Interestingly, she retitled "matriarchal polygamy" as "voluntary polygyny"—initiated by women, with very different sexual politics implications. Always puzzled as to how previously dominant women could have been overthrown, it seemed plausible to speculate that "from a peaceful pro-

miscuity with matriarchal dominance to a voluntary polygyny—the females agreeing to share rather than compete—seems to me a very possible step. And polygyny produces the characteristics which lead to further masculine dominance" (Gilman to Ward, November 6, 1908). No
letter survives revealing any written response from Ward to her hypothesis. From 1908 onward, however, his changing circumstances made him
even less likely to engage with her ideas.

Ward's biographer, Clifford H. Scott, observes that within the voluminous correspondence in Ward's Brown University papers, female correspondents like Gilman account for more than half of the total. This is
a remarkable proportion, given Ward's civil service career as a paleobotanist in Washington, D.C., from 1865 to 1903, and as sociology professor at the all-male Brown University from 1907 to 1913. Ward "had
always been a handsome and virile man" whose woman's rights advoca-
cies "produced a group of women admirers" (Scott 40). These female
correspondents clustered mainly in the last twenty years of his life. They
included journalists, educated and unemployed wives, woman suffragists,
labor and socialist activists, sex reformers, college professors, social workers, African-American educators, philanthropists, schoolteachers, students, and other female members of the general reading public moved
to respond to his publications by writing to him directly.[19] Among his
feminist admirers were Harriot Stanton Blatch, Frances Swiney, Anna
Garlin Spencer, May Wright Sewall, Florence Hull, Helen Campbell,
Antoinette Blackwell, and Mary Chapin.[20] Some of Ward's female correspondents became "regulars" with whom he exchanged considerably
more correspondence than with professional peers and friends whose letters with Ward have preoccupied biographers.[21]

Women, including Gilman, secured less and less of Ward's attention once he became established at Brown. Several circumstances had
changed. First, he was no longer the insufficiently appreciated intellectual founding father of sociology, confined in a Washington, D.C., civil
service position, recipient of voluminous sympathetic female contacts.
From 1907 he lived in Providence, Rhode Island. His wife Rose despised
provincial Providence, returning after only one year to Washington,
D.C., to reside with her sister, Sarah Comstock. Ward visited her errati-
cally. Then suddenly in 1908 she had a stroke, becoming a paralyzed and
bedridden invalid cared for by Comstock. After a dutiful visit in 1908 or
1909, Ward came less and less, for which the family condemned him.

Four years later, Ward died from a sudden heart attack at the age of seventy-two.

After his death, Gilman published a tribute: his legacy would be his books and arguments, most especially for women, for whom "he should stand as the greatest light ever thrown upon their abnormal condition and its results to the world." Reminiscing about Ward at a sociology meeting, where delegates overwhelmingly presented specialized, fragmented studies, she recollects that "Ward rose to his feet, a towering figure, tall, broad, massive, with a noble head that wore the kindness of large wisdom. He . . . said: 'I confess that nothing deeply interests me in social improvement which does not apply to the whole human race'" ("Lester Ward Is Dead" 166).

In her final published sociological book, *His Religion and Hers* (1923), she described his gynaecocentric theory as "the most important single precept in the history of thought," besides evolutionary theory itself (57). Her residual allegiance to Ward made her the target of scathing attacks by critics of feminism.[22] Nonetheless, she always paid tribute to Ward as the era's foremost academic theorist of women's subjugation.

Despite Gilman's longstanding engagement with his work, she held his explanations of women's oppression to be unconvincing. Her explanation of the ending of female supremacy and female-initiated sex selection significantly differed from Ward's. These findings necessitate revision of prevailing accounts of Gilman's particular theoretical legacy and biography, clarifying her original and distinctive inputs into lively contemporary disputes about nature, history, sexual relations, and gender dynamics. Historicizing sex *itself* and demonstrating its plasticity within human sexual arrangements, her qualification of key tenets of Ward's influential theory of women's subordination places the nature of *her* critique of women's situation within a clearer Progressive Era intellectual context. It stands to modify accounts of the intellectual grounding of American feminism.

Finally, Ward, a women's movement celebrity and ladies' man, proved better able to analyze the vertical, unreciprocated, and unequal male-female relations of the era than to overcome them in his own life. Gilman was one of the women from whom he withheld the intellectual reciprocity and respect sought. He made his confidantes among women who served him, emotionally and professionally, giving them their devotion, time, labor, and money. Gilman would not make him any such offer, even if she had possessed the means to do so. She had her own mission and ultimately achieved what she did, warts and all, without much of the respect and acknowledgment she craved from Ward.

NOTES

1. On reform Darwinism and Neo-Lamarckianism more generally, see Stocking, *Race, Culture and Evolution;* Pfeifer, "The Genesis of American Neo-Lamarckianism" 156–67; Burrows, *Evolution and Society;* Hofstadter, *Social Darwinism in American Thought;* and Safford, *Pragmatism and the Progressive Movement in the United States.*

2. Illinois-born Edward Alsworth Ross trained at Johns Hopkins University, married Washington, D.C., artist Rosamond Simon, and became one of the Progressive Era's most prolific and best-known sociologists, one of the famous "Wisconsin Progressives." See the microform manuscript series, *The Wisconsin Progressives,* and the State Historical Society of Wisconsin, *Edward A. Ross Papers.* For discussions of Ross's works and career, see Weinberg, *Edward Alsworth Ross,* and McMahon, *Social Control and Public Intellect.* See also Ross, *Seventy Years of It.*

3. Helen Campbell was Gilman's coeditor of *The Impress* in San Francisco from 1893 to 1895 and was the friend with whom Gilman shared residence in Jane Addams's settlement movement in Chicago, particularly the Unity settlement from 1895 to 1896, which Gilman dubbed "Little Hell." Campbell studied economics with Richard T. Ely and was visiting professor at the University of Wisconsin, where Gilman visited her for a month. See Mary Jo Deegan, "Introduction" 18, 20, and 21.

4. Both Gilman and Ward objected to Kidd's survival of the fittest approach to social Darwinism and his embrace of Weissman's repudiation of Lamarck's theory of inherited cultural traits, evident in Kidd's *Social Evolution.*

5. For biographies and studies of Ward's life and work, see Barnes, "Lester Frank Ward"; Beard, "Lester F. Ward" 119; Burnham, *Lester Frank Ward in American Thought;* Cape, *Lester Frank Ward;* Chugerman, *Lester Ward;* Finlay, "Lester Frank Ward as a Sociologist of Gender" 251–65; Giddings, "Lester Frank Ward" 67–68; Gillette, "Critical Points in Ward's Pure Sociology" 31–67; McClay, "The Socialization of Desire" 65–73; Mitchell, "Some Recollections of Lester F. Ward and James Q. Dealey" 44–47; Patten, "The Failure of Biological Sociology" 919–47; Ross, "Lester Frank Ward" 64–67; Small, "Lester Frank Ward" 77–78; Sniegoski, "Lester Frank Ward" 47–64; Stern, "The Liberal Views of Lester F. Ward" 102–04.

6. His earliest work on the subject dated from the 1870s. See Ward, "The Social Evil" 238–39.

7. In homage to Anthony, he humorously quipped that he would speak neither of "philanthropy nor philandry, much less of their opposites, misanthropy, misogyny, and misandry, for the last of which terms the synonym Miss Anthony is now in common use." See Ward, "Six O' Clock Club Speech" 4, 7, and 8–11.

8. Ward accorded prostitution almost a causal and genealogical function. If man's attempts to evoke desire for coitus failed, appeals to "reason" had a pecuniary or mercenary inflection, as he took advantage of her other "more constant and less capricious desires" in exchange for her submission "to his embraces" (Ward, "On Male Sex Selection" 76).

9. His suggestions included: Dawkins, *Cave Hunting;* Grote, *A History of Greece;* Lubbock, *Prehistoric Times;* Rawlinson, *Five Great Monarchies of the Ancient Eastern World;* Tylor, *Researches into the Early History of Mankind.*

10. A water-colorist obsessed with the female nude, Stetson cast his Bohemian persona in the Byronic tradition, with highly masculinist notions of the necessity for frequent sexual outlet for the creative process to be effective, and what some biographers dub "Victorian" ideals of the permissible activities of his wife and the future mother of his children. Commentators often accept at face value Gilman's later minimizing of the conflicts leading to their final 1888 separation and 1894 divorce. Each partner in this "mistaken mating," as Gilman privately called it, left a diary of courtship, marriage, and relationship deterioration. See Denise D. Knight and Mary Armfield Hill's excellent annotation and editing of the Gilman and Stetson diaries, respectively: Gilman, *The Diaries of Charlotte Perkins Gilman,* ed. Knight; and Stetson, *Endure,* ed. Hill. On Stetson's art, see Eldredge, *Charles Walter Stetson.*

11. By 1904, Gilman's work had appeared in journals and periodicals such as: *Ainslee's, American Fabians, Armenia, Booklovers, Century Club Advance, Chautauqua Assembly Herald, Christian Register, Coming Nation, Cosmopolitan, Current Literature, Independent, Harper's Bazaar, Housekeeper's Weekly, Kansas Suffrage Reveille, Literary Digest, New Nation, New York Times, New York Tribune, Pacific Monthly, Pacific Rural Press, Providence Journal, Puritan, Saturday Evening Post, Scribner's Woman's Column, Signal, Success, Truth, Twentieth Century Home, Union Southern Educational Journal, Worthington's Illustrated.* For examples of Gilman's correspondence with publishers and journal editors, see the letter to Gilman from the editor of the *Saturday Evening Post,* September 26, 1899; Holt *(The Independent)* to Gilman, May 31, 1902; Connelly *(Success)* to Gilman, May 22, July 19, 26, and 29, October 7 and 30, 1902, January 27, February 25,

March 12, 1903; Faber *(Shopping)* to Gilman, September 17, 1908; and Jordan *(Harper's Bazaar)* to Gilman, December 10, 1908.

12. For instance, in 1906 in *Applied Sociology,* Ward noted that human uses and assessments of available resources were fatally flawed by adherence to androcentric philosophy, which amounted to wasting the talents and potential contributions of half of the population—women—simply on the ground of sex (232). He continued to ponder the unsolved aspects of his own and other theories of androcentric culture across the 1900s. In 1910 he critically reviewed Annie Porritt's essay "Woman as a Metonymy" as ahistorical twaddle unwarrantedly ignoring economic factors (Ward, "The Historical View of Women" 356).

13. See for instance, many unidentified news clippings and journal articles in Gilman's papers, penned often as reports on her lectures or responses to her books and articles: "Remarkable Literary Success of Mrs. Charlotte Perkins Stetson," *Oakland Post* (1900); "Babygardens," *New York Evening Post* (1900?); "Mrs. Gilman's Volume on Children," *New York Times—Saturday Review of Books* (January 5, 1901); "The Ideal Home," *New York Times* (December 26, 1903): 98; Olivia H. Dunbar, "Mrs. Gilman's Idea of Home," *The Critic* 43 (December 1903): 568–70; Vernon Lee, "The Economic Dependence of Women," *North American Review* 175 (April 1, 1903): 71–90; "Mrs. Gilman Says It Is 'Cradle of Human Love, but Deathbed of Industry'" (1903); "Mrs. Gilman Arouses Hotbed of Discussion," *Eagle* (February 29, 1903); "The Extension of the Suffrage to Women: Subject of an Interesting Debate before the Outlook Club Last Evening: Gilman vs. Finck"; "The Ideal Mother: Her Place in the World as Defined by Charlotte Perkins Gilman" (1903); "Maternity Mixed with Housework," June 20, 1903; and "Do Women Protect Men?" *Times Democrat* (December 8, 1904).

14. Pressing her knowledge of his critics, she noted that "Mr. Holt has three replies which he calls 'withering.' I don't think they'll 'wither' much; and the matter needs wide and thorough discussion." The reference to "Mr. Holt" concerned a symposium that Henry Holt (1840–1926), editor of *The Independent,* tried to publish in 1906. On Henry Holt's career as editor of *The Independent* and as a book publisher, see Madison, *The Owl among the Colophons.* Ward was chagrined because his work had been given, without consultation or consent, to three professional rivals and critics: G. Stanley Hall (1844–1924), Edmund B. Wilson (1856–1939), and Franklin Giddings (1855–1931). Holt proposed to publish their critiques with Ward's article, inviting him to reply to them. Ward refused, calling Holt's actions "a breach of professional ethics." Eventually, Ward

saw Hall's and Wilson's critiques, which confirmed his decision to refuse. See Ward, *Glimpses of the Cosmos* 6: 223–24.

15. For a critical discussion of Gilman's investment in her Beecher genealogy, see Weinbaum, "Writing Feminist Genealogy" 271–302. Studies of the Beecher family include: Rugoff, *The Beechers;* and Snyder, *Lyman Beecher and His Children.*

16. On patterns in the class background and resources of typical Progressive Era and mid-twentieth-century university faculty, see Adams, *The Academic Tribes;* American Association of University Professors, Yale University Chapter, *Incomes and Living Costs of a University Faculty;* Carnegie Foundation for the Advancement of Teaching, *The Financial Status of the Professor in America and Germany;* United States Bureau of Education, *Salaries in Universities and Colleges in 1920;* L. Wilson, *The Academic Man.*

17. See also Barry, *Gentlemen under the Elms.*

18. Nor was Gilman the only skeptical reader of Ward. Harriot Stanton Blatch, suffragist feminist daughter of Elizabeth Cady Stanton, wrote him to take issue with his account of prostitution, female sexuality, and race relations. See Blatch to Ward, June 23 and September 2, 1903.

19. See, for instance, McAdoo to Ward, May 28, 1898.

20. See, for instance, letters to Ward from: Harriot Stanton Blatch 1902–06, Frances Swiney 1903, Emma Stanton 1910, Anna Garlin Spencer 1906, May Wright Sewall 1900, Florence Hull 1892–94, Helen Campbell 1889–96, Antoinette Blackwell 1882–96, and Mary Chapin 1898, Ward Papers, folders 19, 20, 23, 24, 27, 28, 31, 33, 35, 37, and 38, and reels 12–14.

21. One in particular warrants brief examination: Emily Palmer Cape, who tried to undermine Ward's esteem for Gilman. A Columbia University graduate and wealthy forty-five-year-old lumber merchant's wife and mother of two, Cape was a feminist, suffragist, and writer who was without a career. After hearing a Ward lecture and seeking a project to absorb both her passions and skills, she visited him at Brown and proposed that she become his biographer and the editor of a twelve-volume compilation of his lesser-known writings published since the 1870s. Titled *Glimpses of the Cosmos,* they secured a publisher and set to work. This highly personal partnership absorbed the final years of Ward's life. Cape was to be his literary executor, with sole access to his voluminous lifelong diaries for preparing his authorized biography. Ward's biographer, Clifford H. Scott, contends that the family allegation that Cape and Ward had an extramarital affair cannot be proved beyond doubt. Nonetheless, any rumors and scandal about it would have circulated within their Washington and New York

circles across 1910–11. Ostracized by Ward's relatives, Cape continued the project on the more modest scale of six volumes and published her memoir of her relationship with Ward in 1922 (see Cape, *Lester Frank Ward*).

By contrast with the lack of analysis so far of Ward's relationships with his female correspondents, there has been particular interest in his correspondence with sociologists Franklin Giddings, Edward A. Ross, Albion Small, and Charles Veditz. See, for instance, the following Stern sources: "Giddings, Ward, and Small: An Interchange of Letters"; "Letters of Alfred Russell Wallace to Lester F. Ward"; "The Ward-Ross Correspondence, 1891–1912"; and "The Letters of Albion W. Small to Lester F. Ward," December 1933, March 1935, December 1936, and March 1937.

22. See, for instance, Walsh, *Feminism* 44, 154, 158, 163; Barnett, *Foundations of Feminism* 37–48; Barnett to Gilman, December 28, 1920, March 6, 1921; and Gilman to Barnett, February 26, 1921.

6

Mrs. Stetson and Mr. Shaw in Suffolk

Animadversions and Obstacles

Janice J. Kirkland

Beginning with her criticism of his play and his animadversion on her country, the acquaintance between Charlotte Perkins Gilman and George Bernard Shaw was a process of influences positive and negative, proceeding as much from opposing as from accepting the ideas of one another. It would have been enough if they had met, if she had heard him read one of his plays, and if she had read her poems to him, but more followed. There is minor evidence of his influence on her first nonfiction book, which became an international best-seller.

Her views on him ranged from the imputation of demonic possession to the approval implicit in her lasting ownership of one of his books. Although she did not review his many plays and other works, she must have read him to have condemned his lack of seriousness, which she did in the last issue of her magazine, *The Forerunner.* On his side, he agreed with her in supporting women's suffrage, but they used very different methods of writing about it, as evidenced by their separate responses to a much-publicized book attacking both suffragists and women in general. And most important, several books on Shaw contain admissions that he learned a lesson from her philosophy of overcoming obstacles and that he acted upon it.

Gilman, then the divorced thirty-six-year-old Mrs. Stetson, had her first experience with that English institution, the country house visit, in August 1896. She had arrived in England on the S.S. *Mongolian,* Allen Line, on July 21, to attend the International Socialist and Labor Congress as a delegate from California. Two weeks later, on August 3, she caught an afternoon train north from London's Liverpool Street Station into East Anglia, arriving about 6:30 p.m. in the small village of Sax-mundham. The long English summer day provided several more hours of daylight for her to see the countryside as she was driven three miles to the even smaller village of Stratford St. Andrew, where her host and hostess, Sidney and Beatrice Webb, had rented the rectory.

Gilman had every reason to expect this visit to Suffolk to be a pleasant and memorable occasion. From her earliest years she had heard family stories of the travels in England and Scotland by her great-aunt Harriet Beecher Stowe in the 1850s, when as the author of the immensely popu-lar novel *Uncle Tom's Cabin* she was fêted, followed about by enthusiastic crowds, and entertained by nobility (Charles Beecher 20–140). On one trip Stowe's sister, Mary Beecher Perkins, Gilman's own grandmother, accompanied Aunt Harriet (Hedrick 265). Mrs. Perkins likely told her grandchildren exciting stories about her personal experiences of British travel.

Now Gilman was in England herself, but her first country house party was not the unqualified success she hoped for, and she was to retain uncomfortable memories, particularly of Bernard Shaw. She had met the Webbs, Shaw, and other members of the Fabian Society, "that group of intelligent, scientific, practical and efficient English Socialists," at the Socialist and Labor Congress, where they made her an honorary mem-ber (Gilman, *Living* 203). She later wrote in her autobiography, "I sat with them during the meetings, and was delighted to meet some who were already known to me as writers. I saw a good deal of the 'great G.B.S.' as he was called, Mr. Shaw. He and others of the Fabian group wore knee-breeches, soft shirts, woolen hose, and sandals" (203). In the summer of 1896, however, Shaw had not yet become the "great G.B.S." but was still struggling for recognition. He was known as outspoken, even rude, and he had a record as a womanizer. Even worse, he had just had hopes that one of his plays would be produced in New York but the arrangement had fallen through, so he was not feeling particularly mel-low about America and Americans (Holroyd 321–23).

As the carriage approached the rectory at Stratford St. Andrew via a tree-lined drive, Gilman saw a green meadow on her left and ahead of her an efficient-looking Victorian-style house of grayish brick. One commentator claims the dreary house "was too much for Charlotte Stet-son, who fled" (Pearson 178). This contention, however, is inaccurate. She certainly did not flee; she arrived Monday and left for London the next

Saturday to address dockworkers on Sunday (*Diaries* 633). She soon found, however, that of the seven people staying in the rectory, she was the only American and the only stranger; the others were all well acquainted with one another.

The host, Sidney Webb, eighteen months younger than his wife, Beatrice, had been a civil servant who was able to quit his job in favor of full-time social research after they married, relying on her income to support both of them. He seems to have stayed in the background during the visit, according to Gilman's diary and autobiography. Beatrice Webb was known for her acerbic tongue, which was now exacerbated by the onset of a bad cold. On August 14 Beatrice wrote in her diary about the Socialist Congress in which Gilman had just enthusiastically participated: "A whole fortnight wasted in illness—a rheumatic cold combined with general collapse. This must excuse the absence of the brilliant account which I looked forward to writing of the International Congress! To us, it was, as we expected it to be, a public humiliation. The rank and file of socialists, especially English socialists, are unusually silly folk—for the most part feather-headed failures—and heaped together in one hall with the consciousness that their every word would be reported by the 'world press,' they approached raving imbecility" (99).

In addition to Beatrice Webb and Gilman, there was only one other woman in the house party, Charlotte Payne Townsend. Like Beatrice, she was wealthy and shared the rectory rent with the Webbs; she had been a generous donor to their London School of Economics. Charlotte Payne Townsend was probably unaware that Beatrice intended to secure her economic contributions on a more permanent basis by promoting a marriage for her with another Fabian, Graham Wallas, an intellectual bachelor who had also been invited to stay at the rectory. In the same diary entry for August 14, Webb wrote of Townsend: "We, knowing she was wealthy and hearing she was socialistic, interested her in the London School of Economics. . . . It was on account of her generosity to our projects and 'for the good of the cause' that I first made friends with her. To bring her more directly into our little set of comrades, I suggested that we should take a house together in the country and entertain our friends. To me she seemed at that time a pleasant, well-dressed, well-intentioned woman—I thought she should do very well for Graham Wallas!" (99). Beatrice was to find that she was in error; Wallas, who arrived late and left early, had little time for Townsend. Beatrice may also have thought at first that Gilman was wealthy, as Americans in England often were, in which case she would have learned her error in this regard, too, because Gilman was, as usual, living on a shoestring.

In addition to Sidney Webb and Graham Wallas, two other men were staying at the rectory: young Charles Trevelyan and Bernard Shaw. Trevelyan, heir to a baronetcy and the son of a noted historian, had degrees in history from Cambridge University (Morris 2–16). At twenty-six years of age, he was unmarried and the youngest member of the house party. In 1898 he would visit the United States with the Webbs, and his letters from that trip suggest that in 1896 he might have regarded the American Gilman rather warily. Meeting an American senator in 1898, he notes that his own cool attitude is changing because of the man's "complete friendliness to England. I find in none of them any of *that hostility of which we heard so much,* and I am getting to be very hopeful of the future of our relations" (Trevelyan 23; emphasis added). No doubt others at the rectory expected "that hostility" from Gilman.

Shaw had arrived at Stratford St. Andrew the previous Saturday. At age forty, Shaw was not yet fully launched in his career as a successful playwright. He had written *Candida* and failed thus far to have had it performed in either London or New York; he was currently involved in writing a new play about the American Revolution. Shaw wrote briefly in his diary entry for August 1 that he was going down for six weeks with the Webbs and Charlotte Payne Townsend to Stratford St. Andrew Rectory, near Saxmundham. He had stayed with the Webbs before on other country visits; Sidney was his best friend.

The morning after her arrival, Gilman wrote letters in a tent in the garden. She was finding the visit "most restful and pleasant" and reported trying a bicycle a little "just trying to mount—rather vainly" (Gilman, *Diaries* 633). After lunch she took a long nap. At tea she had some talk with the Webbs. Bedtime was at ten, the end of a restful day and a quiet evening.

On Wednesday, August 5, she again wrote letters in the tent on the lawn; there was also a summerhouse on the other side of the lawn, where Shaw was working on his plays. They had a talk "on literary work—very friendly and useful criticism." Then came lunch, naptime, teatime, and a "little walk with Miss Payne Townsend & Mrs. Webb" (633). In the evening, at Beatrice's request, she read from her first volume of poems,

In This Our World, and a few more recent poems. In her autobiography, she recalled the evening: "The kind interest of these people was all due to the little first book of poems. Mrs. Webb had me read some of them, and later ones . . . and listened attentively. To my great surprise she then advanced this dictum: 'You will do critical work but you will never be able to do original work.' I had always supposed that critical work involved more education than mine, and that if my work had any merit it was originality. But as I studied her cryptic judgment I saw at last what she meant—'original' was research work, and critical was pointing out what was the matter with society, no matter how original was the analysis" (*Living* 204). Gilman's main lifework was "pointing out what was the matter with society," so her explanation of Beatrice's comment may have been accurate; the unsought, tactless and patronizing character of the comment, however (particularly the use of "you will never be able" to a person with whom she was not well acquainted, and who was her guest), certainly seems unwarranted.

One of the poems that Gilman probably read aloud that evening was "An Obstacle," which she had also read to fellow passengers on the ship to England (*Diaries* 631). Evidence that she did in fact read it that evening at the rectory would surface many years later, in a surprising way. The first and last of its eight stanzas read as follows:

An Obstacle

I was climbing up a mountain-path
    With many things to do,
Important business of my own,
    And other people's too,
When I ran against a Prejudice
    That quite cut off the view.

. . . .

    I took my hat, I took my stick,
    My load I settled fair,
I approached that awful incubus
    With an absent-minded air—
And I walked directly through him,
    As if he wasn't there!

(*In This Our World* 103)

Her diary reports that Thursday was rather like Wednesday; she had "more talk with Mr. Shaw—interesting rather." In her discussions with him she noticed "little cubes of wood he placed here and there, visualizing the positions of his characters on the stage" (*Diaries* 203). Shaw sent to London for a copy of his play *Candida* and read it to her, asking her opinion. If he was particularly interested in her response because she was American and represented the audiences he hoped to reach, her opinion must have disappointed him, coming as it did after his failure to have it produced in New York (Holroyd 321–23). Gilman was not impressed by the play, as she candidly informed Shaw: "It did not seem to me at all convincing—the assumption that the puny poet was the stronger of the two men, and that Candida was so superior to her efficient husband. If that impressive lady had had to go out and earn her living she might not have been so impressive" (*Living* 203–04). Since the poet character Marchbanks to some extent represented Shaw himself, he probably did not take this outspoken criticism easily; he may have been sensitive about the play already, since others had also criticized it as containing too much talk and not enough action to keep an audience interested (Ervine 339).

Gilman had read Henrik Ibsen's play *A Doll's House* some years before (*Diaries* 442) and would likely have recognized *Candida* as a reverse response to it, in which the husband rather than the wife walks out of the house at the play's conclusion. To Gilman, as to many feminist admirers of Ibsen, Shaw had missed the point both by this reversal and by giving Candida a choice of men (rather than a choice of a real life as an individual over an artificial life as a wife). Gilman was too polite to tell Shaw this, or at least she does not mention having done so. Interestingly, her suggestion that Candida would have been a different character if she "had had to go out and earn her living" shows Gilman was already considering the influences of economic parasitism and lack of meaningful work for women; these ideas would coalesce eleven months later when she would write in her diary for July 1, 1897, that she had "gotten hold of a new branch of my theory" on the economic basis of the woman question, "the biggest since I saw it. Now I can write the book" that was to become *Women and Economics* (*Diaries* 682).

What she did say to Shaw was enough to irritate him; this is borne out by a later explanation he gave of the ending, making the poet and not Candida the central figure: "What business has a man with the great destiny of a poet with the small beer of domestic comfort . . . at the apron string of some dear nice woman? . . . Morell cannot do without it. . . . To Eugene [Marchbanks, the poet], the stronger of the two, [it is] an atmosphere in which great poetry dies . . . and he goes out proudly into the majestic and beautiful kingdom of the starry night" (Stanton 169). Shaw's belief in the superior destiny of the creative man is important in understanding his behavior that evening in the rectory.

That afternoon the two Charlottes went on a walk by themselves because Beatrice's cold was worse and she was confined to the house. While she was miserable, her male guests were enjoying themselves. "All of these men are funny all the time," Gilman wrote in her diary. "Miss T[ownsend] listens" (663).

Dinners at the rectory were risky affairs, since Beatrice was anorexic and did not indulge her guests with luxurious meals. The house party was far from well nourished, for she "intently scrutinized every mouthful consumed at her table, which rather killed the appetite" (Bee Wilson 40–41). At dinner that particular Thursday evening, perhaps in reaction to Gilman's criticism of his play, Shaw was "bitterly brilliant" and "made jokes about his sister's grave" (*Living* 204). Just once Gilman says she answered him successfully, betraying that many times he got the better of her in front of the other guests. When the table talk took up the subject of "animadversions on the U.S.A.," Shaw turned to her, sitting quietly beside him, and caustically remarked that he supposed she would put all this into the newspapers when she got home. "I assured him that I did not write for the papers, and was not that kind of a writer, anyway. 'Then what were you thinking about?' he demanded. To which I peacefully replied, 'About the effect of geography on the mind.' After a little they all laughed, and made no more remarks about my country" (204).

Gilman's use of the term "animadversions," rather than some milder term, seems deliberate and shows that within the context of dinner-table debate she was being exposed to attacks similar to the previous "you will never" from Beatrice Webb. This time it was Shaw, attacking by using the less personal but no more pleasant method of criticizing her country. This may have been the reason that in her diary she described the evening following the dinner as "rather stupid," although she omits mention of the meal and its unpleasantness (*Diaries* 633). In *Women and Eco-*

nomics she would return to the influence of geography on the mind and make an example of England and the United States as if still trying to explain away the unpleasantness she had experienced:

> Social conditions, like individual conditions, become familiar by use, and cease to be observed. This is the reason why it is so much easier to criticise the customs of other persons or other nations than our own. It is also the reason why we so naturally deny and resent the charges of the critic. It is not necessarily because of any injustice on one side or dishonesty on the other, but because of a simple and useful law of nature. The Englishman coming to America is struck by America's political corruption and, in the earnest desire to serve his brother, he tells us all about it. That which he has at home he does not observe, because he is used to it. The American in England finds also something to object to, and omits to balance his criticism by memories of home. (79)

Stetson's brief diary entry for Friday, August 7, reveals little, reporting only that she received and answered mail from London and went for a walk in a nearby park with Sidney Webb. Saturday she had a morning "as usual" and left from the Saxmundham station to return to London that afternoon by the 3:30 train, having been in Suffolk five nights. But this was not the end of the repercussions from her visit.

One play that Shaw was working on in the rectory summerhouse was *The Devil's Disciple,* written between April and the end of November 1896. It is of particular interest as his extended statement of Anglo-American relations in crisis during the American Revolution includes a portrait of Gen. John Burgoyne, sometimes described as the man who lost the Colonies for the British by his defeat at Saratoga. "Animadversions" against the U.S.A. at dinner were bracketed by the melodrama Shaw was working on: a bitter defeat for the English by colonials to whom they felt superior. It is reasonable to suppose that the other guests knew the subject of Shaw's play; Charles Trevelyan probably discussed its background with Shaw, since his father, George O. Trevelyan, was writing a monumental history, *The American Revolution;* it would eventually reach a length of six volumes, copyrighted between 1899 and 1914.

The romantic drama, *The Devil's Disciple,* like that of *Candida,* involves a woman's choice between two men: Judith Anderson must decide between her husband, Anthony Anderson, and Dick Dudgeon, the "devil's disciple." Judith is a weak character; like a traditional melodramatic heroine, she often bursts into tears. Throughout the play's trial scene she is either silent or sobs convulsively, and she is so impressed by the British General Burgoyne that she gives him an "awe-stricken curtsy."

It would be satisfying to say that Gilman condemned Judith's character as she had that of Candida, but there is no evidence that she read the finished play or saw a performance of it or of any other Shaw play. If she took exception to the sharpness of his conversation during the 1896 visit to Stratford St. Andrew, later portraying a painful experience as rather innocuous in her autobiography, it might explain why she apparently did not see his plays in later years, although they were often performed in New York City, where she lived. She also declined to review any of his publications during the years that she produced *The Forerunner*, 1909–16.

Her most outspoken comment on Shaw appears in a letter to her future husband, Houghton Gilman, written just a year after the Suffolk house party, on August 1, 1897: "Shaw's work is always clever and good reading. *But I do not love the man. He has an evil spirit*" (Hill, *The Making* 289; emphasis added). When she first met Shaw, Charlotte Gilman probably had difficulty accepting the sincerity of a man who professed to respect women but whose behavior often proved otherwise. Her negative reaction to him need not have depended only on his discourteous treatment of her in Suffolk.

During her stay in England, she also became acquainted with two new female friends who had had experience with his philandering and insincerity: May Morris, daughter of artist and author William Morris, and Edith Nesbit, wife of another Fabian and womanizer, Hubert Bland. The stories of their entanglements with Shaw are outside the scope of this essay, except to note that May Morris (then Mrs. Sparling) is first mentioned in Gilman's diary on July 28 and August 2, 1896, before the visit to Suffolk, and that Gilman stayed with Edith Nesbit Bland in Kent October 14–16, two months after she was in Suffolk. She liked them both and saw them again on return trips to England. Either of them could have told her a great deal about Shaw, and they both had reason to suggest that he had "an evil spirit" (DuCann 121–37, 153–70).

Evidence that Gilman did not include other Fabians in her dislike of Shaw appears in her diary entries for October 9, 14, 16, and 20, 1896, when she had dinner and tea with the Webbs at their London house, met Charlotte Payne Townsend there, and went to a Fabian meeting with the latter. Shaw is not mentioned in any entry. Gilman's and Shaw's comments on the October 9 Fabian meeting are instructive in showing their contrasting attitudes; Gilman's focus is on her contacts with other people; Shaw's is on himself.

Gilman wrote: "Go in evening to my first Fabian meeting. Very exciting. J. R. McDonald moves to withdraw 'Tract 70[.]' Animated discussion. The executive wins—tract retained. Mrs. Hubert Bland asks to be introduced & asks me to dinner. Mrs. Webb to tea. Mrs. Steele took me to have a 'Zabbioni.' Rev. Percy Dearmer sat by me." Shaw wrote: "At the Fabian Society I have had a heroic victory. I rashly boasted beforehand that my side would be victorious—that the enemy would be smashed, annihilated, routed, scattered. And it all came off; they were. I made a tearing speech, and was insufferably pleased with myself" (Terry 89; MacKenzie 231–32). One reason Gilman may have been repelled by Shaw was the monumental ego he displayed, as ego was for Gilman inimical to evolution and social service.

A year later in summer 1897, Gilman was back in the States on a lecture tour. On her birthday, July 3, she was in the small town of Eureka, Kansas, staying with the Addisons. Kate Addison was president of the Kansas Equal Suffrage Association; Gilman had been through Kansas lecturing in June 1896 just before her trip to England. Now she was back for a second round (Harper, *History of Woman Suffrage* 4: 647). Her diary notes, "The Addisons present me with a five dollar bill for a birthday present." On July 5 she recorded, "Mrs. A. & I drive in town after dinner" (*Diaries* 683). The drive probably included some shopping during which Stetson bought a book with the five-dollar bill and asked one of the Addisons to inscribe it. The inscription in her copy of Bernard Shaw's *On Going to Church* reads: "Birthday greeting July 5 '97 C.P.S. from A." (Scharnhorst and Knight 212). Perhaps it was curiosity or perhaps ambivalence about his "evil spirit," but however she acquired his book, she kept it.

Time passed and Shaw and Stetson, both highly productive writers, went their separate ways. In 1898 Shaw married Charlotte Payne Townsend; in 1900 Charlotte Stetson married Houghton Gilman and took his name. In 1908, in his preface to a reprint edition of *Fabian Essays,* Shaw noted of Socialists: "Today we neither respect our opponents nor confute them. We simply, like Mrs Stetson Gillman's [*sic*] prejudice slayer, 'walk through them as if they were not there'" (*Fabian* 288). He had not only remembered her poem "An Obstacle" but also assumed that his readers would do the same.

In 1912, a London physician, Sir Almroth Wright, published a letter in the *Times* condemning suffrage activism in terms of the general inferiority of women. Because of many favorable responses to the letter, Wright expanded it into a book in 1913, *The Unexpurgated Case against Woman Suffrage*. Wright was a friend of Shaw's and was his model for Sir Colenso Ridgeon in *The Doctor's Dilemma*. Shaw was in a tight corner: as a defender of woman's suffrage, he had to comment on Wright's book, but his response, "Sir Almroth Wright's Polemic" (*New Statesman,* October 18, 1913), minimized the whole matter by couching criticisms in high praise for his friend's "admirable honesty and splendid lucidity" and by lamenting how "thoughtless and unobservant an exceptionally gifted man can be." He even suggested that Wright made such an easy victim that the suffragist "will be disarmed by the manifest inhumanity of hitting a defenseless antagonist at all." He ends on a cheerful note with the hope that the Duel of Sex "will end over Sir Almroth Wright's book in frank confession and good-humoured laughter" (*Fabian* 243–47).

Gilman, who was not a friend of Wright's and who knew from firsthand experience how debilitating it was to be an intelligent woman in a male-dominated society, was not in the mood for good-humored laughter when she wrote an angry review of "The Unexpurgated Case of Sir Almroth Wright" in the November 1913 *Forerunner* (303–07). She quotes Wright as saying that woman has "stifled discussion by placing her taboo upon anything seriously unflattering being said about her in public" (304). Gilman replies that woman "has been under man-made taboos since most ancient times, but has, herself no power to enforce any. And most especially, when did she succeed in preventing anything seriously unflattering being said about her in public? . . . Seriously unflattering things about women are being said in public and have been said in public ever since men could talk. Literature is full of them, popular proverbs teem with them, club, bar-room and barber-shop reek with them, and the public press is wide open to them" (304). She quotes Wright at length, which Shaw does not, so readers may judge for themselves. Wright says: "The happy wife and mother is never passionately concerned about the suffrage." Gilman responds: "This is . . . quite false.

The suffrage movement knows many wives so happy that their husbands are with them in the work, often their children, too. It would seem that what Dr. Wright feels must be the case he states as fact." Gilman concludes, not like Shaw with laughter but with the view that to Wright "women are inferior to men because they are women; that . . . they have no right to the ballot because they cannot fight (and it is utterly abominable of them to show that they can!) and that the simple reason they want the suffrage is because they are sexually unsatisfied. This argument ought to appeal . . . to the man in the street, and doubtless will" (306). The differences between Shaw and Gilman in these two reviews, although both are pro-suffrage, are those of the sympathetic but superficial observer versus the inescapably involved person sworn to fight discrimination of the "Wright type."

By 1914 as the Great War began, Gilman, as she was now known, had published *The Forerunner* monthly for more than four years. She was a determined pacifist, but this belief did not mean that she failed to differentiate between the motives of the combatant nations. When she read a statement by Shaw in an unknown source, she reacted angrily in print in the August 1915 issue of *The Forerunner.* He had referred to British militarism and German militarism as being similar, and Gilman responded with a vigorous contradiction calling that suggestion ridiculous and absurd. She seems still to have entertained the idea that he possessed an evil spirit: "The preposterous claims of all the dreadful things England, France, and Russia were going to do to Germany become ridiculous in the face of the time it has taken them to develop an efficient opposition to the German assault. In especial become ridiculous the words of Mr. Bernard Shaw, comparing British militarism to Prussian militarism, and describing the British lion as long 'crouching for a spring' upon Germany. The palpable fact of her unpreparedness make[s] this crouching-for-a spring idea patently absurd" (*Forerunner* August 1915, 223).

The following year she stopped publishing *The Forerunner.* In the last section of the last issue, the "Comments & Review" of December 1916, she reviewed a play, *The Road Together,* by George Middleton, which she liked very much, comparing it favorably to Shaw's theatrical output in general and dismissing his plays by trivializing them: "Here is opportunity for sharp tragedy, for poignant melodrama, for an offensive farce, or for Mr. Shaw's inconclusive amusingness. But in the hands of Mr. Middleton we find instead of any of these the strong drama of life, real human life" (334). Thus she disposed of Shaw's "amusing" work (which she must after all have read or perhaps seen) because it did not deal with "real human life."

In 1928 Shaw published *An Intelligent Woman's Guide to Socialism and Capitalism,* opening his "Foreword for American Readers" with the statement: "I have never been in America." He went on to tell all about America anyway, ending by referring to the title of the book: "I have been asked whether there are any intelligent women in America. There must be; for politically the men there are such futile gossips that the United States could not possibly carry on unless there were some sort of practical intelligence back of them" (*Intelligent Woman's Guide* xi). On January 4 of that year, the *New York Times,* which Gilman often read, had quoted him as saying, "I am afraid to go to America. . . . I am, it is true, a master of comic irony, but even I could not bear to see the Statue of Liberty." If Gilman noticed these or any other of his written animadversions upon her country, which were many, she never was offended enough to rid her shelves of his *On Going to Church.*

On Going to Church is just a small book, barely sixty pages and too short to be divided into chapters. He had published it in January 1896 in the Savoy, before he and Gilman met; she may have seen a copy of it in Suffolk, where it is probable that she and Shaw, separately or together, visited the old church of St. Andrew. They at least may have discussed the church, since it was a small village with little else of interest, and they were staying in the church rectory. St. Andrew had admirable features: a Norman nave, a seven-hundred-year-old stone font, a Jacobean oak pulpit, and an Elizabethan chalice of beaten silver. From the tower battlements, strange faces looked down (Mee 370; Pevsner 415). Gilman certainly saw the exterior; if she went inside, it was probably the first English village church that she visited. She may therefore have kept Shaw's book as a reminder of her first English country visit, or because she could smile at Shaw's version of the Athanasian Creed, which he rewrites as, "I believe . . . in the Holy Trinity of Father, Son (or Mother, Daughter) and Spirit" (55). But she is most likely to have kept it because Shaw spoke of something she believed herself: a wider religious feeling to replace narrow doctrine-bound creeds. He concludes the book with the idea that churches are symbols of the universal catholic ideas affecting all humankind, and that we must enter the church "without thought or belief or prayer or any other vanity, so that the soul, freed from all that crushing lumber, may open all its avenues of life to the holy air of the true Catholic Church" (59–60).

Gilman held similar religious beliefs. In *His Religion and Hers,* published in 1923 when she was sixty-three, she wrote: "Seeing God as within us, to be expressed, instead of above us, to be worshipped, is enough to change heaven and earth in our minds, and gradually to bring heaven on earth by our actions" (292). She sees changed roles for men, women, and especially children (who have "an instinctive longing for happiness"), but she does not see a perfected future within early reach: "After a little, a few centuries or so, when we have cleared off all the rubbish from our minds; when the practical lifting of the world is well underway; when health is universal and all of us at the work we love best; when general education has given to every mind its background of common knowledge, its foreground of common hope, then the child's instinct for happiness will be fulfilled" (298). There is an echo here of Shaw's hope, expressed twenty-seven years before at the end of *On Going to Church,* that "the soul . . . may open all its avenues of life to the holy air of the true Catholic Church" (59–60), but Gilman expands Shaw's hope into an all-encompassing vision of a future world in which the liberated soul could operate to its full capacity.

In 1934, when Houghton Gilman died suddenly in Norwich Town, Connecticut, Charlotte Gilman disposed of their property and moved to California to live near her daughter, taking only sixteen pieces of baggage of which five were boxes of books and manuscripts (Lane 350). Among the books she kept on this final move was Shaw's *On Going to Church.*

Shaw, too, clung to something of hers. Nine years after her death he wrote a small item in a book about a friend, which showed that he still remembered her poem "An Obstacle." Among his Fabian friends of many years was Sydney Olivier, civil servant, colonial administrator, secretary of state for India, and eventually Lord Olivier. When Olivier's widow edited his letters for publication in 1944, Shaw wrote an introduction.

Olivier, said Shaw, was a law unto himself, being a frank and outspoken man. In fact, Shaw defined his friend in terms of Gilman's poem, which he had likely heard her read during that long ago visit at the Stratford St. Andrew rectory. Not only did he use the idea of dealing with an obstruction by ignoring it, but he still remembered that the particular obstruction in the poem was "a Prejudice," and he again quoted the concluding line of the poem.

He also remembered Gilman's name as it was then, and her nationality. Although she had been the well-known writer and lecturer Charlotte Perkins Gilman since 1900, she was still to him, in his old age, what she had been in Suffolk, "the American Mrs. Stetson." His comment, within a description of his friend Olivier, was written with the usual Shaw tongue-in-cheek: "[Sydney] had no apparent conscience, being on the whole too well disposed to need one; but when he had a whim that was flatly contrary to convention he gratified it openly and unscrupulously as a matter of course, dealing with any opposing prejudice by the method recommended by the American Mrs. Stetson, of 'walking through it as if it wasn't there'" (Olivier 10).

There is some difference between his use of the "method recommended" and how women readers may have read the poem, however, and that difference is gender-based. Gilman herself and many other women in 1896 were committed to "walking through" the social prejudices that limited their life options and crippled their potential. Those women who were fighting for suffrage and other rights may have identified the obstacle of prejudice in their own lives as principally male-engendered and male-enforced, a deeply serious problem for those negatively affected by it.

Shaw has also changed the sex of the Prejudice to the neuter "it." The final four lines of the poem actually contain masculine pronouns; the Prejudice is male. These lines read:

> I approached that awful incubus
>   With an absent-minded air—
> And I walked directly through him,
>   As if he wasn't there!

Shaw remembers the obstacle as having no gender; for Gilman and her followers the obstacle of gender bias was never neutral; it was an obstacle made for women by men, and this was a basic fact that could not be erased.

After Shaw's death in 1950, his biographer, Archibald Henderson, explained how it happened that Shaw used Gilman's poem and stressed that this was not an isolated incident. "One of the cleverest of American women of her day, a brilliant writer and speaker on social, educational and industrial problems, was Charlotte Perkins Stetson, who was later married to a Mr. Gilman. Shaw could never remember her name (curious idiosyncrasy for one with his phenomenal memory), and always called her Charlotte Stetson Perkins." Henderson quotes a slightly different version of the last six lines of the poem:

> I took my hat, I took my steels,
>   My load I settled fair;
> I approached that awful incubus
>   With an absent-minded air,
> And I *walked directly through him*,
>   As if he wasn't there.

Henderson continues, "Shaw told me that he had taken to heart the lesson of that poem; and the conquest of prejudice had been a vital factor in his life. 'I learned a great lesson,' he would often say, 'from Charlotte Stetson Perkins!'" (Henderson, *Man of the Century* 834–35).

One can regret only that through their long but tenuous acquaintance they did not emphasize what they had in common, especially in their criticisms aimed at improving their respective societies. Then they might have "walked right through" the obstacles of being of different sexes, different nationalities, and to some extent different mindsets. They might have been friends. Shaw may still have the greater reputation, but in Gilman's work to increase opportunity and recognition for half the human race, what she accomplished was of incomparably more value. "Her legacy is greater than many another whose name is better known" (Scharnhorst 119).

7
The Sins of the Mothers and Charlotte Perkins Gilman's Covert Alliance with Catharine Beecher

Monika Elbert

A new standard is rising—the woman's standard. It is based not on personal selfishness but on the high claims of motherhood, motherhood as a social service instead of man-service. This new motherhood shines before us like a sunrise. Women as world builders, women recognizing the need of stronger, nobler people and producing them.

> Charlotte Perkins Gilman, "The New Mothers of a New World" 249

She, who is the mother and housekeeper in a large family, is the sovereign of an empire demanding as varied cares, and involving more difficult duties, than are really exacted of her . . . while she wears the crown . . . [she] professedly regulates the interests of the greatest nation on earth.

> Catharine Beecher, *A Treatise on Domestic Economy* 144

Several months before her death, Charlotte Perkins Gilman wrote and sent a rather striking poem, "For Birth Control," to Margaret Sanger to help her commemorate the twenty-first anniversary of the U.S. birth-control movement at a gala event in Washington, D.C., the Birth Control Comes of Age Dinner (February 1935). Gilman, who had written many stories, essays, and verses celebrating the high standards that accompany voluntary motherhood, reiterates the cause and the need for birth control, "for mothers free to bear strong children willingly" (1–2). She also articulates the upshot of freedom of choice for women, "For mothers in whose power shall be / The lifting of humanity— / A world of improving more and more— / A world at peace from shore to shore" (10–13).

Motherhood for Gilman was a serious (and risky) business, as it had been in the abstract for her great-aunt, Catharine Beecher. Though Gilman did not frame her maternal discourse in the same sentimental tone of her Beecher foremother, her secularized discussion of motherhood was just as energetic, idealized, and impassioned. And indeed, the purpose of motherhood for Gilman, as for Beecher, a proponent of True Womanhood, was to improve the human race. This uplifting of humanity could be measured in two ways: by a stronger breed of children being born, but also by a more enlightened generation of women evolving. Like Catharine Beecher, Gilman felt that disease would beget disease, and the sins of the fathers—and more specifically from Gilman's perspective, the evil emanating from an excess of sexual desire (in the shape of venereal disease)—or imbalance between the physical and spiritual realms, would be passed on to the next generation.[1] For Beecher and for Gilman, physical fitness corresponding with mental health was necessary for good mothering; both women writers were in fact health-conscious; their view of mothering was defined more by the practical aspects of vibrant health than by a sentimental picture of romantic or narcissistic maternal love.

Indeed, Catharine Beecher was as pragmatic as her grand-niece Charlotte in advocating sex education for women; Beecher even preached ready access to knowledge about contraception (Van Why in Beecher and Stowe, *American Woman's Home* 17). Yet both were inclined to discourse publicly at least about sex as a means for procreation, not as pleasure, and in so doing, their writing about children became scientific and clinical. Each woman secularized the discourse of maternity, divesting it of sentimentality but still retaining the dichotomy between "good" and "bad" mothering. It is almost as if the fear of actual mothering compelled Gilman and Beecher to distance themselves by adopting the scientific discourse of physiology and pathology, as they hid behind the veneer of mother worship and the civic duty of women as mothers.

For Gilman, as for Beecher, woman's influence was paramount in shaping the future of her progeny and the destiny of the entire nation, but woman, however much she seemed empowered by this elevation, would have to take a back seat to the children. Many times, for example,

Gilman's female protagonists feel compelled to do certain duties, not for their own sake, but for the "sake" of the child (a word which is repeated in many stories). Children come first; Gilman, like Beecher, presents a child-centered rather than mother-centered (or woman-centered) ideology. Gilman spells out the mother's duty quite clearly: it is not only to breed healthy children—"The duty of the mother is first to produce children as good as or better than herself" (*Women and Economics* 187) but also to educate her children properly—"It is then the duty of the mother . . . to educate her children as to complete what bearing and nursing have only begun" (188).

This essay seeks to examine Gilman's complicity, however inadvertent, with Beecher, in her veneration of motherhood—and her emphasis on the social practice of maternity. Beecher, at times, seems quite advanced in her thinking about the biological well-being of the child and mother and does not blink an eye toward the language of the physical body. And conversely, although it would seem at such times, as in her treatise, *The Home*, as if Gilman is more progressive than Beecher in her views of motherhood, elsewhere Gilman identifies the mother as the highest form of womanhood. It is telling that their choices of titles for their domestic manuals are similar: compare Beecher's *American Woman's Home* (coauthored with sister Harriet) and Gilman's *The Home*. Yet both authors are also concerned about women's relationship to the physical world, or separate sphere of business, as manifest in their titles, *A Treatise on Domestic Economy* (Beecher) and *Women and Economics* (Gilman). Thus, both Beecher and Gilman share in the same veneration of the domestic realm, with the caveat that they elucidate unnecessary nostalgia that goes along with motherhood and that they stress practicality above sentiment.

Even in Gilman's most forward-looking, utopian work, *Herland*, the most revered woman is the great Mother figure, who reproduces asexually, by intellectual and spiritual means.[2] Gilman's most famous utopian vision is based on maternity on its own merits, without the added complexity of a husband and of sex. Indeed, in several of her essays, Gilman complains about modern emancipated women using sexuality wrongly— in an unthinking and lascivious manner, rivaling the promiscuity of the men in their lives. She calls for a more sacred view of sexuality, as the means by which children are begotten. Though Gilman feels that birth control has benefited women in their choice of planning, she also perceives an inherent misuse: it has become "a free ticket for selfish and fruitless indulgence, and an aid in the lamentable misbehavior of our times, affecting both men and women." She adds that this sexual excess or depravity is more dangerous for women. "In all that affects the health and happiness of the race, the mother is the most important factor" ("The New Generation of Women" in Ceplair, *Charlotte Perkins Gilman* 285). In the last analysis, woman was not to prioritize sexuality; her highest calling or duty was to have healthy children.

Quite clearly, this philosophy is child-oriented. In *Moving the Mountain,* the predecessor to *Herland,* Gilman's character Nellie announces "children are people, and the most valuable people on earth. The most important thing to a child is its mother. We made new mothers for them" (Gilman, in Kessler 161). From this passage, it becomes clear that the mother serves primarily as a tool for the child; she is an "important thing" to the child, and her needs are, for the most part, important, insofar as her fulfillment guarantees the happiness of the children, who are, after all, "the most valuable people on earth." Gilman fosters the cult of purity (in terms of health) and of service (or "usefulness," as Gilman's protagonists often say) as much as Catharine Beecher before her did.

Paradoxically, though known for her reformist tendencies, Gilman sometimes lapses into a veneration of motherhood bordering on the sentimental, whereas Beecher, deemed generally more conservative and sentimental, chastises young women for resorting to oversentimentalized or romanticized feelings. Philosophically, the two relatives and authors meet on the ever-shifting line between realism and sentimentalism.

Hildegard Hoeller, in her study of Edith Wharton, has shown how the two terrains often intersect, and what she says about Wharton's fiction can be applied to Gilman. Hoeller shows how realist and sentimental voices are in dialogue with each other and that in her later works Wharton actually shows the shortcomings of realism and tries to negotiate "the ideology of sentimental fiction" (Hoeller xii). Gilman, who is generally viewed in the realist tradition, also has forays (or lapses) into sentimentalism, as she waxes poetically about a future race of perfect mothers and the contemporary woman's ultimate happiness being linked to maternal duty. Part of this convergence of literary traditions might stem from Gilman's own confused maternal experience; as Denise D. Knight asserts, "Certainly Gilman's lingering doubts about her own maternal competence shaped her views" (Knight, *A Study* 63). Gilman's relationship with her mother also figures in her resorting at times to late-nineteenth-century realism and at others to mid-nineteenth-century sentimentalism. Gilman's sense of bonding with her mother was derived partly from "commiserating their way through sentimental novels." Even though her mother's invalid condition would later make her see the mother-daughter bond as oppressive (Hill, *The Making* 60), this sharing of a female-based sentimental text would influence Gilman in her later writing. Carol Farley Kessler, referring to Nina Baym's work on the sentimental heroine, shows how these novels could be empowering and attributes Gilman's later elevation of motherhood in her fiction to this bonding with her mother: "This reading with her mother was a positively formative influence upon her later utopian writing, one of which Gilman seems to have been unaware" (Kessler 18). Gilman seems to purge the sexual act and the excess of romantic feeling (which might make women make foolish choices) by indulging in the sentiment of maternity.

Beecher also seemed to sublimate sexual feeling, either by preaching physical exercise (much as Gilman later would do) or by prescribing maternal bliss as woman's highest goal. Though not prudish about contraception (true of her niece as well), Beecher condemned the popular trend among young women to mope and languish, as they find "a charm in Byron's misanthropic repinings" (*True Remedy* 43). Beecher decried "that restless longing for excitement, that craving for unattainable good, that morbid action of the imagination, that dissatisfaction with the world, that factitious interest in trifles, and those alterations of high excitement and brooding apathy" that she associated with the new type of "highly-cultivated female mind" (42, 43).

Maternity seemed a safe refuge from overstimulation of romantic feelings for both Gilman and Beecher; yet, it also served, paradoxically, as a way to express deep, even passionate, feelings in an acceptable and pragmatic fashion.[3] Gilman definitely negates the presumption that women are by nature good mothers when she decries the myth of sentimental motherhood: "She [modern woman] still believes, and her husband with her, in the infallible power of 'a mother's love' and a 'mother's care'; and our babies are buried by thousands and thousands without our learning anything by the continual sacrifice" (*The Home* 242). Sentimentalism turns to sensationalism as Gilman goes on, in journalistic style, to offer recent newspaper headlines as evidence exposing the lack of maternal instinct in contemporary woman. These headlines testify to women's negligence, incompetence, and physical or psychological incapacities; they range from "Mother and Baby Both Badly Burned," "Choked in Mother's Arms," "Escaping Gas Kills Baby," "Insane Mother's Crime," "Drowns Her Eight-Year-Old Daughter," to a most curious "The Mother of Twenty-Five Children . . . of these only three sons and four daughters are now living" (246). While Gilman uses these headlines to show the poisonous and claustrophobic environment of the modern private home, she also tries to define a "new science," which she calls "Child Culture" (243).

As Gilman announces in *Women and Economics*, motherhood could be reduced (or promoted, depending on one's view) to a science: "Motherhood is but a process of life, and open to study as all processes of life are open. . . . Motherhood, like every other natural process, is to be measured by its results" (178). Beecher, too, shares in this scientific bent, as she spends much time in her domestic handbooks discussing ways in which women could become better mothers by giving very factual accounts of the function of the human body (short lessons in biology and physiology), a quasi-scientific view of home economics, a compendium of exercises to maintain good health, a manual for gardening and cooking, and nonsentimental advice on rearing children.

In comparing Gilman's work with Beecher's, one notes that the most striking similarity is their view that there is not a maternal instinct, but that maternity is acculturated and learned—often through a period of trial and error. Yet both writers indicate that mothers can be held accountable for the mistakes they make in choices of partners or in their methods of bringing up babies, as mothers create the genetic and social environment for children's development. If the child is puny, sickly, or diseased, then the adage *"cherchez la mère"* could obtain. If motherhood was the most sacred of institutions, then mothers could be blamed for their mistakes. Thus, instead of telling quaint and sentimental stories about the joys of motherhood, these writers often resort, if not to scare tactics, then to guilt-trip tactics (how motherly!), in order to convey the same message that the more sentimental school of women writers exemplified by Harriet Beecher Stowe (Gilman's great-aunt, and Beecher's sister) promoted: that mothering is woman's most defining experience and most significant vocation.

Both writers are preoccupied with women's health and consequently the health of their children. Beecher warns of the deterioration of the American people and points to the debility of contemporary American mothers, which is passed on to the children: "And so American women every year become more and more nervous, sickly, and miserable, while they are bringing into existence a feeble, delicate, or deformed offspring" (*Physiology and Calisthenics* 151). She traces the sickness of women back to an imbalance in their mental and physical activity. "One portion of the women have all the exercise of the *nerves of motion,* and another have all the *brain-work,* while they thus grow up deficient and deformed, either intellectually or physically, or both" (150–51). A sick mother will beget sick children.

Gilman agrees that the balance between mind and body creates a healthy child: "A right motherhood . . . should understand with an ever-growing power the best methods of developing, strengthening, and directing the child's faculties of body and mind, so that each generation . . . would . . . show a finer, fuller growth, both physically and mentally, than the preceding" (*Women and Economics* 188). And in her essay "The New Generation of Women," Gilman goes so far as to advise women to have medical examinations before marriage for the protection of the unborn.

Moreover, Gilman worries about the health of the women of the lethargic middle- and upper-level classes whose health has deteriorated. After comparing them with the mothers of the "lower social classes" who can bear children easily and naturally, Gilman condemns the modern woman for her fragility, and says not to find blame for the vices of the father but to hold the mother responsible. "The more women weaken themselves and their offspring, and imperil their lives by anti-maternal habits, the more difficulty, danger, and expense are associated with this natural process, the more do women solemnly take credit to themselves and receive it from others for the glorious self-sacrifice with which they risk their lives (and their babies' lives!) for the preservation of humanity" (*Women and Economics* 201).

Similarly, Beecher in her treatises many times condemns the mothers of the degenerate middle and upper classes for relying so heavily upon servants and thus forsaking their own good health and that of their children; she paints an idyllic picture of mother and children working together at tasks around the house and thus maintaining good health by getting sufficient physical exercise (see, for example, *Physiology and Calisthenics* 121; *Treatise on Domestic Economy* 151).

Beecher's and Gilman's rhetorical styles are similar; they expose the problems that mothers have created by unhealthy habits or by improper ways of raising children, and then offer remedies for improvement. Their points of condemnation and the manner in which they express their censure often sound indistinguishable. For example, both writers attack middle-class and upper-class women for their vanity in following fashion and their folly in imposing their dangerous tastes in diet and dress onto their children. Gilman complains that women, as slaves to fashion, jeopardize their children's health by not allowing them to wear comfortable clothes: "She whose condition of arrested development makes her unquestionably submit to the distortion, constriction, weight, and profusion of fashion in clothing for her own body, is not likely to show much sense in dressing a child" (*The Home* 240).

Gilman goes on to show how mothers nourish their children improperly and also deprive them of vented, well-lit rooms. The same kind of Foucauldian surveillance which so maddens the protagonist of Gilman's "The Yellow Wall-Paper" is relevant to the situation of the child. She condemns this "constant watching," which stunts the child's mental and physical development: "We bar our windows and gate our stairs in some cases; but our principal reliance is on unending watchfulness and a system of rigid discipline. 'Children need constant care!' we maintain. . . . Convicts under sentence of death are in their last hours kept under surveillance like this, lest they take their own lives" (*The Home* 247).

Beecher likewise draws upon the folly of mothers in choosing bad clothing, nourishment, and ventilation for their children, and she shows the unhealthy impact such choices have on future generations. About clothing, Beecher laments, "A large majority of the mothers and daughters of the nation adopt a style of dress that is exactly calculated to produce disease and deformity" (*Physiology* 122). She also points to the ways in which mothers and teachers accelerate the deterioration of children's muscular and bone structure by allowing poor posture. "Some children are made to sit still for hours on seats at schools that do not properly support the body. . . . Other children are allowed to sit so many hours in wrong positions, either while reading or writing, as to bring on deformity by a similar process. Other children sleep on high pillows and in such uniformly wrong positions as induces deformity" (123). Elsewhere, she describes how "fashion in dress can . . . distort the bones, and misplace the most delicate organs, and interrupt every health function" (*Letters to the People* 110).

Beecher points out that the only remedy for such evils involves "proper exercise, diet, and fresh air" (123). She suggests that the children of wealthy mothers are at higher risk than those of the underclass, since they are deprived of fresh air and exercise. The purpose of Beecher's *Letters to the People on Health and Happiness* is to show how the present generation of children is being raised "to be feeble, deformed, homely, sick, and miserable" and how girls especially are having their health destroyed systematically (7). She compares the children of her generation (who were not sickly) to the children of the current generation, in both urban and rural areas—"a great portion of them either have sallow or pale complexions, or look delicate or partially misformed" (9). She warns that when this generation grows up, "they will have a still more puny and degenerate offspring" (10).

Time and again, Beecher indicates the need for wholesome (and not excessive) nourishment, exercise in fresh air, and proper sleep as the antidote to these evils. She warns of the dangers of the widespread practice of "pouring down medical liquids and pills" peddled by quacks (101) and condemns fad diets or cures, though she was much taken by the Water Cure.

Beecher also feels that mothers who show the virtues of patience, cheerfulness, and benevolence will teach the same to their children. Beecher, like Gilman, shuns the practice of being too strict and disciplinary with children; she disapproves of the "stern, unsympathizing maintenance of parental authority, demanding perfect and constant obedience, without any attempt to convince a child of the propriety and benevolence of the requisitions" (*Treatise on Domestic Economy* 227). Like Gilman, she believes that mothers are the guardians of the nation's health and will ensure the progress of the nation: "But it is to woman, to whom, as wife, mother, educator, nurse, and home-keeper, the training of the human body in infancy and the ministries of the sick-room are specially committed, who has the most direct and immediate interest and responsibility in this effort. . . . Woman is the Heaven-appointed guardian of health in the family" (*Letters* 186). She maintains that all women, not just biological mothers, should be committed to the health of others, since women, in their nurturing roles, all have this responsibility;

indeed, in her mind, Providence has designated that women should sustain "the family state, in all its sacred and varied relations and duties" (*Letters* 188).

Her injunction to the people in her *Letters to the People* is really a wake-up call to mothers to perform their duties with dignity and with the proper healthy attitude. In a rather patriotic fashion, which Gilman sometimes also indulges in, Beecher pronounces that "Our Country" depends upon the work of women. "But are not the most responsible of all duties committed to the care of woman? Is it not her profession to take care of mind, body, and soul?" (*Treatise on Domestic Economy* 30).

Catharine Beecher, a teacher, though not a biological mother, was known for her pioneering role in woman's education, as in her work at the Hartford Seminary, which sought to prepare women to be teachers —and to further the mission of women as guardians of health.[4] Apparently Beecher felt that women should be educated specifically for those nurturing professions—"their 'true profession' as educators and homemakers" (Sklar 222). Beecher also believed that even if women did not become biological mothers, there were only a few of "those who are unconnected, by family ties, friendship, or sympathy, with the children of others" (*American Woman's Home* 265).

Gilman's fictional characters, if not teachers or mothers per se, are involved in educating and maintaining the health of those around them. In "Fulfilment," the protagonist, Irma, brags to her sister, Elsie, a married woman with a family, that Elsie need not continue to feel sorry for her because she, Irma, has had a fulfilled life. Irma's definition of being fulfilled and having lived is by the maternal service she has rendered to an extended community. Though not a biological mother, she has been able to support herself by becoming a larger-than-life mother:

> "The kind of work I've done has helped people—lots of people —especially children. I've been a sort of foster-mother to hundreds of them, you see, some fifteen years, averaging twenty new ones a year—that's three hundred, besides those in the first five beginning years.
> Also—I adopted some." ("Fulfilment" 251)

Though the married Elsie is a complacent woman who has defined herself throughout life by her domestic responsibilities to her children and husband, Irma seems to validate her existence by showing her allegiance to a maternal ideal, even though, as she says to her sister, "The one thing I haven't got is the husband—there you are ahead" (252). They are both involved in affirming the values of, if not Beecher's Cult of True Womanhood, something very analogous to it.

In Gilman's story "Mrs. Beazley's Deeds," another woman is inspired, not to lethargy (as in "The Yellow Wall-Paper") but to action, as she is convinced by a strong female mentor to abandon her abusive husband and to "make a stand" for "the children's sake." The mentor (female boarder) of the story depicts how Mrs. Beazley "could make a home for the children" (*Yellow Wall-Paper and Other Stories* 171) and in some detail shows how each child's lot would improve with the new arrangement. Motherhood, once again, is the motivating factor for the woman's development and growing self-reliance. Many mothers in the Gilman canon are inspired to improve their condition by their preoccupation with their children or with their maternal roles. This accords with Beecher's idea that healthy women would become the best mothers.

In "Martha's Mother," Gilman portrays an invalid woman who is inspired to reclaim her initial vigor and "usefulness" (Solomon 222) by becoming the mother to young women in a boarding house. Moving from lethargy to domestic usefulness, and from rural retirement to the sinister city, she no longer relies on her daughter's efforts to support her. Indeed, she is finally able to protect the daughter, Martha, in mother hen fashion, by staving off her lecherous boss, who comes seeking Martha out in the mother's new extended home.

If women are not healthy enough to be good mothers, they are chastised in the Gilman canon; Beecher, too, called for women to muster up all their vital energies to become good mothers. For Beecher, a type of neurasthenia sets in when women are remiss in taking up regular exercise, which consequently leads to a type of mental and emotional stagnation. And bad health practices would be fostered among the children of such misguided women. In all of her treatises on home and health, Beecher encourages women to teach balance and good health to their children. Indeed, time and again, she encourages women to be physically fit—even in the limited capacity of keeping house—to maintain their own health and the happiness of their children. "Bad" mothering in Gilman could be understood as giving in to depression or lassitude, even when it is imposed upon them through rest cures, as in "The Yellow

Wall-Paper," or by making wrong choices of husbands, who might pass on bad genes or worse, venereal disease, to the unborn children.[5]

In "Joan's Defender," Gilman presents another portrait of a woman, Madge Marsden, who is advised by her physician brother to relinquish for one year her sensitive daughter, Joan, into the safekeeping of his wife, a better mother. As a perfect companion piece to "The Yellow Wall-Paper," this story shows how an invalid woman is forced into further invalidism and is, essentially, preempted by the expert, in this case, her physician brother, who promptly points out her flaws as a mother.[6] Though the brother knows that Joan's bully of a father has a great deal to do with her mother's passive condition, he does not try to meddle in their domestic affairs. Instead of giving his sister the benefit of the doubt, he blames her. "For the children's sake," he says, "you ought to be stronger, Madge. See here, suppose you lend me Joan for a long visit" (*Yellow Wall-Paper and Other Stories* 317). As in "The Yellow Wall-Paper," the physician-expert deprives her of her maternal rights; this request to "borrow" her child is preposterous (318). Madge suffers from the same type of neurasthenia as the narrator in "The Yellow Wall-Paper," but her brother basically gives up on her and chooses instead to focus on her daughter, whom he feels he can refashion into the woman his sister can never be. Joan, the daughter, "was a different proposition . . . she had no serious physical disability as yet" (317). The mother, though, seems doomed:

> Nothing in particular was the matter with his sister except the fretful temper she was born with, idle habits, and the effects of an overbearing husband.
>
> The temper he could not alter, the habits he could not change, nor the husband either, so he gave her up—she was out of his reach. (317)

This censure sounds much like the initial indictment by the narrator, which we hear in the first two sentences: "Joan's mother was a poor defense. Her maternal instinct did not present that unbroken front of sterling courage, that measureless reserve of patience, that unfailing wisdom which we are taught to expect of it" (314). One could perhaps take this indictment ironically, except for the fact that Joan does thrive when she is taken away from the mother, and the mother remains a pathetic woman. It is obvious that the brother's child-centered philosophy comes at the expense of the mother's welfare, and that type of thinking recurs in many of Gilman's stories. Dr. Warren is not "severe" with the children: "He believed in giving a child the benefit of every doubt, and especially the benefit of time" (316). But he begrudges his sister this time and patience. In the end, if a woman has sickly children in the Gilman canon, it is because she herself is overly sensitive or feeble, she has been promiscuous, or she has made a bad choice of a husband. In either case, the woman is blamed for the condition of the children.

Several stories by Gilman, such as "The Vintage," "One Way Out," and the novel *The Crux*, serve as cautionary tales to show how women are punished for falling in love with men who have venereal disease. As Gilman laments in "The New Generation of Women," modern woman has become as licentious and excessive as men, and this requires "medical examination before marriage" (288). Indeed, Gilman insists on woman's responsibility in the reproductive process: "This effort to protect the unborn from the worst of diseases requires knowledge, courage, and a high sense of woman's responsibility" (288).

In *The Crux*, Gilman's spokesperson, Dr. Bellair, instructs the innocent Vivian, "Marriage is motherhood. . . . That is its initial purpose" (121). Dr. Bellair laments her own childless situation and takes the blame upon herself. "I married a man who had gonorrhea. In place of happy love, lonely pain. In place of motherhood, disease" (120). She laments the fact that young women are not instructed in sex education. "Girls aren't taught a word of what's before them till it's too late" (120). In her own admission, Dr. Bellair explains how she has transferred her maternal feelings to her profession: "When I found out that I could not be a mother, I determined to be a doctor, and save other women, if I could" (120). Thus, her career is based upon a desire for motherhood, not on some other rational impulse.

Dr. Bellair appeals to her charge, Vivian, by projecting her own maternal failure; she appeals to Vivian's maternal aspirations to thwart her intended marriage to a man with venereal disease. She asks of Vivian, "You love children, don't you, Vivian?", to which Vivian responds with a "heavenly smile on her face . . . Better than anything in the world" (Gilman, in *Reader*, ed. Lane, 120). In order to convince Vivian completely about her potential tragedy with a diseased man, she resorts to the rhetoric of sentimentality: "Think about their lovely little soft helplessness—

when you hold them in your arms and have to do *everything* for them"
(120). It is almost as if Dr. Bellair has transferred her maternal aspirations
(she was not able to have children, as her husband had gonorrhea) onto
a surrogate daughter.

The cycle is made complete through the vision of maternity; the
bonding between surrogate mother and daughter is made possible. But
then rather sensationally, in the vein of sentimental literature, Dr. Bellair
subverts the image of cute, pink-cheeked babies to paint a grim picture
of babies inheriting venereal disease. They appear in various ways, as
"crippled," "idiots," "blind," or stillborn. The discourse of disease leaves
as great an impression on women as the sentimental language of blissful
mothering; it serves as a cautionary tale for women to be vigilant in their
selection of husbands and in their own sexual practices.

Remarkably, these depictions of stunted babies depend upon the same
pathos as pictures of bouncing babies in sentimental literature. The images are emotionally evocative and as manipulative as any tableaux of
motherhood that Stowe could have created. Indeed, in Gilman, Stowe,
and Beecher, the impetus is on the child, not on the woman. In her dec-
laration of fitness for parenting, "The New Mothers of the New World"
(1913), Gilman states in no uncertain terms that the future of the country
depends on women's proper choices. "We will marry only clean men,
fit to be fathers. . . . We will breed a better stock on earth by proper
selection—that is a mother's duty" (248).

A woman's poor choice of a mate in terms of eugenics is evidenced
in Gilman's "The Vintage." Here, Leslie, a "vigorous girl" of "blazing
health" (104), bears a crippled child and has various stillborns, until she
herself succumbs to death—all as a result of her improper choice of a
husband, a man who had contracted syphilis. So "Again and again she
undertook the mother task, to mould and fashion with long love and
patience another child" (106), but all of her attempts are aborted. When
Leslie's son grows up, he is not allowed to marry, for he himself would
pass on the disease; the sins of the fathers have been visited upon the
next generation. In a different take, in "One Way Out," a woman uses
the pretext of bad genes to avert a marriage she is not impassioned about.
After taking her cousin/fiancé to a lecture on heredity and consumption,
she warns him about the consumption which runs in the family and advises a termination of their engagement.

On another note, Gilman, at her most ethnicist, depicts a woman who has chosen a spouse unwisely. Ellen Burrell, moved by passion, "let herself go by marrying an Italian lover, a successful man enough, but hopelessly a 'Dago'" ("His Mother" 73). Ellen's punishment is to have a son equally as seductive and charming as her husband. When the son abandons a girl he has gotten pregnant, Ellen Burrell finds her redemption in helping "ruined girls" in "Magdalen asylums." She recognizes "the father" in her irresponsible son and blames herself: "That's my fault for giving him such a father" (76). Finally, she has him arrested for his involvement in getting girls involved in prostitution, basically disowns him, and devotes her life entirely to the fallen women, her new children.

Gilman's fables and poems also contain similar lessons in eugenics—and in the Darwinian impulse to breed strong children. In "Improving on Nature," for example, Mother Nature chastises Man for wanting to select the smallest, most fragile, helpless, and ornamental woman as his wife; as she puts it, "Picks out the weak timid ones, does he? And what does he inherit then?" (214). In a rather complementary but stereotypical way, Mother Nature then looks at the perfect specimens of women, those who have developed physically and are strong and wise—the African woman, the American woman of the Far West, the German peasant woman, and the woman from India (216). Her final command is to follow the course of nature, which is for women to do the choosing of their mates, not vice versa. Scolding the male, she advises, "She is not your female—you are her male! Go study your biology!" (217). To woman, she places a higher command: "Resume your natural function of choosing—and make the kind of man you like—that is your especial duty to the race" (216). Again, there is no talk of love here; it is practical advice which revolves around the welfare of the children.

In two of her most important treatises for women, *Women and Economics* and *The Home,* Gilman finds fault with woman's emphasis on her superficial role as sex object and as consumer, linking the two, and attributing the evils of excess in sex or in consumerism to Freudian psychology or to a capitalist economy. In "The Lady Oyster," Gilman alludes to what she often refers to in her stories, the need to make children woman's mission. "Think of the world your children have to live in. Think of the diseases we die under, unnecessarily. . . . Rouse up and do something for your children after they are reared—and for other people's children" (212). In "Wild Oats and Tame Wheat," one finds the recurrent theme that a naïve woman might contract venereal disease unwittingly, and there is a major condemnation of man: "He shared with her what he thought fit, including his diseases" (219).

Finally, in the fable "Freed," Gilman shows her propensity to clean up the human race through good mothering. "All of the women in the world, free, proud, strong, saw with new eyes the duty of women, and re-populated the earth with a *clean* people . . . " (209; emphasis added).

This emphasis on a sterile-clean environment and on Amazon-like health and strength for women, as well as an obsession with purity, racial or biological, is also manifest in Gilman's many poems. Though one might have expected a more political stance from Gilman's *Suffrage Songs and Verses,* one finds, instead, a mother and child-centered ideology, appealing to women in almost a religious way, to carry on the important task of breeding, for the good of the nation. In "Song for Equal Suffrage," the speaker makes an almost anti-suffragist statement: "Woman's right is woman's duty . . . We are half of every nation! We are mothers of them all!" (23). This frenetic pitch is achieved in many of her verses; in "The Housewife," woman is seen as the "Mother of Nations!" (9). In "We As Women," the speaker talks about woman's ability to "purify politics" (12).

This purification of the state by maternal women, as we shall see shortly, is also true of Beecher's discourse. Gilman's "She Who Is to Come" presents a spiritual type of goddess mother (the "Beloved") who will redeem the world: "A mother—with a great heart that enfoldeth / The children of the Race . . . " (24). In "Mother to Child," the speaker imagines a new type of communal motherhood, in which "loving mothers" stretch from land to land and hold "all" children dear. Reminiscent of the moral of Gilman's stories is the speaker's injunction, "Love all [children] for the child's sake!" (7).

The tone of Gilman's poems in *In This Our World* is not very different from those of the suffrage poems, except for the fact that there is more emphasis on woman's biological role in the Darwinian sense. In the poem "Motherhood," the speaker discusses the need for woman to remain healthy and strong in her mission: "A clean, strong body, perfect and full grown, / Fair for the purpose of its womanhood, / Not for light fancy of a lower mind" (134). Here, as in "Girls of To-Day," the speaker sounds disturbingly like Walt Whitman in his rhapsodizing about the mothers producing a new breed of sons, or in Gilman's words, a "glorious New Mother of New Men" (135) or "makers of men" (147).

Gilman's and Catharine Beecher's concerns about womanhood truly converge—in the practical matter of woman's health issues. And when one discusses health, one inherently becomes less sentimental than if one simply discusses the glories of motherhood. Beecher is just as concerned about women's mental and physical fitness to become mothers, though Gilman's access to Darwinian concepts about heredity were not yet available to Beecher. Yet that troublesome tendency which Gilman pressed—the obsession with purity, and the need to make over men, who are seen as less than healthy in their desires and in their health—is also true of Beecher.

By looking at Beecher's domestic treatises as well as her handbooks about health, such as *Letters to the People on Health and Happiness* (1855) and *Physiology and Calisthenics* (1856), one can see the centrality of the material realm. The physical and practical realm of physical fitness and mental health is as important to Beecher's sense of good mothering as any sentimental image her works might sometimes evoke. Catharine Beecher, as an upholder of True Womanhood, is not as prudish about the physical realm as has been frequently suggested; in her exercise and health manuals, she goes into great detail about the functions of the body, even to the extent of including diagrams and illustrations.

In her essay "The New Generation of Women," Gilman sounds much like her great-aunt Catharine Beecher in her assertion that a "strong, active, well-muscled body is a blessing to a woman as much as to a man" (280). Like Beecher, Gilman felt that physical education should be required of girls and young women at school. Beecher maintains that a woman cannot take "rational care of the health of a family, except by communicating that knowledge in regard to the construction of the body and the laws of health which is the basis of the medical profession" (*American Woman's Home* 104). Bad morality may breed pestilence, as the sins of the fathers are visited upon the next generation. The mother's influence is of paramount importance for both Gilman and Beecher. Beecher felt that "nothing has a greater influence to secure" a child's happy and healthy temperament "than a mother's example" (215) and cautions strongly against any other interpretation:

> When sons and daughters grow up sickly and feeble, parents commonly regard the event as a visitation of Providence. They assume that these evils come without cause, or that the evil is super-

natural. Nothing of the kind. In some cases causes are inherited, but in most cases foolish management is the cause. Very generally parents themselves are responsible for this pain, this debility, this depression, this misery. . . . In utter ignorance of the simplest physiological laws, they have been . . . undermining the constitutions of their children, and so have inflicted disease and premature death, not only on them, but also on their descendants. (*American Woman's Home* 264)

The antidote to this sad chain of events is for the woman to be properly educated in the management of babies early on in life. Beecher also suggests that a healthy and active body will ensure the healthy mind needed for good motherhood. In a passage concerning the connection between body and mind, Beecher might well have instructed Gilman's narrator in "The Yellow Wall-Paper" on the meaning of self-reliance and the power of mobility in the realm of health: "The indications of a diseased mind, owing to the want of proper exercise of its powers, are apathy, discontent, a restless longing for excitement, a craving for unattainable good, a diseased and morbid action of the imagination. . . . " (262). Like the negative Gilman protagonist, this type of woman might give in to alternating states of "languor" and "over-excitement." Beecher, like Gilman, is especially worried about the woman who will indulge in sensuality to elevate a sense of excitement; certainly, Gilman does inherit this Beecher prudishness.

Finally, both Gilman and Catharine Beecher see the possibility of the mother/woman effecting social change within the nation; this vision is more than obvious in this chapter's introductory epigraphs. Beecher goes so far as to compare woman's influence to that of the statesman. And in her *Treatise on Domestic Economy*, Beecher points to the mother's influence over her children and her husband—suggesting that the security of the nation resides upon the rule of the mother. This rhetoric is very similar to that of Gilman, especially in her collection of suffrage poems.

The paradigm of cleansing the nation requires that the women have something or someone to purify, and for both Gilman and Beecher, they do: first themselves, next the children, and then, of course, men. As Beecher maintains, "American women . . . more than any others on earth" have "the extended privilege of extending over the world those blessed influences, which are to renovate degraded man" (*Domestic Economy* 13).

This need to "degrade" men so that women can have a regal and superior position as wives and mothers is problematic in Beecher's as well as in Gilman's constructions of motherhood.

It comes as a surprise, then, that critics have made Gilman out to be such a radical feminist, especially in her depiction of motherhood—since it resonates with definitions of a bygone era. But critics then and now have recognized Gilman's basic conservatism. Gary Scharnhorst tries to make sense of her reactionary and elitist tendencies and points to her fears of miscegenation and of sexual freedom. He explores her distrust of contemporary feminists and asserts that in her later essays "Gilman seemed petulant and prudish, scarcely a progressive at all" (*Charlotte Perkins Gilman* 70).

Amy Wellington, a contemporary of Gilman's, felt that it was odd and unjust that the popular consensus of Gilman was that she was "dangerous" and "erratic" and sought to destroy family life (67–68). In Gilman's defense, Wellington portrays Gilman as a reformer who believed in "permanent monogamous marriage" (68) as well as a "'thinking motherhood'—a motherhood free, at last, not only from economic and political, but from sexual subjugation" (72). At least this one contemporary acknowledged that marriage and motherhood were of prime importance to Gilman.

Another contemporary, Annie L. Muzzey, defends Gilman in a short essay: "So far from undervaluing the vocation of maternity, which has been conceded as the one unquestioned right of womanhood, it must be acknowledged by even her severest critics, that Mrs. Stetson exalts and broadens the office and power of motherhood" (89). Though critics have seen Gilman's treatment of motherhood as harsh, Muzzey asserts that Gilman shows "an unusual reverence for all that is deepest, purest, and holiest" in motherhood and wifehood, only leaving out the "false sentiment" often associated with the institution of motherhood (89). It is not comprehensible how critics of her time saw her as a "dangerous meddler," dangerous because, in her book *Women and Economics,* she "gives small encouragement to women to stay by the hearthside" ("Charlotte Perkins Gilman" 2).

As this essay has shown, Gilman did venerate motherhood, often to the point of writing sentimentally about it, especially in her stories and poems, and this veneration aligns her with her great-aunt Catharine Beecher. In her essays, she is more rational in her promotion of motherhood. However, even there, she sounds a bit hyperbolic. For instance, at the conclusion of her essay "The New Generation of Women," Gilman evokes an image of the Great Mother and insists that women in her generation as in those of prior generations will always be best defined as mothers, partly because of their biology: "No honest thinker need be alarmed by the new status of women. The laws of nature are apt to have their way. Women are first, last and always mothers, and will so continue." She juxtaposes the rhetoric of censure with that of the sublime when she returns to the image of the mother. "We may look over and beyond the physical indecencies of our misguided young people, as well as of the older generation, and the mental indecencies of a sex-ridden psychoanalysis, and see before us the same dutiful and affectionate mother, whom we have always loved, with a broader outlook and larger powers." This redemptive, larger-than-life mother seems to be the ballast of society, for as Gilman concludes, "Motherhood will keep" ("The New Generation of Women" 288).

This opinion is not very different from Catharine Beecher's assessment about the saving grace of the American mother and of the institution of motherhood, dedicating her first treatise on domestic economy "to American Women, who, as housekeepers, mothers, and school teachers, are to decide the safety and prosperity of our country." In the domestic handbook she coauthored with Stowe, *American Woman's Home,* the dedicatory inscription is similar, even though the book was published almost thirty years later, after the nation has experienced the great discord of a "House Divided" (that public event is described with domestic terminology) in the Civil War.[7] Even then, mothers are seen as the country's salvation. The book is dedicated "to the women of America, in whose hands rest the real defense of the republic, as moulded by the early training and preserved amid the maturer influences of home" (iii). In her prefatory poem ("Two Callings") to her domestic treatise, *The Home* (1903), Gilman also maintains that motherhood, albeit a new form of liberated motherhood, will save the world: "But Mother—the World's Mother—come at last / To love as she had never loved before / To feed and guard and teach the human race" (xxiii). Though she might have relinquished her daughter to her husband in her personal life, Gilman, as a national spokesperson, could not relinquish her maternal duty in her writings.

Beecher and Gilman had similar reasons for writing their domestic treatises and for setting the mother on the altar of the nation. The entire Beecher clan felt that woman's most important responsibility was child-rearing, and their books try to educate future mothers. The main difference is that the Beecher great-aunts celebrated housekeeping duties for a wife, whereas Gilman tried to shirk those earlier domestic duties of the "Cult of True Womanhood." For both Gilman and her great-aunt, the material realm is juxtaposed with the cultural myths of motherhood to debunk or downplay the mysterious and mythologized views of woman-hood promulgated by the cult of domesticity. Gilman, though, is able to use the frenzied high pitch of sentimental discourse and transform it into a Darwinian discourse, infused with Gilman's passionate plea for healthy parents and children. Both the sentimental and the Darwinian discourse affect the reader by inspiring the horror of loss (in the senti-mental) or the horror of disease. Thus, the spiritual and the secular con-verge in a grotesque manner in Beecher's and in Gilman's notions of mothering.

Notes

1. As Cynthia J. Davis discusses, Gilman was inspired by the evolutionary theories of sociologist Lester F. Ward, who felt that woman, and not man, was the first and primary life force; his "female-centered theory allowed Gilman to give full voice to her essentialist understandings of women as mother without risk of pathologizing taint" (Davis 149). Also, see Dale Bauer, who examines Edith Wharton's problematic views toward genetics and race at the turn of the century. Recently, after my writing this essay, Dana Seitler published an article on eugenics in Charlotte Perkins Gilman's writings—about how Gilman's no-tion of natural selection for good "moral" mothers privileged white middle-class motherhood and fed into the racist notions of eugenics and degeneration popu-lar at the time.

2. Sandra Gilbert and Susan Gubar discuss Gilman's "misreading" of the maternal and also her misapplication of Lester Ward's injunction for men to "fecundate." In *His Religion and Hers*, Gilman "essentialized and biologized race . . . conflating physical evolution with moral improvement in often sinister or ludicrous ways" (Gilbert and Gubar, "'Fecundate! Discriminate!'" 214). Gilbert and Gubar associate Gilman's ambiguity about motherhood with modern femi-nists' equally ambiguous constructions of maternity.

3. In her own estimation, Charlotte Perkins Gilman felt that she inherited the "Beecher urge to social service" (*Living* 6) as well as the family predisposi-

tion to depression, for Dr. S. Weir Mitchell told her scornfully that he had already treated two other Beecher women (*Living* 95). Not many critics have traced Gilman's ideological roots back to her Beecher family tree. Several critics have dwelt in passing upon superficial similarities and, in insisting upon Gilman's radical nature, have emphasized the differences—and thus missed the striking and deeper similarities. Robert Shulman points out that Gilman, like her great-aunts, used fiction as a tool for reform to try to "re-vision" a new life for women. However, Shulman feels that Gilman challenged the "domestic ideology" promoted by her great-aunts (xxvii). Polly Wynn Allen maintains that Gilman tried her entire life to overturn "the domestic ideology so sacred" to Catharine Beecher and Harriet Beecher Stowe, but that ultimately she owed her analysis of the "socioeconomic organization of domesticity" to their influence (*Building Domestic Liberty* 83–84). Gillian Brown mentions how Catharine Beecher and Gilman were both interested in refashioning domestic architecture to liberate women, though Gilman's utopian vision was far less agoraphobic (*Domestic Individualism* 177–78). Dorothy Berkson believes that both Stowe and Gilman looked to a "maternalized religion" to overcome the evils of cold patriarchal thinking ("So We All Became Mothers" 108–09). Milton Rugoff, biographer of the Beecher family, maintains that Gilman shares the Beecher commitment "to a social ideal." He likens "Catharine Beecher's early campaigns for women's education and financial independence" to "Charlotte's efforts to live as a liberated woman in the 1890's" (*The Beechers* 593). Ann J. Lane discusses the depression shared by the Beecher family and passed on to Charlotte. Catharine Beecher had a nervous breakdown at twenty-nine and then again at thirty-five and was sent to a sanitarium for the then-famous water cure; Harriet Beecher Stowe would later also spend time in the same sanitarium for depression (Lane, *To Herland* 110–11). Mary A. Hill remarks that the Beecher women, whom Gilman visited as a child, were Charlotte's earliest role models and that her feminist and social consciousness developed as a result of her connection to them (*Making of a Radical Feminist* 14–15). Carol Farley Kessler aptly notes that Gilman's "diverse paternal legacy" (which included Catharine Beecher and Harriet Beecher Stowe) presented her "with challenging, albeit conflicting, models for being a woman" ("Dreaming Always" 16). Valerie Gill points out that Catharine Beecher and Harriet Beecher Stowe "attacked 'domestic femininity' while glorifying it" ("Catherine Beecher and Charlotte Perkins Gilman" 16); I feel that Gilman is similarly paradoxical and subversive, always maintaining high regard for maternity even as she shows the overwhelming burden attached to it.

4. Curiously, Beecher felt that what was lacking at some of the institutions for the Water Cure, which she patronized, was the mother figure, who would offer a holistic approach to health: "Another defect in such institutions is the want of an intelligent, refined, and sympathizing matron to fulfill the offices of a mother in the care and superintendence of the whole concern" (*Letters* 147). Note also that she praises the type of female seminary that allows girls to engage in household management and physical domestic work while a motherly woman supervises; there are "thirty or forty merry girls, superintended by a motherly lady, chatting and singing, washing and starching, while every convenience is at hand, and every thing around is clean and comfortable" (*Treatise on Domestic Economy* 32).

Compare Gilman's notion of a maternal, utopian establishment for women's recovery of health, as depicted in "Dr. Clair's Place." Dr. Clair, who has two children of her own, becomes a communal type of mother as she opens up a "psycho-sanitorium," called "The Hills," to help nurse women who are ailing (neurasthenic) back to health. This treatment is not like S. Weir Mitchell's "rest cure." Instead, like Beecher before her, she promotes a variety of activities—intellectual, physical, and domestic—to help with women's recovery. Among these activities were "basket-work, spinning, weaving, knitting, embroidery" and "gardening" (Gilman, in Shulman 298). Beecher envisioned an ideal establishment for recovery as a "Temple of Health," whose environs were to be about as large in size as Washington, D.C. This institution was to merge "the atmosphere of a water-spa, a college, and an amusement park" (Burbick 102). Her utopian conception was unfortunately a bit classist and totalitarian, with "health police" in charge (103), and in this particular plan for the future, Beecher seemed less maternalistic than in prior conceptions.

5. See Janet Beer's studies on the centrality of health in Gilman's fiction, although she focuses on the imagery of disease and sickness as it pertains to the diseased institution of marriage.

6. See Barbara Ehrenreich and Deirdre English for an early and still valid study of the male expert's influence on women in the health and medical fields.

7. According to Joseph Van Why, Catharine Beecher penned most of *American Woman's Home*, but she included Stowe as one of the authors so that the book would seem more acceptable and sell better: "Catharine was shrewdly aware that the public might question a spinster woman in her late sixties writing authoritatively on such subjects" (iii). It is interesting that Catharine as "spinster" and Gilman as divorced mother might both be seen as pariahs writing

about something that they did not understand—hence the danger perceived by the critics. Both finally tried to be scientific about the concept of motherhood, but vestiges of a romanticized motherhood remain. In their attempt to be factual or scientific about motherhood, they might have tried to seem as if they could be authorities on the maternal experience that neither could fully claim.

8

Gilman's *The Crux* and Owen Wister's *The Virginian*

Intertextuality and "Woman's Manifest Destiny"

Jennifer S. Tuttle

The American Western has long been considered a genre inhospitable to women. Its valorizations of masculine individuality, male homosociality, violent physical struggle, and public, outdoor life are frequently mentioned in feminist critiques of the genre. Indeed, some critics, most notably Jane Tompkins, have asserted that the Western arose precisely as a rejection of the values espoused in the most popular literary form of the nineteenth century, the so-called domestic novel, which was written largely by women and made women's experience central to the plot. In the conventional Western, women are either erased entirely from the landscape, or cast (at best) as supporting characters or (at worst) as impediments to male heroism.[1] In *The Crux,* a novel first published serially in *The Forerunner* in 1911, Charlotte Perkins Gilman provides a middle-class white woman's answer to the Western, combining this nascent masculinist tradition with long-established "female" literary modes. Building on the recent work of scholars such as Deborah Evans and Judith Allen, who have noted the novel's invocation and transformation of traditional Western themes and devices, I explore here an intertextuality between *The Crux* and the prototypical Western, Owen Wister's *The Virginian,* which was one of Gilman's favorite novels (Scharnhorst, *Charlotte Perkins Gilman* 98).[2] In *The Crux,* Gilman does not simply respond to the Western genre with a tale of female heroines in the West; she invokes Wister's novel explicitly and in multiple ways, telling her story not from the point of view of a male hero but from the perspective of the eastern white woman who, like Western women and women of color, conventionally is silenced, objectified, or obliterated altogether from mainstream representations of the Western experience. In doing so, Gilman intertwines two seemingly incompatible genres, appropriating elements of both the domestic novel and the Western to forge a powerful articulation of what she called elsewhere "Woman's 'Manifest Destiny.'" This generic combination allows Gilman to critique traditional gender roles and social organization, and to offer a new vision of individual and social health.

Gilman's choice of the Western as her touchstone was especially powerful because this new genre was beginning to provide a vehicle for exploring issues of national import, including social organization, race relations, and American nationalism and imperialism. *The Virginian,* first published in 1902, is often recognized as the first novel to formulate the Western plot that would become so popular in the twentieth century, and is noted for its concern with such national issues.[3] The story's narrator is a sickly, eastern white man who flees the exhausting and feminizing social obligations of the East for the supposedly free and masculine West. Through his eyes, readers meet the novel's eponymous cowboy hero, whose masculinity the narrator attempts to emulate in hopes of regaining his own vigor. This title character, the Virginian, is an icon of Western manliness, and the story presents his transformation from a young embodiment of the West's promise of freedom, independence, and individuality, to a masterful leader of a renewed American civilization reborn in the West. This rebirth is made possible by the Virginian's courtship of the eastern schoolmarm, Molly Wood. Throughout the novel, Wister makes great sport of Molly, a spinster and somewhat reluctant "New Woman" whose New England, "civilizing" ways ultimately are mastered and coopted, through marriage, by the Virginian.

In *The Crux,* Gilman retells this conventional Western plot from what is in effect Molly Wood's point of view, recasting Wister's schoolmarm as her own character, Vivian Lane. The story revolves around a group of women, with Vivian at its center, who leave behind the stagnant and oppressive New England way of life to migrate westward on the advice of a woman physician, finding growth and establishing an enlightened community in Colorado. Whereas in their hometown of Bainville, Massachusetts, with its repressive traditions, excess of unmarried women, and scarcity of marriageable men, such women languish out of duty to the old ways, in the West they form the heart of a thriving new world founded on many of Gilman's principles for progressive social change.

Vivian's recovery in the West is the centerpiece of this story, for she suc-ceeds not only in narrowly avoiding marriage with a syphilitic man (which affirms her need to reject outmoded models of feminine "inno-cence" and to embrace sexual self-determination) in favor of a more suit-able betrothal, but also in finding economic independence in the profes-sion of her choice.

Not surprisingly, as the plot of *The Crux* suggests, Gilman's novel is grounded firmly within a number of literary trends associated with American women writers. As a cautionary tale that "fulfilled the social function of testing some of the possibilities for romance and courtship—testing better conducted in the world of fiction than in the world of fact," Gilman's novel reinvents the late-eighteenth-century seduction novel, in which, as Cathy Davidson argues, women were encouraged to take more control over their own lives in their dealings with men (*Revolution and the Word* 113). Similarly, the novel contains many of the hallmarks of so-called domestic fiction popular in the mid-nineteenth century. Gilman grounds her plot in women's lives and struggles, centering on the trials and triumphs of her young heroine, Vivian. Indeed, she bases the book's vision of community on women's moral authority and supposedly essen-tial female virtues.[4]

Finally, Gilman's novel speaks to much of turn-of-the-century wom-en's fiction with its focus on the New Womanly pursuits of professional fulfillment and economic independence.[5] Yet Gilman also seeks to reach beyond traditional "feminine" modes of expression in *The Crux,* and she does so through her allusions to Wister's novel and her appropriation of the Western plot more generally. Women had, of course, long been writ-ing about the frontier, and Annette Kolodny has suggested that the last part of the nineteenth century marked a new era in such writing, in which women could fulfill both the role of "domesticator" and that of "adventurer" (Kolodny, *Land before Her* 240).[6] While she was not the first to write such a tale, Gilman's invocation of, and response to, Wister's novel allows her to mold the newly developed Western genre to her own literary and social agenda.

That *The Crux* is in part a rewriting of *The Virginian* becomes clear upon comparison of the two novels' central women characters, Vivian Lane and Molly Wood. One of the most significant similarities between them is the fact, noted by Gary Scharnhorst, that both women are New England blue bloods distinguished by their "Pilgrim" ancestors (*The*

Crux 121; Scharnhorst, *Charlotte Perkins Gilman* 38). Both young spin-sters, the two women also venture West in hopes of becoming school-teachers among the Anglo-American settlers there. In *The Virginian,* Molly leaves her home in Bennington, Vermont, "with a spirit craving the unknown" (69); yet it soon becomes clear, in the chapter titled "The Spinster Meets the Unknown," that Wister intends to make sport of Molly's presumption that she, as a woman, is suited to undertake such an adventure. The narrator describes her train journey: "Molly Wood sat bravely up in the through car, dwelling upon the unknown. She thought that she had attained it in Ohio, on Tuesday morning, and wrote a letter about it to Bennington. On Wednesday afternoon she felt sure [that she had achieved it], and wrote a letter much more picturesque. . . . [W]hen she left the train at Rock Creek, . . . she knew that she had really at-tained the unknown, and sent an expensive telegram to say that she was quite well." However, Molly soon finds herself the passenger of a drunken stage driver who careens the wagon into a ditch; at this point, the narrator reveals, "After four days of train and thirty hours of stage, she was having a little too much of the unknown at once" (73). Wister invokes Molly's battle with "the unknown," parodying her departure from her "place" as a conventional New England woman, her journey West serving as mere comic relief for the more serious drama unfolding for the book's male characters.[7]

In describing Vivian's anticipation of her journey West, Gilman al-ludes to Molly's brush with "the unknown," though Gilman's Vivian is both a more serious and a more admirable character. Raised, like Molly, to embody traditional New England womanhood, Vivian seems on the surface to be "restrained and courteous" (*The Crux* 104); yet she finds herself "boiling with rebellion" against the traditional ideals and attitudes of her culture (105). Prohibited by her father from attending college, Vivian "long[s] for occupation." Convinced that "[h]er work must be worth while," Vivian feels that her strong mind is being "held in dumb subjection" (106). Early in the novel, the narrator expresses Vivian's frus-tration in a line that echoes Molly Wood: "Change she desired, she longed for, but dreaded the unknown" (108).

Soon enough, however, Vivian's malaise is diagnosed, along with that of several other women, by a woman physician named Jane Bellair, who urges the whole group to migrate to Colorado. Significantly, she prom-ises to help Vivian begin her career there as a kindergarten teacher, freeing her from the silenced and duty-filled existence she had been leading at home. Thus, in a final rejection of Molly's ignorance and incompetence in the face of "the unknown," Gilman's narrator explains that, having stepped down onto the train platform on arrival in Colorado, "Vivian lifted her head and faced the new surroundings as an unknown world" (125)—a world in which, having escaped a repressive eastern life, she will, with her head lifted high, pursue meaningful work and achieve self-determination.

Having established her heroine's comparison with Molly Wood, Gilman transforms Wister's eastern schoolmarm; rather than dismissing her journey West and relegating her to a supporting role in the plot, Gilman celebrates Vivian's quest for adventure and change, placing it on center stage. Indeed, Vivian experiences the kind of personal transformation in the West that Wister had reserved for his male narrator. While the journey west was often prescribed to men as part of what I have called their "West Cure," in *The Crux* it is Vivian, not a male character, who undergoes such a cure.[8]

The West Cure involved a variety of outdoor pursuits, including hunting, camping, and rough living on dude ranches or in the wilderness (often in the West). Its purpose was to aid middle- and upper-class men from the northeastern cities, exhausted and supposedly feminized by applying themselves too vigorously to business concerns, to regain health and vigor through emulating the more "masculine" traits and pursuits embodied in a Western model of manliness. Part of a widespread and varied phenomenon in the nineteenth and early twentieth centuries, this treatment was prescribed by Gilman's rest cure physician, S. Weir Mitchell, most often to his male patients. "[T]he working capacity of numberless men" was in jeopardy, Mitchell warned in a volume aptly titled *Wear and Tear, or Hints for the Overworked,* in large part because "the man of business" has "no inducement to abandon that unceasing labor" of the brain and the office. "He does not ride, or shoot, or fish, or play any game but euchre," he laments (74–75). The cure Mitchell proposed was to live "the out-door life of the camp by silent lake or merry river, or far in the noiseless deeps of northern forests" ("Camp Cure" 47). Hunting or fishing to provide his food, sleeping in a tent or, better yet, out in the open, the patient would find himself renewed and ready once again to pursue his professional obligations.

The Philadelphia aristocrat Owen Wister was one of Mitchell's best-known West Cure patients, in large part because Wister fictionalized his cure in *The Virginian*. The novel's sickly eastern narrator finds a degree of health through imitating the manliness of the book's title character, learning to ride a horse, hunt, and survive in the outdoors. Through this apprenticeship in Western masculinity, the narrator undergoes a transformation, which he considers in the second half of the novel: "Remembering my Eastern helplessness in the year when we had met first, I enjoyed thinking how I had come to be trusted. In those days I had not been allowed to go from the ranch for so much as an afternoon's ride unless tied to [the Virginian] by a string . . . ; now I was crossing unmapped spaces with no guidance. The man who could do this was scarce any longer a 'tenderfoot'" (246).

Having escaped the airless and "civilized" East both literally and figuratively, Wister's narrator is cured of his feminine malaise. The New England women Gilman sketches in *The Crux* are oppressed by the same cultural obligations to tradition, propriety, and gender-based codes of behavior that threaten the well-being this narrator and other white men celebrated in Westerns, as Deborah Evans has noted ("'Come Out to Colorado'" 5). Like male West Cure patients, these women have been sickened, figuratively, by a stifling environment, a fact that is made explicit when the aptly named Dr. Bellair diagnoses and treats the problem: the "whole town," she complains, has "*arthritis deformans* of the soul," causing women to suffer from "bed-ridden intellects" and "arrested development" (*The Crux* 109–10, 114). She offers a West Cure—that is, change, mobility, and freedom in the West, a journey into the unknown —as a prescription. "Come out to Colorado with me," she urges, "—and grow" (110). Whereas a male physician like Mitchell would have prescribed a rest cure for such women, Dr. Bellair urges that they regain their vigor by "roughing it" in the fresh air of the West (219).

Vivian, in particular, ventures into the "wild, rough country," where she "cook[s] in primitive fashion," sleeps long and deeply in the outdoors, and swims in a pristine mountain lake, pursuits that call strikingly to mind Mitchell's West Cure prescriptions.[9] It is revealed upon her return from this camp that, indeed, "she was well," cured of the malaise that had subdued her in Bainville (219–20). Like male West Cure patients and Wister's narrator, Vivian is cured through a rejection of her traditional duties to the old New England ways, immersing herself in the healing landscape and symbolic freedom of the West, a treatment which allows her to devote herself to her profession, as a kindergarten teacher, with renewed vigor and purpose.

Though Vivian's West Cure and new life in Colorado are central to Gilman's plot and are clear rewritings of Molly Wood's role in Wister's Western, Vivian travels West with a multigenerational cohort of women, all of whom are revived by the move. Deborah Evans has made the important point that this in itself is a significant revision of the Western: while Wister valorizes masculinist individualism, Gilman links her vision of female heroism to the well-being of the entire community (Evans 8).

This analysis can be taken one step further in examining the central symbol of community in *The Crux:* a boardinghouse, run and inhabited by the Bainville women, called the Cottonwoods. Like the boardinghouses and apartment hotels in Gilman's other work, this communal living space becomes the domestic, civilizing center of a "family of twenty-five," thus embodying Gilman's trademark progressive model of community (129). As Ann Lane has written, the boardinghouse in Gilman's fiction "is not for the private service of a single family; it is socialized, servicing many people and offering independence to those who run it and work in it" (Lane, "Fictional World" xxvii). Indeed, the Cottonwoods provides economic independence for Orella Elder, the woman who owns and operates it, and its socialized housekeeping frees Vivian and Dr. Bellair to pursue their own professions. Not surprisingly, such independence for these white, middle-class women is enabled by the labor of the cook, Jeanne Jaune, and her supporting staff; the story's lack of concern for the working class is fairly typical of Gilman's later reformist theories and is one of the milder examples of her class and race bias in the book.[10]

Nevertheless, the Cottonwoods and the progressive social change it represents embody a striking revision of Wister's West as portrayed in *The Virginian,* transforming one of his most potent symbols. In *The Virginian,* the cottonwood tree stands for masculinist, violent frontier justice, for it is from such a tree that the Virginian, as ranch foreman, is obligated by a code of manly responsibility to lynch a friend of his, named Steve, who had turned to rustling cattle. In the aftermath of the deed, chronicled in the chapter called "The Cottonwoods," the Virginian laments the costs to friendship and emotional ties necessitated by such a masculinist ethic. Anguished over having executed his friend, the

Virginian initially rationalizes the act: "A man goes through with his responsibilities," he says, no matter the emotional cost (258). Yet he keeps returning in conversation to the subject of Steve, "los[ing] his bearings in a fog of sentiment" and "sob[bing]," "utterly overcome" with loss. "I knew Steve awful well," he cries (260). Wister places considerable emphasis on this crisis, an emphasis enabled in part through the narrator's repeated references to the haunting image of the cottonwood tree, which "loom[s]" in the narrator and the Virginian's path as they seek to leave the area of the hanging, causing the two men to go out of their way to avoid it (258).

Gilman's boardinghouse appropriates this symbol, replacing its associations with violence, individualism, and masculinity with cooperation, communal values, and femininity. As Evans explains, Gilman "deflates the western expectation that women are unwelcome representatives" of domesticity, family, and civilization, "and instead represents them as welcome additions who win the admiration of the lonely young men" who presumably are in need of such institutions (8). The centrality of the Cottonwoods to Gilman's idealized West effects a significant revision, then, of the conventional Western. Her domestic Western absorbs Wister's symbolism in order to advocate a new set of values.

However, though my emphasis here has been on Gilman's modification of Wister's text and worldview in favor of her own, it is precisely in her call for New England women's centrality to the national project of westward expansion that, ironically, she is most similar to Wister. Like him, Gilman avidly invoked contemporary theories postulating "the frontier" as a zone of freedom, opportunity, and (white) racial regeneration, even as she offered a feminist challenge to male-centered paradigms of the West and society as a whole. In her advocacy of what she called "Woman's 'Destiny'"—which posited the West as a haven for New England "stock" fleeing, by implication, the influx of immigrants to the eastern cities—she was, in fact, in complete agreement with Wister. The model community Gilman proposes in *The Crux* relies upon the classic notion of the West as a locus of social and racial regeneration.

Both Gilman's and Wister's eastern schoolteachers, as descendants of Pilgrims, represent a eugenic hope for the future, serving as vessels through which the West would be populated with a revitalized, white American identity. Wister argued that flight to the West was necessary in part because "hordes of encroaching alien vermin . . . turn our cities into Babels and our citizenship into a hybrid farce" ("Evolution" 331). He therefore ends *The Virginian* with a vision of Molly and the Virginian's fruitful marriage that symbolically will regenerate the white race in a West free of "tainted" bloodlines. The Virginian, boasting "old stock in Virginia English and one Scotch Irish grandmother," becomes "an important man, with a strong grip on many various enterprises, and able to give his wife all and more that she asked or desired" (243, 327). Molly, who proudly traces her ancestry back to "flaxen"-haired, Anglo-Saxon colonists, serves as the pure-blooded mother of "many children," who presumably will form the center of this new Western ruling class (210, 327). Both sides, Wister argues, contribute to "the making of our country" (326), to regenerating Eastern, Anglo-American hegemony on the frontier.

Gilman's argument in *The Crux* is quite similar. One of the central plots of this novel features Vivian's education about her responsibility in such matters. Women such as Vivian had a duty to choose their mates well in order to improve the quality of human stock. Gilman's West is a locus for renewal and regeneration, in terms not only of gender and social organization but also of what she calls "the race" (202). Certainly, her most overt argument in the novel presents the need to revitalize the *human* race, which she sees as decaying because of both the waste of marriageable women in the East and the alarming prevalence of men and women infected with venereal disease. With women's increased education about infection and consequent sexual self-determination, along with their entry into a favorable marriage market as exists in the West, she sees an opportunity to improve society. Warning Vivian that she must not marry a man with venereal disease, her grandmother reassures her that "[o]ur girls are mostly clean, and they save the race, I guess" (202). She then insists that "our girls," meaning, of course, white, middle-class, New England women, in refusing to marry infected men, can "rid the world of all these—'undesirable citizens'"; that is, of people infected with such illnesses (203).[11] Gilman's language here suggests a slippage between the discourses of disease and those of racism and xenophobia. The race can be saved, *The Crux* argues, through eugenic means, and Vivian learns that she has a central role to play in this racial revitalization in the West.

It is worth remembering here that, from its first use, the term *Manifest Destiny* was inflected by race, invoking a sense not just of American entitlement to expansion and conquest, but of "Anglo-Saxon" rights to dominance.[12] When Gilman penned her story of American—and more fundamentally, human—revitalization in the idyllic West, therefore, she was writing within a tradition that conceived of the West in precisely these racialized terms.[13] Like Molly, Vivian is rewarded for her commitment to eugenic bloodlines. While not yet married at novel's end, she is betrothed to a transplanted white easterner presumably free of disease. Having linked herself with a "desirable citizen," Vivian has completed her personal renewal and promises a cultural renewal out West through her marriage and her participation in the Cottonwoods' newly established community.

The Crux's eugenicist argument for westward expansion and for women's central role in this phenomenon is made more overtly in Gilman's 1913 *Forerunner* essay called "Woman's 'Manifest Destiny,'" first published in the *Woman's Journal* in 1904.[14] In this piece, she asks, "Why do not the women who really believe that marriage is their mission, go forth in bands of maiden emigration to the frontiers, where lonely men grow hard and bad for lack of 'women's influence'?" She then declares: "If we [women] are in truth citizens, let us get about our duties. The upbuilding of our country, the overcoming of evil tendencies, the fostering of all social improvements—these call for the increase of good people, and the influence of our best civilization." "Let the conscientious surplus of women go West," she says, "like the young man." Gilman's essay expresses, then, the same argument enacted fictionally in *The Crux*. With what is in essence an appropriation of the well-worn call "Go West, young man!" Gilman claims for New England women the duty to civilize the West with "the increase of good people" (385); hand in hand with this racialized nationalist project goes her claim on behalf of such women to the freedoms and privileges conventionally offered to men in the West, among them mobility, regeneration, heroism, adventure, and an active part in constructing American national identity. She does so in her novel by converging the genres of domestic fiction and the Western, linking her novel explicitly to *The Virginian*. In blending these genres, Gilman also exemplifies the ways in which so-called domestic fiction contributed to "the imperial project of civilizing": in *The Crux*, the men and women in the new America "become," as Amy Kaplan has theorized in her work on earlier domestic discourse, "national allies against the alien, and the determining vision is not gender but racial demarcations of otherness" ("Manifest Domesticity" 184). In both its visionary and its regressive aspects, as in its generic allusions, then, *The Crux* signifies that Gilman was deeply in conversation with national policies and mainstream figures of her time.

NOTES

1. In contrast (and reaction) to the domestic novel, argues Tompkins, the Western attempts "the destruction of female authority"; its plots, she points out, replay "the plot of the domestic novels in reverse; Westerns either push women out of the picture completely, or assign them roles in which they exist only to serve the needs of men" (*West of Everything* 39–40). The Western's reductive portrayal of women has been widely noted. A classic example of such scholarship is Annette Kolodny, *The Lay of the Land.*

2. See also Gary Scharnhorst and Denise D. Knight, "Charlotte Perkins Gilman's Library."

3. For an excellent recent analysis of the Western's engagement with these topics, see Barbara Will, "The Nervous Origins of the American Western," 293–316, especially 311 n.5. In her essay, Will also examines *The Virginian*'s groundbreaking elements as well as its debt to earlier, perhaps proto-Western, literary forms.

4. Nineteenth-century middle-class women writers valorized female experience and moral authority (and simultaneously manipulated the discourses of domesticity and True Womanhood) in what has variously been called "domestic fiction," "literary domesticity," "woman's fiction," and "exploratory" and "didactic" novels. See, for example, Nina Baym, *Woman's Fiction: A Guide to Novels by and about Women in America, 1820–1870,* 2nd ed.; Susan K. Harris, *19th-Century American Women's Novels: Interpretive Strategies;* and Mary Kelley, *Private Woman, Public Stage: Literary Domesticity in Nineteenth-Century America.*

5. One of the best known studies of turn-of-the-century women's fiction is Elizabeth Ammons, *Conflicting Stories: American Women Writers at the Turn into the Twentieth Century.*

6. While Kolodny's study focuses on the domesticating impulse in women's frontier writing through 1860, she anticipates that such writing after that era will assert more adventurous plots. Certainly, however, women had long been troubling conventional representations of gender on the frontier. Recent scholarship exploring these and other impulses in women's Western writing includes Vera

Norwood and Janice Monk, eds., *The Desert Is No Lady* and Georgi-Findlay, *The Frontiers of Women's Writing*. See also Kolodny, "Letting Go Our Grand Obsessions" 1–18.

7. Many readers have noted the fact that Molly is a flat, unsympathetic character. Frances W. Kaye, for example, describes her as "squeamish" and "worth fleeing from," an embodiment of the "feminization of American culture" bemoaned by Ann Douglas in her book by the same name (Kaye 167–68); while Madelon E. Heatherington remarks that Molly represents all of the "trivialities" of civilization that Western plots reject ("Romance Without Women" 653).

8. For more discussion of the West Cure and its relevance to Wister, and of the West Cure's portrayal in *The Virginian*, see Tuttle, "Rewriting the West Cure" and Will, "The Nervous Origins of the American Western."

9. Deborah Evans has analyzed in more detail this last scene, in which Vivian swims in the mountain lake, arguing convincingly that it resembles a similar scene in *The Virginian*.

10. See my introduction to *The Crux* 73–74 n.151 for more discussion of this issue in the novel.

11. As Judith Allen has argued, "The eugenic and feminist projects interlink on Gilman's Western frontier" ("Reconfiguring Vice" 190).

12. See Reginald Horsman, *Race and Manifest Destiny* 219–21.

13. Along with Horsman, G. Edward White discusses the Anglo-Saxonism in eastern ideals of the frontier in *The Eastern Establishment and the Western Experience,* 197.

14. The full citation for this article is: *Woman's Journal* (June 4, 1904): 178.

9
Creating Great Women

Mary Austin and Charlotte Perkins Gilman

Melody Graulich

Mary Austin enjoyed lecturing male writers about their failures in creating women characters. After her move to New York in 1910, she wrote to her friend Jack London, "Yes I have a grouch against you. . . . Not against you so much as against all men writers" for failing to capture "the note of feminine power which is quite as powerful in its way as the power of men. . . . I notice in your work—thank heaven that you haven't pretended at any time to know much about women,—but I notice that though they show an increasing naturalness, your women are never really *great* women" (qtd. in Stineman 46–47; emphasis added). Apparently Austin believed London capable of creating an independent, powerful woman, for she offered him models for future heroines. Her first example was Charlotte Perkins Gilman.

Austin's suggestion was astute. Gilman could easily have held center stage in one of London's novels, for he filled his fiction with narrative digressions about social theory and philosophy, the kind of work she was best known for, having published the influential *Women and Economics* in 1898.

In 1911, shortly after Austin's letter to London, Gilman published *The Man-Made World*, where she, too, explored the shortcomings of male authors in a chapter titled "Masculine Literature." With its "preferred subject matter . . . the Story of Adventure and the Love Story," reflecting the "two essential features of masculinity—Desire and Combat—Love and War" (94–95), "fiction, under our androcentric culture, has not given any true picture of woman's life, very little of human life, and a disproportioned section of man's life" (102). Yet because of the "humanizing of women," she suggests, "life is [being] discovered to be longer, wider, deeper, richer than those monotonous players of one tune would have us believe," leading to "fresh fields of fiction" (104–05). Among the new plots Gilman listed were: "First, the position of the young woman who is called upon to give up her 'career'—her humanness—for marriage and who objects to it. Second, the middle-aged woman who at last discovers that her discontent is social starvation—that it is not more love that she wants, but more business in life: Third, the inter-relation of women with women—a thing we could never write about before because we never had it before, except in harems and convents" (105).

In 1911 Gilman was living on Riverside Drive in New York City, not far from the apartment of her friend Mary Austin. "I saw a good deal of her," Austin later wrote in her autobiography (*Earth Horizon* 326). While Gilman was writing *The Man-Made World*, Austin was writing a novel, *A Woman of Genius*, published in 1912. "If only I could have [my husband] and my work," declares Austin's heroine, Olivia Lattimore, "I should ask no more of destiny; I do not now see why I couldn't" (191). Calling Austin a "great artist," Gilman expressed her admiration for *A Woman of Genius*, in which Austin attempted to write about the struggles of "great women" (Gilman, review of *A Woman of Genius* 279). Having gone through those struggles herself, Gilman could respond with insight to the novel's treatment of the social forces that retard the development of genius in women, with personal understanding of the difficulties of uniting work and marriage, and with generosity to a heroine she realized most readers would find "unwomanly."

A Woman of Genius is about an exceptional woman, but unlike Cather's *The Song of the Lark*, written a few years later, it explores the importance of support from other women. Olivia's sister tells her that the risks she has taken in her life will help other women to have "the courage to live lives of their own," while her best friend says that her honesty will "help other women to speak out what they think, unashamed" (*A Woman of Genius* 261, 290). In both Austin's and Gilman's fiction and feminist thought, women repeatedly come to the aid of other women, just as for a number of years the two authors offered each other support and admiration. With remarkably similar backgrounds, the two developed parallel feminist analyses that they expressed in social critiques, fiction, and other genres, with considerable bravery and defiance. Believing that, as Austin said, "what women have to stand on squarely [is] not their ability to see the world in the way men see it, but the importance and validity of seeing it in some other way," they helped each other speak unashamed of taboo subjects. In their own middle years, they repeatedly exposed the "social starvation" of the unhappy middle-aged woman and offered her alternative life choices (*The Young Woman Citizen* 19). While their artistic goals differed and they grew apart in the last decades of their lives, the autobiographies they wrote in the early 1930s shortly before their deaths confirm their shared struggles.

Austin might be speaking for both women when she describes in *Earth Horizon* the childhood "determination" that led eventually to her writing. Writing about herself in the third person, Austin notes that she "was never much taken with the wish of many girls of her acquaintance that they had been boys. She thought there might be a good deal to be got out of being a woman; but she definitely meant neither to chirrup nor twitter. She meant not to remit a single flash of wit, anger, or imagination. She had no idea of what, in her time, such a determination would entail. She was but dimly aware of something within herself, competent, self-directive; she meant to trust it" (157–58).[1] Unwilling to appropriate a male point of view to achieve "greatness" or speak in the chirrups and twitters expected of the woman writer, unaware of what Austin later called "their prophets," both Austin and Gilman found ways to liberate their wit, anger, and imagination ("Greatness in Women" 197). Their mutual influence deserves exploration because more than any other women at the turn of the twentieth century, they demonstrated in their lives and works new ways of understanding what could "be got out of being a woman" (*Earth Horizon* 157–58).

When Austin died in 1934, two of Gilman's books were in her library, *Women and Economics* and an edition of "The Yellow Wall-Paper," inscribed: "To Mary Austin—with real admiration and interest. Charlotte Perkins Gilman 1910."[2] But their relationship began some thirty-five years earlier.

Both Austin and Gilman moved to California in 1888, following severe episodes of depression. When they met in Pasadena in 1899, Austin was immediately attracted to and identified with Gilman, who had been publicly vilified as an "unnatural mother" for sending her daughter to live with her former husband: "I had been invited to meet her, and been struck by her beauty, the fine lines of her head and the clear look of her eyes, the carriage of her shoulders so erect and precise. I was for her, and the freedom from convention that left her the right to care for her child in what seemed the best way to her" (*Earth Horizon* 293). No doubt their conversations helped them to see how their depressions and struggles with motherhood were the result of constrictive gender roles and expectations.

Both women felt abandoned by fathers they associated with intellectual achievement. Both grew up with repressive, rejecting, and dissatisfied mothers who expressed clear preference for their brothers. They emphasize particularly their mothers' lack of physical affection and describe themselves as starved for love and support. Each presents herself as an isolated lonely child who turns to her imagination, to making believe, for solace; each re-creates with considerable bitterness more than fifty years later a scene where her mother sought to silence her creativity. Austin's mother told her "storying was wicked" and "she'd have to punish you or you would grow up a story-teller" (*Earth Horizon* 42–43), while Gilman's mother ordered her to "shut the door on [imagination, on the inner life], on happiness, and hold it shut" (*Living* 23–24). Each describes her mother as making her feel unlovable, and, in Austin's words, as "falling short . . . as a young lady" (*Earth Horizon* 169).

Yet each woman ultimately struggled to see the forces that inhibited her mother's life. "Mother's life was one of the most painfully thwarted I have ever known," wrote Gilman (*Living* 8); Austin realized that much of her mother's anger stemmed from having "always wanted another sort of life for herself. . . . It was what most women wanted; time and adventure of their own" (*Earth Horizon* 177). One can see the beginnings of their feminist understanding in their attempts to understand their mothers' unhappy lives.

Struggling with expectations of "true womanliness" (as Austin called it) and their own thwarted ambitions, both women also suffered severe breakdowns in young adulthood. Gilman had published "The Yellow Wall-Paper" in 1892—based on her experience in undergoing the rest cure for neurasthenia—and Austin had her own experience with a nervous breakdown from overwork at school. The doctor's diagnosis was that "it might have something to do with the natural incapacity of the female mind for intellectual achievement." According to Austin, he held "the deep-seated conviction that all illnesses of women were 'female' in their origin, and could best be cured by severe doses of housework and child-bearing. 'The *only* work,' said Dr. Hankins, 'a female should do is beside her own fireside'" (*Earth Horizon* 152).

Both women felt liberated by the move west, seeing the West as a healing landscape and portraying it as such in their writing. Like other unconventional women who moved west during this period and later, both associated it with what we might now call alternative lifestyles and with autonomy.[3] In many of Gilman's stories and novels, women find adventure and achieve economic independence in the West, perhaps most notably in *The Crux* (1910), in which a Colorado woman doctor, who has made her own escape from a constricting New England town, returns to inspire an oddly disparate group of women to follow her lead. In one of Austin's finest stories, "The Walking Woman" from *Lost Borders* (1909), the main character is an unnamed desert wanderer who had "begun by walking off an illness" and was "healed at last by the large soundness of nature" (97). The western backcountry offers her multiple trails toward self-definition and spiritual wholeness. Assessing her life, the narrator concludes in one of Austin's most memorable lines, "She was the Walking Woman. That was it. She had walked off all sense of society-made values, and, knowing the best when the best came to her, was able to take it" (*Western Trails* 97).

As suggested more fully at the end of this essay, "The Walking Woman" can serve as a parable for the life stories of Austin and Gilman. In their autobiographies, they suggest in parallel metaphors that the West offered something they hungered for. Pasadena's natural landscape and climate "were meat and drink to me," says Gilman (*Living* 107). Suffering literally from malnutrition but "plagued with an anxiety to know . . . the things of the wild," Austin describes her discovery of the leaves of the wild grape far up one of the Tejon canyons and how she got "well on something grubbed out of the woods." "But there was more to the incident than that; that was the beginning of the notion in Mary's mind of a poor appetite of any sort being cured by its proper food; that there was something you could do about unsatisfactory conditions beside being heroic or a martyr to them, something more satisfactory than enduring or complaining, and that was getting out to hunt for the remedy. This, for young ladies in the eighteen-eighties, was a revolutionary discovery to have made" (*Earth Horizon* 195). Revolutionary indeed. One remedy was stimulating company who would support her writing, which led Austin to Pasadena in 1899.

Rustic and rural, its character influenced by its Indian and Spanish history, Pasadena was known for its bohemianism, artists, and social critics. Gilman had spent two crucial years there from 1888 to 1890, during which time she established herself as an economically independent writer. As part of her lecture tour after publishing *Women and Economics* in 1898, she returned to Pasadena to visit her daughter, Katharine, who was living there with her father and Gilman's close friend, Katharine's stepmother, Grace Channing Stetson. Gilman was a member of the congenial "Arroyo Seco" group that Austin met at Charles Lummis's adobe hacienda, El Alisal: writers Gwendolyn Overton, Margaret Collier Graham, Sharlott Hall, Edwin Markham; scientists and anthropologists David Starr Jordan and Frederick Webb Dodge; artists Maynard Dixon and William Keith. This avant-garde group, all focusing as early as 1899 on representing the multicultural West as offering the United States both a rich history and a model for a healthier future, anticipates in many ways later more famous groups in Santa Fe and Taos, of which Austin was also a member. Although she is seldom thought of as a Western writer, Gilman insisted humorously upon claiming that role in a letter to Lummis dated, perhaps significantly, April 1, 1898. Her "feelings are hurt," she says, at not being included in his "galaxy of [Western] authors": "Don't I still sign 'Pasadena' in hotel registers! Am I not introduced on platforms as Mrs. Stetson of California! Don't I write everything I can think of for that blessed country. . . . "[4] In fact, Gilman did publish frequently in Lummis's magazine, *The Land of Sunshine,* as did Austin.

Perhaps Austin saw Gilman as a model, for when the two women met, Gilman had confronted and made decisions with which Austin was still struggling. Unhappy and frustrated in her marriage, with its "pattern of male dominance and feminine subservience," Austin would summon her courage and leave her husband a few years later (*Earth Horizon* 271).[5] She was eager to commit herself to her writing, as Gilman had, and Gilman probably echoed the encouragement Austin had already received from Eve Lummis and Ina Coolbrith, Gilman's neighbor in Oakland, to submit her stories for publication.

Most poignant, Austin had also gone through a difficult childbirth and postpartum depression, with poor medical care, and when she met Gilman had begun to acknowledge that her daughter Ruth was severely retarded. When she defended Gilman against charges of unnatural motherhood, she also defended herself, for almost everyone, including Austin's own mother, blamed her for her child's problems. After their meeting, with the aid of a young woman doctor who began to practice in the region, and perhaps thinking of Gilman's right to care for her child in the best way, Austin made the difficult decision to institutionalize Ruth. In the autobiographies the two women wrote many years after their friendship began, their pain at "losing" their children still remains fresh. Describing the painful decision to send her child to live with her former husband, Gilman concludes that "this seemed the right thing to do":

> No one suffered from it but myself. This, however, was entirely overlooked in the furious condemnation which followed. I had "given up my child."
>
> To hear what was said and read what was printed one would think I had handed over a baby in a basket. In the years that followed she divided her time fairly equally between us, but in companionship with her beloved father she grew up to be the artist that she is, with advantages I could never have given her. I lived without her, temporarily, but why did they think I liked it? She was all I had. (*Living* 163)

After describing her attempts to smile cheerfully as her daughter departs on the train, she says:

> That was thirty years ago. I have to stop typing and cry as I tell about it. There were years, years, when I could never see a mother and child together without crying, or even a picture of them. . . .
>
> What were those pious condemners thinking of? (*Living* 163–64)

Austin also focuses on misunderstanding, on pain and loss suffered alone:

> It was not long after that she put Ruth in a private institution in Santa Clara where the difference between herself and other children, which was beginning to trouble her, would not be felt, where it would not be known. Here the inability of other people to bear her cross would not be taxed; where one could say if questioned, "We have lost her"; . . . where the pain could be borne alone, as it was for another twenty years. It is a relief to speak of it now, of the cruelty, the weight, the oppression of its reality, the loss of

tenderness, of consideration, the needless blight and pain. (*Earth Horizon* 295)

Both women describe wounds that never healed; they remained fresh years later. Their mutual support for each other's decisions must have greatly comforted them.

Only late in their lives, in their autobiographies, could Gilman and Austin speak out about this subject, and even then both passages suggest unresolved conflicts. But the theme emerged, deflected, in much of their writing. Austin wrote several stories about women who lost children, including *A Woman of Genius*, "The Walking Woman," and "The Castro Baby" (1899), about the sympathetic response of a group of white Protestant women to a poor Mexican woman whose child is dying. Though she never argued that having a baby completes a woman's life, women in her stories often long for children. Gilman wrote many works attempting to redefine motherhood, including *Herland* (1915), where she explores shared childrearing, and the highly ironic "An Unnatural Mother" (1894), where a woman must choose between devotion to her child and to the needs of her community.

These shared life experiences informed their fiction, as did their struggles to depart from unhappy marriages. Both wrote their way out of these marriages. In "The Yellow Wall-Paper," Gilman, like many other women writers, sheds the self that might have been, the self that she had to let go in order to achieve. She could then go on to offer her readers affirmative resolutions, to write her many, many positive stories where women manage to overcome obstacles and find meaningful work, stories like "Making a Change," "An Honest Woman," and "The Widow's Might." (It is ironic that most contemporary readers find the tragic story of entrapment more powerful than the upbeat stories of liberation.)

Austin also wrote a haunting story about her marriage and its effect upon her, a story that owes a debt to "The Yellow Wall-Paper" and to her relationship with Gilman. Like "The Yellow Wall-Paper," "Frustrate" is narrated by an unnamed, restless, baffled woman whose marriage left her feeling "just kind of hungry . . . *always*" (*Western Trails* 229). With naive faith in the Sleeping Beauty myth, she believes only a man can awaken her imagination, thinking that if she "could get to know a man who was big enough so [she] couldn't walk all around him, so to speak—somebody that [she] could reach and not find the end of,—[she]

shouldn't feel so—so frustrated" (233). Her repressed and inexpressible yearnings, so well conveyed by her wandering uncertain tone, make her seem a bit "crazy," rather like Gilman's narrator in the early part of "The Yellow Wall-Paper." Neither narrator has an outlet for her imagination, a way to make sense of what she intuits about her life. Both stories are autobiographical, narrated by the women their authors might have become had they not escaped their marriages. While Gilman abandons her heroine to madness instead of allowing her to escape into health and creativity, as she herself did, Austin suggests there is a way out by creating a double for her frustrated heroine, a woman writer who has achieved an ironic viewpoint on her own frustrations.

Written during the years Austin and Gilman were closest and published in 1912, shortly after Gilman's gift of a copy of "The Yellow Wall-Paper," "Frustrate" is one of Austin's best stories, but she decided never to reprint it in a collection, perhaps because it is too autobiographical, for the narrator expresses Austin's own insecurities. Possibly she was scarred by her experience with her editor, who, she claimed, attempted "to determine what should and should not be written" about "the experiences of women, as women," an argument Gilman also frequently made. "I wrote a story for 'The Century,'" Austin commented in *Earth Horizon,* almost certainly "Frustrate," "in which a woman tells what she suffered in finding that she was not attractive looking. The paragraph in which she described herself was deleted. 'I couldn't bear,' said the editor, 'to have a woman with such beautiful thoughts, looking like that'" (320).[6]

In "Frustrate," Austin creates sympathy for this consciousness struggling to grow and implies the waste of her narrator's imagination, yet at the same time suggests that while she is not to blame for her resignation, it is not the only response to her situation. In *Earth Horizon,* Austin describes herself as never having "surrendered" to "resignation," as seeing life as "essentially remediable, undefeatable" (268). As both she and Gilman often do, Austin uses paired heroines in "Frustrate," in this case to explore the close relationship between the woman she might have been and the woman she became, the great writer with her own game.

Read this way, "Frustrate" appears a thinly veiled comment on Austin's years in Carmel, where she was the "plain" woman writer among a group of sexually promiscuous male comrades, including London, poet George Sterling (with whom biographers contend that Austin may have had an affair), and others. The narrator lives in Castroville, California, not far from Carmel-by-the-Sea, fictionalized as the artist colony "Fair-shore." Austin was simultaneously attracted to the sexual liberation at Carmel and suspicious of it; she certainly felt pain and bitterness at the "bohemians'" rejection of her for her "thick waist" and "plain looks."[7] In the fantasy utopian novel she wrote about the years in Carmel, *Outland* (1910), she ignores that pain and imagines for her main character a satisfying personal relationship. One wonders if her title influenced Gilman's choice of *Herland* (1915), in which she imagines a world where mothers don't have to experience the pain she had undergone when she could not care for her daughter.

Yet "Frustrate," like much of Austin's other fiction, focuses on a moment of recognition between two women, and in considering the importance of Gilman to Austin it becomes possible to read it in quite another way. While "Frustrate" can be read as having been influenced by "The Yellow Wall-Paper," and even as a revision of it, where Austin uses her paired heroines to explore the constrictions of marriage *and* to offer readers a way out, perhaps the paired heroines are two women who met at another artist colony, Lummis's adobe in Pasadena. Perhaps the woman writer the narrator meets *is* Charlotte Stetson (Gilman) rather than an older and wiser version of Austin herself. Gilman, who also never surrendered to resignation, offered Austin a game plan for becoming a great writer. Austin grants her fictional "woman writer" the ability to see "how it was with me." She also grants her generosity, as the narrator believes that the woman writer talks of herself only to help the narrator look at her own longings and dilemmas from another angle. But perhaps the woman writer really *was* talking about herself. The passage then obliquely insists upon one of the most profound—and transformative—feminist truths: we learn to identify and articulate our feelings, and our selves, in moments of identification with others.

Austin and Gilman remained friends throughout the first two decades of the century, when both lived off and on in New York. Both were active in feminist causes and crusades, and, as illustrated in this essay, their theoretical feminist writings present similar critiques of the culture they both described as "androcentric." In *The Man-Made World*, Gilman makes an argument very similar to the one Austin later made in *The Young Woman Citizen* (1918), succinctly voiced in this line: "Civilization as we now have it is one-eyed and one-handed. It is kept going by man's way of seeing things and man's way of dealing with the things he sees"

(17). Both women wanted society to have the benefit of both hands, believing, in Austin's words, that "[w]omen, in their hundred thousand years of managing the family have developed a genius for personal relations," a genius for cooperation and affiliation that should be put to use for the public good ("Woman Looks at Her World" 69). "This is the mother's century," Gilman wrote, "the first chance for the mother of the world to rise to her full place, her transcendent power to remake humanity, to rebuild the suffering world—and the world waits while she powders her nose" (*Living* 331).

Yet as these last sentences imply, their view of "women" was often fundamentally essentialist, focusing on difference. Although Gilman opens and closes *The Man-Made World* with chapters on humanity, arguing that the "common humanity" between women and men "has largely escaped notice" (13), her work supports Austin's later assertion: "I have always believed that there is a distinctly feminine approach to intellectual problems and its recognition is indispensible to intellectual wholeness. All that I have ever, as a feminist, protected against is the prevailing notion that the feminine is necessarily an inferior approach" (Austin, response to review by Lewis Mumford).

The women eventually moved in different directions when, after World War I, Austin soured on socialist politics and the "Young Intellectuals" and moved to New Mexico to focus on how the regional ethnic cultures of the United States offered a regenerative vision to a world seemingly entrapped in modernist despair. Although describing Gilman in *Earth Horizon* as one of the friends she kept "pace" with most "faithfully" and *Women and Economics* as a "notable book," she added a critical comment on Gilman's politics and writing:

> About 1908 she began to publish a magazine on the subject [women and socialism], called "The Forerunner." The worst of it was that she wrote it all herself—articles, stories, reviews, poems—and she couldn't write. . . . Everything she wrote was in the same key. She lectured interestingly, but invariably. She talked well, but without illumination. We all liked her; she was friendly and cheerful and hospitable. . . . But we could not keep together; we did not read alike, and we could not write alike. I had to drop her magazine with its terrible sameness, its narrow scope. I could not get her interested in writing. After a time I lost touch with her; so did her other

friends. Time went on and left her standing at the old corner, crying the same wares. She had become a Socialist of the narrowest mould. (*Earth Horizon* 325–26)

Gilman was aware of Austin's criticism many years earlier. In January 1922 she wrote a note to "AW," her friend Amy Wellington, suggesting that she read Austin's *The Land of Little Rain*. With her note she enclosed a "Pretty good parody" that she had apparently written based "on Mary Austin who said [to Gilman] 'I do think, however, that if you gave your mind to it you could write.'" Titled "Without Bo[a]rders," the parody is an allusion to a collection Gilman had earlier praised, *Lost Borders*, and, as those who have read Austin will recognize, it effectively mocks her sometimes strained and earnest diction. I quote the final paragraphs:

> Then, when your eyes open with new-born fiction, all swims in the blue glory, blue with the comfortingness of summer skies and the short-necked nestling nemophilia, warmed with the gold glow of heaven.
>
> Orange blazes with it, the orange pool in the marshes, the orange door-slab, the curdled orange and crimson with the peacock in the midst of it.
>
> Only to those who live there is the knowledge of inner delighting beyond the eye, of the calm bed-places, even one for the stranger, and the glad necessities for time of eating.
>
> All in all you shall not find better, no, not on Belgrave Square nor all 5th Avenue, so think we who are indwellers.
>
> Joke, for a Husband, 8 Jan. 1922
>
> (Gilman Papers, Schlesinger Library)[8]

Austin was certainly an "indweller," while, as Ann J. Lane points out in *To Herland and Beyond*, Gilman was not particularly introspective. Austin was obsessed with style and originality; as early as the 1890s she told a friend, "I worked four hours today . . . trying to get the right word to describe the hills to the east. But I got the word—puckery—and it is right!" (qtd. in H. Doyle 211). As Gary Scharnhorst has observed, Gilman "wasted little patience on works whose authors tinker with point of view or turn well many a felicitous phrase"; she wrote as clearly and directly as possible for didactic purposes (*Charlotte Perkins Gilman* 12). Austin saw herself as an artist; Gilman saw herself as a reformer.

Gilman recognized a certain prickly arrogance in her friend, for in her 1912 review of *A Woman of Genius* she wrote of the novel's heroine: "Olivia is not a loveable person—as is often the case with geniuses. In the pursuit of her work, or perhaps we should say, in her works' pursuit of her, she is forced to sacrifice not only much that was dear to her, but the dearest wishes of others. This also is frequently the case with geniuses. We are quite used to its expression in men" (280). Yet Gilman also believed that Olivia is "far from happy personally" because she has never achieved a "mingling" of "affection" and "passion" (280). While she attributed that unhappiness to social forces, there is an undertone in the review that suggests Olivia has contributed to her own isolation.

Certainly one key difference between the two authors was Gilman's long and apparently happy marriage. Austin had a few significant affairs but writes in *Earth Horizon* that she never remarried because it was clear in each case that any sacrifices would have to be hers. She left an unpublished manuscript when she died titled "Love Is Not Enough," and she, like Olivia, was unwilling to sacrifice work or autonomy for love. Yet in *Earth Horizon* Austin expresses regret that her generation of feminists' belief that it would be possible to reshape marriage to fit their needs "was by no means as easy as it promised" (144); the tone of regret sometimes, perhaps often, turns into bitterness in her work.

Despite their differences and occasional irritation with each other, for many years Gilman and Austin had a mutually beneficial and influential friendship. In her review Gilman also praised Austin's earlier book, *Lost Borders* (1909), which ends with "The Walking Woman," the story that can be read as a parable for Austin's relationship to Gilman. The unnamed narrator, herself a desert wanderer, has heard stories of the mysterious Walking Woman, and she seeks her out, hoping for answers to the undefined things she "wished to know" (*Western Trails* 93). Despite the rumors that the Walking Woman is "cracked," the narrator finds that "in her talk there was both wisdom and information," and she admires her independence, captured in the crucial line quoted before: "She was the Walking Woman. That was all. She had walked off all sense of society-made values and, knowing the best when the best came to her, was able to take it" (93, 97). The story's final image suggests that the narrator believes the Walking Woman is a pathfinder: she remembers the rumors that the Walking Woman is "twisted," but she discovers that "the track of her feet bore evenly and white" (98). Throughout her long career Austin created many women like the Walking Woman, artistic, searching women who went their own way, who defied social convention, who offered her wisdom and information. Charlotte Perkins Gilman surely helped her find this path.

One wonders if Austin recalled her comment to Jack London that Charlotte Perkins Gilman was the best model of a "great woman" when she wrote "Greatness in Women" in 1923, with its key line: "Not to know their own prophets is rather a serious predicament for women" (197). Writing in *Earth Horizon* nearly thirty-five years after her initial meeting with Gilman, Austin recalls an encounter with a society woman which imagistically implies her admiration for Gilman. "When I had asked her what she thought about Charlotte Perkins Stetson, she had replied by telling me that Mrs. Perkins, Charlotte's mother, had started the fashion of using English ivy as an indoor decoration in American houses, which she somehow charged up against Charlotte. I never lost the association, but continued to see Charlotte with a decoration of ivy leaves, a flat wreath of them about her head and over her breast" (293). Although she comically replaces laurel with ivy leaves, in this passage Austin places a crown on a great woman.

Notes

An earlier version of this essay appeared in *Jack London Journal* (1994), 148–58. Reprinted by permission.

1. Gilman did write a story, "If I Were a Man" (1914), in which she imagined a woman who wished she was a man, but significantly the main character is "a beautiful instance of what is reverentially called 'a true woman'" who learns what men really think of women like her (*Charlotte Perkins Gilman Reader* 32).

2. A record of Austin's books, including inscriptions, is contained in the Austin collection at the Huntington Library.

3. For more information on such women of Austin's and Gilman's generation, see Bernadin et al., *Trading Gazes: Euro-American Women Photographers and Native North American Indians*. For women who moved West around World War I, see Lois Rudnick, *Utopian Vistas*.

4. Here is an excerpt from the letter:

Here's "Tomorrow" again—you needn't apologize, I'm all the better pleased to have it come out in the fine June number. But my feelings are hurt at not being asked to participate in your Western Writers League! Don't I still sign "Pasadena" in hotel registers! Am I not introduced on platforms as Mrs. Stetson of California! Don't I write everything I can think of for that blessed country and delight to put things in your magazine because it is California's—even if it doesn't "pay" much! People [illegible] me for sending "Their Grass" to you—said I could have done better. I told 'em I couldn't—that it was Californian and belonged there, and that was all that mattered. And here I'm not even mentioned in your galaxy of famous authors!

O hear my cries! Behold my tears! . . .

This is a condition of pardon for forgetting that I am Californian as much as Grace Channing—to say nothing of the ten minutes time I've sacrificed to copying this poem again!

Sincerely—and with suspended hostilities—

Charlotte Perkins Stetson

I would like to thank Joe Staples, University of Arizona, for permitting me to reprint this letter, from his research at the Marion Parks collection at the Braun Research Library, Southwest Museum, Pasadena, California.

5. In *Mary Austin: The Song of a Maverick,* Esther Lanigan Stineman has suggested, "In many ways Charlotte's divorce provided a blueprint for Mary's" (63). In her afterword to *A Woman of Genius,* Nancy Porter also suggests that Austin met Gilman in a "formative stage" of her life and was "deeply drawn" to her (300).

6. Although Gilman frankly commented on her difficulties getting her work published, she did not press this analysis nearly as fully as Austin, who wondered "what obligates us most to impeach the validity of a woman's experience at the points where it is most supported by experience" and described herself as "suspicious of the social estimate of women [because of] the general social conspiracy against her telling the truth about herself" (*Woman of Genius* 4). She also described women as having been silenced by a "wall of men, a filtered, almost sound-proof wall of male intelligence, male reports, critics, managers, advertisers . . . men editors, men publishers, men reviewers" (*No. 26 Jayne Street* 6).

7. Apparently Austin was often mocked by the male bohemians and dismissed as a possible sexual partner. See, for instance, Franklin Walker, *The Sea-*

coast of Bohemia, who summarizes what he sees as Austin's role at Carmel by describing her variously as "dumpy," "flat-chested," "too homely and assertive," and "almost purring at being included in the inner circle" (26, 27).

8. I would like to thank Denise D. Knight for directing me to this letter to me from her work on the Gilman Papers at the Schlesinger Library.

10
From Near-Dystopia to Utopia

A Source for *Herland* in Inez Haynes Gillmore's *Angel Island*

Charlotte Rich

Several sources are thought to have influenced the writing of Charlotte Perkins Gilman's utopian novel *Herland,* from Jonathan Swift's satirical adventure tale of 1726, *Gulliver's Travels,* to Edward Bellamy's Nationalist utopia published in 1888, *Looking Backward.*[1] However, a previously unconsidered inspiration for *Herland* may lie in Inez Haynes Gillmore's 1914 novel *Angel Island.* Gillmore was a Greenwich Village author and editor who became friends with Gilman through the Heterodoxy Club, and her novel *Angel Island* was serialized in *American* illustrated magazine and brought out in book form in 1914, the year during which Gilman began writing her utopian novel. Gillmore's text reveals many resemblances to Gilman's, from premise to characterization to themes, which suggest the probability of its influence on the writing of *Herland.* However, *Angel Island,* while considered a "feminist fantasy adventure" by the publishers who reprinted it in 1988, also contains sharp distinctions from Gilman's novel that nearly render it a masculinist dystopia, allowing for the possibility that Gilman read the novel and was inspired to write a more truly feminist work based on similar speculative premises.

Current evidence makes it difficult to verify that Gilman read *Angel Island,* though we do know that she read magazines that offered serialized fiction, such as *Harper's* and the *Atlantic Monthly,* and that in her hurried, prolific composition she sometimes appropriated ideas without correctly acknowledging her sources.[2] Furthermore, Gary Scharnhorst and Denise D. Knight have observed in discussing Gilman's library that she was fond of popular fiction, fantasy novels, and utopian romances.[3] The many striking similarities between the two texts, as well as the friendship of the authors, make a particularly strong case for Gilman having encountered this novel, while *Herland*'s distinctions from *Angel Island* could reflect Gilman's desire to draw upon elements of Gillmore's text in shaping a feminist utopia. As Sandra Gilbert and Susan Gubar have observed of the relationship between British author Rider Haggard's 1888 imperialist romance *She* and Gilman's *Herland,* "Masculinist dystopias, *Herland* demonstrates, fuel feminist utopias" ("Home Rule" 72). Furthermore, regardless of whether Gillmore's novel is a direct influence on Gilman's, the similar cultural work performed by both of these texts, which emerged in such close temporal proximity, offers a significant commentary on the historical and cultural moment in which they were composed.

Biographical Contexts: Gilman and Gillmore's Relationship

Inez Haynes was born in 1873 to American parents in Rio de Janeiro. After her family moved back to New England, she attended Radcliffe College, during which she became involved in the suffrage movement and married a journalist, Rufus Gillmore. Living in Greenwich Village, she published her first novel in 1908 and soon became the fiction editor of Max Eastman's left-wing magazine *The Masses.* After divorcing her first husband, in 1916 she married journalist William Irwin, and she went to Europe as a war correspondent during World War I, continuing to write fiction as well. Gillmore also authored a history of the suffrage movement in 1921, *Story of the Women's Party.*[4]

Charlotte Perkins Gilman came to know Gillmore through the Heterodoxy Club, a dining club for "unorthodox women" that was established in Greenwich Village in 1912. Founded by reformer Marie Jenney Howe, the group was composed of many women well known today, including journalist and suffragist Rheta Childe Dorr, editor and peace activist Crystal Eastman, labor organizer Elizabeth Gurley Flynn, and authors Zona Gale, Susan Glaspell, Helen Hull, and Fannie Hurst. The members met every other Saturday for lunch, a speech, and conversation on issues of the day; though they varied widely in lifestyles and in views on various issues, according to historian Judith Schwartz, "feminism was the one belief that united every member" (*Radical Feminists of Heterodoxy* 25).

Gilman and Gillmore's friendship apparently began shortly after their joining Heterodoxy in 1912, but Charlotte Perkins Gilman left the club a few years later over the most divisive issue that the group encountered: the United States' position on World War I. Many of Heterodoxy's members, such as Eastman and Flynn, were outspoken pacifists, and some members who were supportive of the war soon left the group over this difference of opinions.

Gilman abandoned the Heterodoxy Club for this reason as well, but she did reestablish her friendships with Marie Jenney Howe, Gillmore, and others during the 1920s. Among Gilman's papers at the Schlesinger Library at Radcliffe are three letters from Gillmore, written in the summer of 1921, that eagerly anticipate Gilman's impending visit to her house in Scituate, Massachusetts, as well as a reply from Gilman to Gillmore, composed as a poem.[5] Indeed, the two women had much in common that would have sustained a friendship over the years: both worked as lecturers on women's rights and as prolific authors of creative writing and journalism; both edited journals; both were involved with the National Woman's Party, which existed from 1916 until 1920; and both experienced an unsatisfactory first marriage and a satisfying second one.[6] With their similar interests in writing fiction and in questioning conventional gender ideologies, it seems highly probable that Gilman would have been aware of her friend Inez Haynes Gillmore's novel.

THE NOVELS: CONGRUITIES AND DIFFERENCES

Gillmore's *Angel Island* is a tale of five men who are shipwrecked on a remote semitropical island and discover it to be inhabited by five beautiful winged women. In their desire for these women, the men resort to treacherous, violent means of capture, cutting off the women's wings and proceeding to force their assimilation, in imperialistic fashion, to the men's Victorian ideals of womanhood. Though the women capitulate for a time to this subjection, marry the men, and bear them children, they eventually rebel by learning to walk, escaping to a remote part of the island, and growing their wings back to the degree that they can fly again. When they threaten to take the children and fly away from the island altogether, the men submit to the women's demand that their children's wings will never be clipped.

The many striking resemblances of the two texts that suggest *Angel Island*'s influence on the writing of *Herland* begin with their similar premises, wherein a group of men find themselves in an unfamiliar, semitropical environment at the mercy of a community of strong, self-sufficient women who exhibit a miraculous ability. As Batya Weinbaum has demonstrated in her study *Islands of Women and Amazons: Representations and Realities,* myths of islands or communities of women, particularly strong or militant women such as Amazons, have arisen on nearly all the continents of the globe for many centuries, indicating an enduring fascination with mythic spaces, whether nurturing or threatening, that consist exclusively of women. Gillmore's and Gilman's texts differ in the uses to which they put this archetypal premise, for while Gillmore's novel traces the almost complete conversion of this community of women to the imported cultural mores of the men, Gilman's novel instead recounts the conversion of the male visitors (with the exception of Terry) to the values of Herland. However, what is notable about these analogous premises is that both authors draw on mythic archetypes of communities of women to interrogate gender relations in their own cultural moment.

Moreover, Gillmore's varied characterizations of the five men who find themselves on Angel Island anticipate with exactitude the contrasts Gilman draws between the three sojourners in Herland, and with similar intent: to articulate the heterosexual politics of their day by invoking a triad of perspectives through which men tend to view women. Both Gillmore's Frank Merrill and Gilman's Van Jennings are sociologists, possessing a contemplative, intellectual cast. Gillmore's narrator says of Frank Merrill that "his conversation, both in subject-matter and in verbal form, bore towards pedantry," but also that he is "a man of impeccable private character, solitary, a little austere" (*Angel Island* 22). Frank, like Van in *Herland,* quickly becomes the leader and chief decision maker among the band of men. Similarly, Gilman's Van describes himself as fascinated by scientific approaches to human life, but also sometimes possessed by "airs of sociological superiority" (8). Furthermore, both of these men show at least the potential to view the women they encounter in a more enlightened, progressive manner than their companions, but herein a significant difference arises between the two. In *Angel Island,* Frank ironically rescinds his initial egalitarianism by marrying the most sexually alluring and submissive of the women, while in *Herland* Van submits to the dictates of the tactful yet assertive Ellador in their marriage.

Both novels also include male characters who regard women as sexual objects of pursuit and as irrational beings that require men's control.

Angel Island's Ralph is described thus: "He presented the anomaly of a man scrupulously honorable in regard to his own sex, and absolutely codeless in regard to the other. . . . Woman, first and foremost, was his game. Every woman attracted him. No woman held him" (15). Likewise, in *Herland*, Van reflects on how Terry envisions that mythic place as "a sort of sublimated summer resort—just Girls and Girls and Girls—and that he was going to be—well, Terry was popular among women even when there were other men around, and it's not to be wondered that he had pleasant dreams of what might happen" (7). The similarities between Ralph and Terry abound; both are handsome men who easily attract the opposite sex, and both voice misogynistic, sexist views about women at the same time as they are deeply drawn to them—Ralph's comment "'Our duty [to women] is to tame, subjugate, infatuate, and control them'" (*Angel Island* 88) sounds eerily similar to many of Terry's comments in *Herland*. Furthermore, both of these characters come up with the idea of capturing the women by appealing to what they believe to be part of women's essential nature: an inclination for pretty objects of adornment.

In addition to these analogous pairs of men who suggest the broad spectrum of heterosexual masculinity by representing the (supposedly) egalitarian, nonsexist intellectual and his contrast, the hypermasculine, sexist womanizer, both Gillmore's and Gilman's novels also portray a third type of man in order to interrogate turn-of-the-century perspectives on gender: the man who idealizes women, in the tradition of the nineteenth-century Cult of True Womanhood. In Gilman's novel, the sensitive and poetic Jeff Margrave elevates women on a pedestal "in the best Southern style. He was full of chivalry and sentiment, and all that" (*Herland* 9). In Gillmore's novel, however, two of the male characters reflect such attitudes. Billy Fairfax is a wealthy, charming, yet shy man who believes women are fragile and must be protected, while Pete Murphy is a witty, artistically inclined Irishman whose tendency is "to underestimate men and to overestimate women," viewing the latter as angelic inspiration (*Angel Island* 35). The fifth male character in Gillmore's text, Honey Smith, does not have as direct a counterpart in *Herland* as the other men, but his good looks and charm attract women in the same way that Terry Nicholson's do, though he is possessed of a more amiable, innocent nature than Gilman's character.

The female characters of *Angel Island* similarly foreshadow Gilman's descriptions of the three Herlanders whom the men marry. These women anticipate Gilman's characters both physically and behaviorally —the latter with a great deal of qualification, as will be discussed further on—though the women's appearances are sensuously described in a manner diametrically opposite from Gilman's approach. Indeed, the way in which the lengthy descriptions of the women's physical selves in Gillmore's novel reify the patriarchal gaze on women is distinctly revised by Gilman's emphasis on the "human" rather than "feminine" attributes of her female characters.[7]

Nonetheless, the physical similarities of these characters to Gilman's Herlanders are too striking to miss. The Angel Island woman whom the castaways name "Peachy," with hair of "a sheer golden blondeness" (110), eyes that are "a blue as limpid as the sky" and lips that are "the pink of the faded rose" (111), anticipates Herland's Celis, whom Van describes as a "blue-and-gold-and-rose person" (91). The Angel Islander whom the men tellingly identify as "Chiquita," because she resembles a Spanish woman with her "raven black" hair, "dusky cream" skin, and lips that are "a splash of crimson" (105–06) anticipates the Herlander Alima, whom Van describes as "a blazing beauty" with "black-and-white-and-red" coloring (91). Chiquita also anticipates Gilman's characterization of Alima because she displays the most conventionally feminine behavior of the Angel Islanders, just as Alima, despite her great physical strength, is described by Van as having "a far-descended atavistic trace of more marked femaleness" (130). The winged woman whom Honey Smith christens "Lulu," though unique for her vaguely Asian look, has brown hair, tawny skin, and brown eyes that physically anticipate Herland's Ellador. However, the latter's personality instead correlates with the most feminist, assertive Angel Islander, the woman whom Billy Fairfax christens "Julia." Julia is the only one of the women who is not distracted by the clothes and jewelry that the men use to trap them, and while her companions soon marry their captors, she remains unmarried until near the end of Gillmore's novel.

Julia's feminist awareness of the limiting roles that the men are imposing on them is illustrated by a scene in which she convinces her companions to learn to walk properly so that they need no longer rely on the men's help. When Peachy bitterly complains of the men's treacherous exploitation of their "ignorance of earth-conditions" (294), Julia's response is significant: "'Be fair to [the men]! Tell the truth to yourselves! If they took advantage of our innocence and ignorance, it was we who tempted them to it in the first place. As for our innocence and ignorance—you speak as if they were beautiful or desirable. We were innocent and ignorant of earth-conditions because we were too proud to learn about them, because we always assumed that we lowered ourselves by knowing anything about them. Our mistake was that we learned to fly before we learned to walk'" (195). Here Julia criticizes her companions' subscription, in metaphoric terms, to the nineteenth-century myth of women's moral superiority to men, an ideology that affirmed the socialization of young women to be passive, dependent, and above all "innocent." Within the metaphors of flying in the air versus walking on the earth, Julia invokes the contrast between a woman's harmful ignorance of her society and her critical understanding of its unpleasant realities such as the sexual double standard and venereal disease, a theme that pervades Gilman's canon of work.

It is ironic that this metaphor also reverses itself in Gillmore's novel; when the women are "brought down to earth" by the men, it is not to lead them to an enlightened, egalitarian perspective on the world but instead to force them into caricatured roles of the innocent, passive Victorian Angel in the House. Nonetheless, throughout Gillmore's novel Julia continues to be depicted as the most cognizant of the limitations that the male castaways on Angel Island have imposed on their female companions. In this sense, she anticipates Gilman's Ellador, who in her many conversations with Van, repeatedly enlightens him to the errors of his received notions about what is "feminine."

Despite these profound similarities between Gillmore's and Gilman's texts, the many differences between *Herland* and *Angel Island* are yet more thought provoking. Most obviously, the men in the first novel *succeed* in capturing the women whom they desire, proceeding to mutilate and incapacitate them and then to assimilate them to their ways, in direct contrast to the Herlanders' usually peaceful assimilation of the captured Van, Terry, and Jeff. The brutality of the men of Angel Island is disturbingly enacted in the scene in which they lure the women into a house filled with clothing and jewels, lock the doors, and then tie them down and cut their wings off. That this mutilation is a metaphoric rape is clearly indicated in the following passage:

They had thought the girls securely tied.

Clara fought like a leopardess, scratching and biting.

Lulu struggled like a caged eagle, hysteria mounting in her all the time until the room was filled with her moans.

Peachy beat herself against the wall like a maniac. She shrieked without cessation. One scream stopped suddenly in the middle— Ralph had struck her on the forehead. For the rest of the shearing session she lay over a chair, limp and silent.

Chiquita, curiously enough, resisted not at all. She only swayed and shrugged, a look of strange cunning in her long, deep, thick-lashed eyes. . . .

Julia did not move or speak. But at the first touch of the cold steel on her bare shoulders, she fainted in Billy's arms.

(197–98)

If any further evidence were needed to indicate that the "shearing" connotes not only mutilation but forced sexual domination too, we need only recall Ralph's earlier comment: "'Marriage by capture isn't such a foolish proposition, after all. Look at the Sabine women. I never heard tell that there was any kick coming from them'" (86).

Gillmore's metaphoric means of representing rape here again anticipates *Herland* thematically, for it is Terry's narrowly averted attempt to rape Alima that brings focus to the final part of Gilman's novel. Indeed, all five of the men on Angel Island, in their feverish pursuit and treacherous capture of the beautiful winged women, exhibit the behavior of Terry preceding his attack on Alima, which Van describes: "To hear him rage you'd not have believed that he loved Alima at all—you'd have thought that she was some quarry he was pursuing, something to catch and conquer" (131). In this sense, despite the contrast between the men's successful sexual domination of the women in Gillmore's novel and Terry's failed rape attempt in Gilman's work, both authors dramatically foreground women's sexual autonomy, or the lack thereof, to interrogate their autonomy in general.

Furthermore, in contrast to the male visitors to Herland, who initially bluster colonialist rhetoric but ironically soon find themselves the objects of the Herlanders' assimilation, the male visitors to Angel Island consistently represent a patriarchal colonizing force, imposing their own ideals on their newly conquered subjects. They teach their shorn captives to speak English and help them practice their new language with stories such as the Cinderella fairy tale, a telling choice of cultural narrative. They dress the women in long, flowing gowns recovered from the shipwreck flotsam, reducing these formerly strong, Amazonian creatures to the epitome of Euro-American turn-of-the-century womanhood, painfully tottering on their atrophied feet and having to be half-carried by their husbands. Most significantly, the men's communications with the Angel Islanders are patronizing and intolerant of any resistance on the women's part, in contrast to the dialogues between the male visitors and the Herlanders that structure much of Gilman's novel. This contrast is illustrated by a scene in Gillmore's novel in which Lulu attempts to question her husband's thinking, when he assures her that "'you're much more healthy and normal without wings'" (298). As she meekly tries to protest, he continues, "'It's not natural for women to fly. God never intended them to.'" When she reflects, "'It is wonderful . . . how men know exactly what God intended,'" he laughs, assuming her to be incapable of sarcasm, and reiterates that "'we know better than you; the man's life broadens us'" (269). Lulu begins, "'Then I should think—'" but she does not finish her sentence. In contrast to the way in which Gilman's trio of female Herlanders so often have the last word in their discussions with the men, having allowed the latter to back themselves into corners with their essentialized notions of "womanhood" or "society," Gillmore's text enacts not only the patriarchal silencing of women but also the internalization of that practice, through Lulu's complicity with such structures of power.

In a similar conversation in Gillmore's novel between Ralph Addington and his wife, Peachy, she appeals to him to let her fly again, proving flying to be a metaphor for female autonomy by relying on arguments that echo those made by Gilman for the right of women to work outside the home. She pleads, "'I'd always be here when you came back. You'd never see me flying. It would not prevent me from doing my duty as your wife or as Angela's mother. In fact, I could do it better because it would make me so happy and well,'" but Ralph's response is a curt dismissal: "'Couldn't think of it, my dear. The clouds are no place for my wife'" (276). In both scenes, Gillmore's metaphoric inscription of flying as a transgressive act of autonomy is richly ironic, for the image of wings might otherwise connote the submissive Victorian Angel in the House. On another level, Gillmore's metaphor is apt, for in the genre of New

Woman fiction at the turn of the century, a bird's power of flight is often invoked to suggest a woman's freedom, as it is in Kate Chopin's *The Awakening*.[8]

And indeed, Gilman herself repeatedly mined the metaphoric significance of flying both in order to critique the Angel in the House and to offer allegories of independent womanhood. In 1891, she published a satiric piece titled "An Extinct Angel," which undermines the Victorian notion of the angelic True Woman by describing this species, which eventually became extinct when its members "found and ate the fruit of forbidden knowledge" (50). The essay also discusses what happened when an angel "fell," attacking the sexual double standard that condemned such women as unredeemable, yet did not punish the men who were partners in, and often agents of, their fall. Furthermore, Gilman published an allegory titled "Two Storks" in 1910 in her own magazine, the *Forerunner*, which recounts a female stork's awakening desire to fly alongside her husband in the "Great Flight" of life. Though he responds with shock that she is an "'unnatural Mother'" and tells her that she has "'forgotten the Order of Nature,'" when she demonstrates that she and their children can fly just as well as he can, he is impelled to acknowledge that she too was "'a Stork before [she] was a Mother'" (12–13).

As the Angel Islanders' failed attempts to gain their husbands' support for their flying suggest, in contrast to the preponderance of conversations in Gilman's text between the visitors and Herlanders that reveal blind spots in patriarchal cultural assumptions, Gillmore's novel's critiques of status quo gender ideology are far more circumscribed. Until the end of the novel, when the Angel Islanders successfully confront their husbands, such criticisms are articulated only among the women themselves. In fact, we do not even hear them speak until over two hundred pages into the novel, when they have been duly assimilated into a Victorian ideal of womanhood, thus privileging the men's orientalist view of them as exotic sexual prey to be captured and "tamed." Moreover, despite the rebellious sentiments they express, some of the Angel Islanders, particularly Lulu, Clara, and Chiquita, also uphold stereotypes about women that are the very attitudes that their leader Julia is fighting to overcome, such as being vain about their appearances, flirting, or succumbing to the "spell" of the men (*Angel Island* 248).

Furthermore, in the final part of Gillmore's novel when the Angel Islanders do assert themselves, their rebellion is for a goal that will benefit future generations more than it will them; they request that the wings of their children never be cut so that the young ones may both walk and fly, but the women do not ask this for themselves. As Julia, their spokesperson, tells the men, "'There is [a] kind of happiness of which when you cut our wings we were no longer capable—the happiness that comes from a sense of absolute freedom. We can bear that for ourselves, but not for our daughters'" (338). While the denizens of Gilman's Herland subscribe to a humanitarian philosophy that similarly emphasizes the welfare of future generations, her characters are nonetheless concerned with the quality of their own lives in a way that the Angel Islanders are not.

In perhaps the most problematic contrast between the two novels, Julia, the feminist leader of Gillmore's winged women, dies at the end of the novel after giving birth to the first male child born with wings, thus relapsing into a conventional, sacrificial feminine role. Like other instances in which patriarchal discursive constructions of women emerge in Gillmore's novel, this moment is ambiguous; it is difficult to tell whether Gillmore is relying on the narrative convention of the self-sacrificing woman in earnest or ironically. However, that ambiguity leaves open the possibility that Gillmore's text is fundamentally conservative, valorizing such representations of women, while Gilman's utopian fantasy clearly and consistently subverts such conventions in order to create an innovative vision of female empowerment.

The Novels' Cultural Significance

In a larger perspective, even if *Angel Island*'s influence on the writing of Gilman's *Herland* cannot be proven, the simultaneous emergence of these two texts, intertwining myths of exclusively female communities with the adventure-tale genre in order to critique patriarchal society, provides a unique commentary on the historical and cultural moment in which they were composed and against which they speak.

First, these adventure novels' occurrence shortly after the turn into the twentieth century allows insight into an era consumed with narratives of the conquest of new lands. Following the short-lived Spanish-American War in 1898, the United States had annexed the Philippines, Guam, Puerto Rico, and, for a short time, Cuba, while growing military and corporate interests in the Hawaiian Islands led to their annexation by the United States the same year. Alongside such political conquests, the

United States was also pursuing economic imperialism in many parts of the world at this time; for example, exploiting the instability of the years just before and during the Mexican Revolution that began in 1910, U.S. business interests pursued a dominant presence in the Mexican economy.[9] When considered in the context of rapidly changing gender roles in American culture at the turn of the twentieth century, these imperialistic enterprises could be regarded as a gendered phenomenon wherein male anxieties over women's growing autonomy at home found release in a traditionally masculine enterprise: the conquest and domination of new lands whose populations were often culturally constructed as a feminized, exotic Other.

Gillmore's and Gilman's similar linking of colonizing impulses with the masculine in their novels supports such an interpretation of American imperialism at the turn of the last century.[10] Besides the way in which the male characters function as mouthpieces for colonialist rhetoric in both texts, the settings of the two novels also suggest ties to American imperialistic activities during that era. Herland's vague location in a "semitropical" region (11), in the "enormous hinterland of a great river" (2), suggests it to be somewhere in South America, a continent where American capitalists were heavily investing in agricultural and natural-resource industries in the late nineteenth and early twentieth centuries. Indeed, Inez Haynes Gillmore's own family epitomizes such economic imperialism, for she was born on a coffee plantation in Brazil, where her New England parents unsuccessfully attempted to prosper as coffee exporters.

Similarly, Gillmore's novel, by describing the setting as a tropical island apparently somewhere in the Pacific, suggests a link to the United States' political imperialism in this era. The Angel Islanders' appearances problematize this implication, for while two of the winged women are described as being of color—Chiquita's physical description likens her to a Latina and Lulu's to an Asian woman, in a fortunate contrast to Gilman's disturbingly all-white Herland—the other three women are described in terms that suggest them to be Caucasian. However, perhaps this is an implicit point in Gillmore's text. While white women were unquestionably in a position of privilege in comparison to women of color in the "real" world at that time, in the dystopic, fantastic world of Gillmore's text they might indeed suffer equally at the hands of a patriarchal system run out of control.

Even more interesting, Gillmore's novel may resonate with another historical reality of the time of its composition: the increasing contact of white Americans on their own soil with individuals of color from across the oceans. "Angel Island" was the actual name of a detention center in San Francisco Bay established in 1910 to hold new immigrants from China for questioning.[11] Perhaps Gillmore's novel, with its descriptions of the Angel Islanders' painfully learning to walk on their small, atrophied feet that suggests the image of Chinese women's bound feet, is signifying upon the cultural resonance of Asian immigration to America that has also been seen as an influence on the writing of Gilman's most famous text, "The Yellow Wall-Paper."[12]

In a literary context, Gillmore's and Gilman's texts also respond in similarly innovative ways to the scene of American letters in the early twentieth century. That both authors turned to speculative modes and mythic tropes to express feminist ideas in these novels suggests that both the prevailing naturalistic strategies and the nascent Modernist strategies of literary representation dominating the outset of the twentieth century may not have been sufficient for their objectives. Batya Weinbaum's ethnohistoric study of mythic communities of women notes, "In modern times, particularly over the last 150 years, many works have used imagistic symbols of Amazons in various historical contexts. These theoretical uses represent the range of psychological states of the authors, as well as the political struggles, contests for meaning, and intellectual currents of their times" (*Islands of Women and Amazons* 10). As fantasies that draw upon ancient myths of self-contained communities of women to explore and critique gender relations in their own era, both Gillmore's and Gilman's texts suggest how prevailing literary practices of their cultural moment may have constrained them, causing them to look to other techniques of representation. The tenets of the male author-dominated genre of naturalism, an offshoot of American realism that pervaded the literary scene at the turn of the century, were often associated with a "masculine" literary ethic. For example, Donna Campbell has considered naturalism a "gender-based countertradition" to the female-dominated local-color writing—interestingly, a genre often concerned with homosocial female spaces—that constituted a large part of the late-nineteenth-century realist movement (*Resisting Regionalism* 7). Thus, though Gilman's interest in using allegory and fantasy as means of articulating feminist critiques was already well established by the time she wrote

Herland, perhaps both she and Gillmore were also writing fantasies concerning female spaces in a gesture against the literary grain of the time: the hardscrabble, masculine world of the naturalist novel.

The years of the First World War also saw the rise of literary Modernism, constituting a reaction against the Genteel school of the late nineteenth century that was now often construed as effeminate and outdated. While Gillmore's and Gilman's novels do not coincide with the naturalist tradition, neither do they anticipate this rebellion, often a gendered gesture of masculine resistance to the perceived "softness" of the Genteel tradition. Rather, they shared feminist concerns that later reemerge, if quite differently, in the work of such female Modernist novelists as Gertrude Stein and Virginia Woolf. Thus, we might view Gillmore and Gilman in the years 1913 to 1915, caught between the rock and the hard place of what were often masculine-gendered imperatives in the existing naturalist movement and the fledgling Modernist one, as transcending both paradigms with speculative narratives focused on female spaces.

In another sense, in their play with fantasy and allegory in *Angel Island* and *Herland,* Gillmore and Gilman may have found themselves turning to the antirealistic modes so frequently employed a few years before by women writers at the turn into the twentieth century, particularly to articulate women's unique subjectivities in a new way and to mine feminist themes. As Elaine Showalter has noted in her introduction to the fiction anthology *Daughters of Decadence: Women Writers of the Fin-de-Siècle,* a collection that includes works by authors such as Olive Schreiner, George Egerton, and Kate Chopin, as well as Gilman's "The Yellow Wall-Paper": "[Women writers] described their sense of transition [at the turn of the century] in feminist allegories which acknowledge the failures of the present and the dangers of the future, but which refuse to turn back" (xviii). In the tradition of turn-of-the-century women writers, Gillmore's and Gilman's mutual use of antirealistic modes to articulate feminist critiques may be seen to contribute to a tradition in women's writing that continues today, particularly in the realm of utopian and science fiction.[13]

In the final analysis, while the direct influences of Gillmore's novel *Angel Island* on Gilman's writing of *Herland* cannot be definitively proven, both texts attempt, as Denise D. Knight has written of Gilman's fiction, to expose "the absurdities and limitations of patriarchal practices and institutions" ("Introduction," *Herland* xii). However, the eruptions of patriarchal discourse and even outright misogyny within Gillmore's novel, whether in order to critique these practices or out of complicity with them, render her text ambiguous in a manner very different from Gilman's confidently articulated feminist utopia. Ursula K. LeGuin's introduction to the reprint of *Angel Island*, in the only previous critical linking of these two texts to date, notes: "If [Inez Haynes Gillmore] didn't see through the patriarchal constructions of gender as clearly as Charlotte Perkins Gilman did in *Herland*, at least she was trying to poke some peepholes in the wall" (x). With the likelihood that Gilman was familiar with Inez Haynes Gillmore's novel *Angel Island*, *Herland* may constitute an intention previously unacknowledged in Gilman scholarship: to rewrite the patriarchal discourses that the former fantasy novel unfortunately betrays in an unambiguous vision of female empowerment and self-sufficiency.

Notes

1. For discussion of Swift's novel's connections with *Herland*, see Keyser's "Looking Backward"; for discussion of the influence of Bellamy's novel and theories on Gilman, see Lane, *To Herland and Beyond* 161–62, and Scharnhorst, *Charlotte Perkins Gilman* 20–23; also, see Gubar, "*She* in *Herland*" for discussion of *Herland* as a "utopian feminist revision" of Rider Haggard's 1886 imperialist romance, *She* (192).

2. I am grateful to Catherine Golden for the insights she offered on Gilman's reading and writing practices.

3. See Scharnhorst and Knight, 182.

4. All biographical information on Gillmore comes from Judith Schwartz's sketch in appendix C of *Radical Feminists of Heterodoxy* or from the biographical sketch of Gillmore in the frontispiece to the reprint edition of *Angel Island*.

5. Series III ("General Correspondence"), section C (Chronological), folder 143, of the Charlotte Perkins Gilman Papers, Schlesinger Library.

6. Biographical information on Gilman comes from Ann Lane and from Gary Scharnhorst.

7. This exoticizing emphasis upon the appearance of the Angel Islanders is magnified by the text's presentation in its original publication, serialized in *American* illustrated magazine in 1914; the chapters are accompanied by vivid color illustrations, usually depicting the winged women.

8. Other American works with New Woman themes that metaphorically or

symbolically connect the female protagonist to a bird, sometimes caged or with a broken wing, include Elizabeth Stuart Phelps's *The Story of Avis* (1878), Ellen Glasgow's *The Wheel of Life* (1906), Willa Cather's *The Song of the Lark* (1915), and Edith Wharton's *Summer* (1917).

9. For further discussion, see Stefoff 92.

10. Gilbert and Gubar's essay acknowledges the complexities of this use of colonial rhetoric, pointing out that "women's use of the colonial metaphor threatens to invalidate itself by replacing or effacing those who are literally colonized" (78).

11. For further information, see Ronald Takaki, *Strangers from a Different Shore.*

12. See Susan Lanser's essay, "Feminist Criticism."

13. Lane's introduction to *Herland* lists several feminist utopian novels written in recent years (xx).

11
Charlotte Perkins Gilman's
With Her in Ourland

Herland Meets Heterodoxy

Lisa A. Long

While Charlotte Perkins Gilman's noted feminist utopia, *Herland* (1915), has garnered critical attention in recent years, her sequel to the novel, *With Her in Ourland* (1916), languishes still in relative obscurity. The latter novel's coeditor, Mary Jo Deegan, contends, "*Herland,* taken by itself, stops mid-story, leaving readers with an erroneous understanding of Gilman's social vision and feminist worldview" (*Ourland* 2–3). Whether or not one considers *Herland* a complete text in and of itself, continuing on with Ellador and Van as they travel back to "Ourland" leads readers to a different geographical, political, and emotional space than the one settled on at the end of *Herland.* Though *With Her in Ourland* is still narrated by Van, his gaze is firmly focused on Herland's sole explorer, Ellador, and her painful, alienating confrontation with the world Gilman's readers inhabited—one that was obscured by Herland's very concrete perfections. As Ellador and two of the three male explorers prepare to leave Herland, the woman country is made immediately mythic: they look forward to returning to the "Real World" and Ellador is now called Van's "Wife from Wonderland," likening her to the bemused Alice of Lewis Carroll's fiction and relegating Herland to the realm of fantasy (*Ourland* 62). Thus, in some sense the beginning of *With Her in Ourland* undoes Gilman's meticulous rendering of Herland and its inhabitants. What seems a possible reality in *Herland* becomes a distant dream in *With Her in Ourland.*

Yet Ellador persists into Ourland. While *Herland*'s Van was securely flanked by his compatriots, Jeff and Terry, during his imprisonment in Herland, Ellador is conspicuously alone on her trip into the world.

Though Ellador comes to appreciate Van's devotion, she seems constantly to feel surrounded by "others"—through her eyes, the various cultures of the bisexual world seem willfully ignorant and inconceivably barbaric. Ellador proves a superior being whose outsider status accords her a seemingly clear and sweeping vision of the weaknesses of the cultures she visits. Her "alien point of view . . . gave her advantages as an observer far beyond our best scientists," Van tells us (*Ourland* 87). However, it is by virtue of her singular vision that Ellador remains a "Her" apart from those residing in Ourland—and, most conspicuously, apart from us, citizens of this world, who are implicated in the horrors of "our" land every time we utter the title of this novel. Extracted from the solid wall of homogeneity and unanimity that had sheltered and completed her in Herland—a "multitude actuated by a common impulse"—Ellador moves from being a comfortable "we" to a solitary "her" (*Herland* 44).

While *Herland* optimistically envisions a community of women in complete harmony with one another, we might read *With Her in Ourland* as depicting the alienating reality of a radical feminist worker in the early twentieth century. Ellador is a brave and visionary woman whose foresight keeps her apart from those with whom she might seem to have the most in common. Indeed, Ellador's empathetic response to the suffering she views threatens to obliterate her, and her journeys through Ourland also chart her efforts to cultivate the distance necessary for her survival. The intense interrelationships of Herland women caused no pain because the women were of one mind; Gilman implies that such complete unions are impossible in the "Real World," for the heterogeneity of modern Americans in particular makes uneasy companions of even the most like-minded people. By employing rhetoric that makes Ellador into an idealized social worker/doctor, Gilman links her own sociological and activist work to Ellador's plight. In this way Gilman posits that while her female ideal must operate literally among others, she must also remain apart from those others, a distant presence who is impervious to the various diseases that infect and compromise the cultures she observes. Only in this way is Ellador able to diagnose social ills and proffer treatments.

A brief look at Gilman's relationships with other feminists during the time she was composing the Herland saga suggests that she wrestled with the issues of debilitating identification and disappointing difference that Ellador faces. In 1912 Gilman became one of the charter members of New York's Heterodoxy Club, a group of unorthodox women who met for lunch every two weeks to eat, commiserate, and debate pressing political issues. Herland might be read as an idealized version of the club, which attracted some of the brightest and most progressive women activists of the day. In 1914 Margaret Sanger addressed the Heterodoxy Club, hoping to find support for her campaign to legalize the distribution of birth-control information. As this essay will demonstrate, Gilman's and Sanger's views at this time coincided on very basic issues: both saw progress in terms of public health, advocating the control of reproduction as the means of ensuring economic stability and human evolution. They founded periodical publications—Gilman's *The Forerunner* and Sanger's *Woman Rebel*—to control the dissemination of their views.

Yet Sanger later wrote that she was unable to strike a "responsive chord" from Gilman, for Gilman's attitude toward the proper expression of female sexuality was at odds with Sanger's (Sanger, *Autobiography* 108). Eventually, Gilman became disillusioned with the possibilities of organized female community, resigning from the Heterodoxy Club when members disagreed with her support of U.S. involvement in World War I and her neo-Victorian views of sexual mores. Gilman continued to associate with Heterodoxy members and even came to support Sanger's cause, speaking in a public forum for the last time in her life at one of Sanger's birth-control conferences. Yet she seemed never to find the community she desired. While Ellador returns home at the end of *Herland,* Gilman struggled along in Ourland.

ELLADOR AMONG OTHERS

Ellador courageously embarks on her trip into the unknown territories of Ourland, eager to "meet and learn a whole new world, and perhaps establish connections between it and her own dear land." However, the limited nature of those "connections" soon becomes apparent, for Herland's representative must continually negotiate her difference from those who inhabit Ourland. What distinguishes Ellador most from the people she encounters is her vision. She does not live in the moment, but functions with "her eyes ahead, far ahead, down the long reaches of the winding stream" (*Ourland* 63). Van repeatedly refers to her perspicacity as a "searchlight," or as the "bird's eye view" (107).

Gilman uses physical metaphors to express Ellador's intellectual and visionary range. This figurative language is also influenced by the advent of airplanes, which initially make Herland visible to Ourland and offer the bird's-eye view Ellador intuitively cultivates. Metaphorically speaking, however, one air flight is not enough to provide insight into the lands below: it is Ellador's prolonged travels, her protracted homelessness, that nurture her perception. As Val Gough also notes, Gilman "views travel as both a means of and a metaphor for acquiring the 'far-seeing' utopian vision" (133).

Gilman posits that one's distance from "home"—physically and psychically—allows one a larger and more synthetic social vision. She practiced what she preached in this regard, in depictions of her own life linking a rooted sense of "home" with a narrow and near-sighted view. In her autobiography Gilman proclaims, "Never having had a settled home, but always feeling perfectly at home anywhere, in this country or others, I have been better able to judge dispassionately and to take a more long-range view of human affairs than is natural to more stationary people" (*Living* 294). Ironically, it is her immersion in others' homes that produces the distance necessary for social reform. Ellador, too, insists that her ability to diagnose and prescribe cures for social ills derives simply from the principles of "perspective." "The farther a thing is away from you the smaller it is, the less well you can see it, the less you are able to understand it, and by the 'law of nature' you look down upon it!" (*Ourland* 143). In an apparent contradiction, Gilman asserts that it is Ellador's close proximity to the pain and suffering she encounters in Ourland—indeed, her fine-tuned ability to feel it herself—that enables her singular and distant vision.

Given Gilman's personal views on travel and progressive thought, it seems inevitable that her novelistic saga continue beyond Herland—and beyond *Herland*. In a feat of Herland-like social engineering, Gilman asserts that she encouraged her own natural proclivity for sociological thought through her travels: "Inheriting a far-focused mind and educating it in a general study of humanity which takes in all races and all times, this wandering life of mine has increased the natural breadth of vision and constantly added to its power" (*Living* 294).

Gilman initially had tried to imagine such a "wandering life" within the confines of Herland. Herlanders do not ascribe to familiar notions of personal property or familial possession; they do not have "homes"; and they see domestic travel as a key component of their children's development. It is because Herland children are "taken all over the country, shown all its arts and crafts, taught to honor its achievement and to appreciate its needs and difficulties" that they grow up "with a deep and vital social consciousness" (*Ourland* 71). However, though Herland does not have discrete, capitalist homes, the whole country is homelike, or *heimlich*, to borrow from Freud ("The Uncanny"). Thus Ellador must leave her narrow and comfortable homeland and, instead, circle the globe in order to adhere to Gilman's dictums. Yet Herland ghosts the novel, for Ellador defines Ourland by what it is not—by the ways in which it is not home, not Herland, *unheimlich*. While Ourland is in many ways "familiar and congenial" to Ellador, it is also uncanny, as the more unsavory elements of the culture that had remained "concealed and kept out of sight" are brought to light by Ellador's investigations (Freud, "The Uncanny" 156). And thus Ellador remains uneasily home-less throughout the novel.

Gilman herself was often easily homeless; she could rejoice in an 1899 letter to her future husband, Houghton, during their lengthy—and distant—courtship, "What a wonderful life it is—to go everywhere—to meet everyone—to eat and drink so largely of human life" (qtd. in Hill 12). And yet, by 1916 she imagined the consequences of such a complete peregrinatory binge; despite the requirements of her social work, Ellador is unable to be fully and completely with the others of Ourland. Gilman posits a complex of kinship and distance necessary for the advancement of civilization. While one must always be immersed in the company of others, one must also cultivate an alienation from those others that allows for insight and self-protection. Gilman graphically expresses the ambivalent push and pull of connection in descriptions of her most intimate relationships.

It is, perhaps, a commonplace that "the experience of living within a supportively communal environment and of enjoying supportive mothering both as daughter and as mother had not been part of her childhood life," as scholars including Carol Farley Kessler ("'Dreaming Always of Lovely Things Beyond'" 95) and others have noted. Many are familiar with Gilman's remembrances of her distant mother, a stern disciplinarian whose devotion "was not the same as petting, her caresses were not given unless we were asleep, or she thought us so" (*Living* 23). Gilman's ability to engage in fulfilling personal relationships with men as well as women remained vexing throughout her life. Writing to Houghton about her mixed feelings toward their commitment to each other, Gilman agonized, "I don't wholly like to be held—and yet I do!" "Makes me kind of angry too. Seems a weakness. To be so tangled up in another person" (qtd. in Hill, *Journey from Within* 14). Her love for Houghton and then her willingness to become extricated in his affairs and emotional life "drags [her], tears [her], pulls [her] toward" him. Love and commitment are perceived by Gilman here as physical assault, as coercion. Too, based on the emotional breakdown that accompanied her first, disastrously traditional marriage, Gilman feared that the gender expectations that inevitably come with her impending second marriage would make her unable again to "harmonize" her work and her private life. "I suppose it is only the essential pain of the woman nature forced out into world service," Gilman concludes (14). Thus the demands of personal intimacy were always in tension with public work for Gilman.

Gilman neatly erases this particular dilemma in *With Her in Ourland*. Van becomes a perfect mate (perhaps an idealized version of her beloved Houghton) who subsumes his own physical and emotional needs to the demands of Ellador's work. However, Ellador's experiences in Ourland still demonstrate the high costs for those naively willing to become completely tangled up in others' affairs.

The first stop on Van and Ellador's global tour is Europe, where World War I is raging. While Van is disturbed by the horrific events, the "atmosphere" of "suspicion, distrust, hatred, of ruthless self-aggrandizement and harsh scorn" nearly kills Ellador. She is initially eager to understand the war fully; as the sole envoy of her country, she feels it her duty "to see, to know . . . to really *know*" (*Ourland* 73). True to her Herland training, Ellador goes on several excursions, touring hospitals and viewing the war's destruction from Terry's biplane. However, Ellador has been trained to the extent that to truly know she must become one with the individuals and the culture. As Van notes, "We feel these horrors as happening to other people; she felt them as happening to herself" (74). Apparently, Ellador is able to garner total knowledge because she is able to completely open herself to others.

However, in Ourland this full and complete melding threatens to destroy her. As her knowledge of war grows, Van notes that she grows "paler and harder" daily, as if the war's brutality is sickening her body, draining away its color and pliancy. After viewing a battlefield she hits a psychological breaking point, becoming "like a woman of marble, cold, dumb, sitting still by the window where she could rest her eyes on the far stars" (74). She is literally paralyzed by what Van notes is her first "experience of pain"; since feeling with these people brings only pain and suffering, she ceases to feel and ceases to speak (74). Later, Van and Ellador visit China, where they hear the tortured cries of a girl whose feet are being bound. Ellador is infected by the girl's pain, lying silent and staring with "long shudders running over her from time to time" (93).

Throughout the novel, Ellador is sickened again and again by the neglect, cruelty, and suffering she sees on her travels (145). Van counsels, "You can't afford to feel our sorrow—you'd die of it," and offers a variety of the talking-cure as a way of managing the pain that her work in Ourland will surely bring. To deflect intense emotional detachment and yet continue to gather the information she so desperately desires, Ellador must present "an amiable but absolute impermeability" to the people and problems she encounters (66).

We can see that Gilman's initial depiction of Ellador's research method takes issue with familiar masculinist notions that sever intellect from emotion. Van writes, "We are so used to seeing our learned men cold and solemn, holding themselves far above all the 'enthusiasm of youth'" that it is difficult to associate a "high degree of wisdom and intellectual power" with the "vivid interest" that Ellador almost childishly manifests in the new world she encounters (62). Thus feeling and intellect are initially connected in Ellador, but American, patriarchal ideals of scientific objectivity eventually prevail in the novel.

In Herland, everything Ellador and her compatriots study—the theories of history, geography, agriculture, education, medicine, etc., they produce—resonates in their minds, emerging, as they do, from the homogeneous population of which they are all a part. Symbolically, Ellador's interactions with her Herland sisters and mothers are no different from interactions with herself; there is little risk of pain or rejection in those relationships. Conversely, American notions of scientific method emphasize difference; the disease, poverty, and ignorance that Gilman, through Ellador, sees all around her must be treated from a distant, mildly sympathetic height. Ellador reasons, "I'm trying not to feel about these particularly awful things, and not to judge, even, till I know more. These things are so; and my knowing them does not make them any worse than they were before" (101). In this way she strives to make herself a conduit; information will flow through her, and she will resist its effects on her.

In fact, it is her outsider status that allows her to be the ultimate scientist, best able to cure social ills and compromised bodies. Thus *With Her in Ourland* charts Ellador's transformation from "alienated" to "alien," a shift, Gilman suggests, that is necessary for the productivity and mental well-being of modern women reformers. The exchange of information eventually becomes a one-way street for Ellador; she learns to extract intelligence from Ourland's inhabitants without letting their emotions infect her. While the thoughts and feelings of Ourland's citizens are all too visible to Ellador, Van reiterates that the opaque "power and clarity" of her mind is beyond his comprehension. Indeed, as Ellador continues to amass information about Ourland, Van notes the subtle way that she elicits it from the people she encounters on her travels: "These were not 'smart' questions, with a flippantly triumphant and all-too-logical demand at the end, leaving the victim confused and angry. He never realized what was being done to him" (107). It's almost as if Ellador's "sympathetic perception" allows her to psychically probe others' thoughts and emotions (147). Indeed, Van claims her "free, strong, and agile mind" has special powers because it is not full of "all the associate ideas and emotions ours are so full of" (159). Ellador learns to distinguish between identification and sympathy. Gilman implies that emotion weakens and calcifies the intellect, while disassociation frees and strengthens it.

Ellador's special mental powers lead Van to describe her literally as an "alien" as often as Ellador uses that word to characterize the immigrant hordes whom she sees as sucking the lifeblood out of the United States. Van notes that she acts "as if she came from Mars, and was studying the rest of humanity in the mass" (87). Thus Gilman insists that an unbridgeable distance must be nurtured between those who reform and those who must be reformed; the objects of study must not be individuated, for it is easier to disassociate from the "mass." Ultimately, the ideal woman reformer is not of this world. Van functions, in part, as a plot device allowing us to see the alien invader who would, otherwise, be invisible to us. "Here are you, as extramundane as a Martian. You are like an Investigating Committee from another world," he marvels (110).

Gilman's use of the alien trope prefigures later depictions of alien abductions; Ellador's gentle yet insidious attentions ferret out Ourland's secrets against the wills of its inhabitants. However, while Ellador's "alien point of view" is a strength, allowing her to treat the nation's ailments, according to Van the "injections of alien blood" from immigration weaken the body of the nation, infecting it with physical and social diseases (106). Yet Ellador is uneasily linked to those immigrants through the alien imagery, suggesting that her presence, too, will alter the shape of the national body and, then, the course of events.

Gilman links Ellador's need to remain removed from the subjects of her study, as well as the palpable impact she will most certainly leave on the national body, to the matters of public health that compelled her and contemporaries such as Margaret Sanger. Descriptions of Ellador's work rotate between social worker and doctor. Such linkages appear earlier in Gilman's career; in an 1898 essay she claimed "the physician, the agitator for hygienic reform naturally sees disease and overlooks health, and the agitator for social reform must of course do likewise" (qtd. in Wegener 56). Van begins to associate Ellador's otherworldliness with the vocation of social worker, claiming she "seemed like an enthusiastic young angel 'slumming.' I resented—a little—this cheerful and relentless classification—just as poor persons resent being treated as 'cases'" (*Ourland* 79). Thus Ellador becomes the typical social worker, a selfless and ministering creature who condescends to aid those whom she deems in need of her help. In this way, Gilman also classes Ellador's cultural differences, naturalizing the dissimilarities between the enlightened vision of the educated reformer and the density of the poor and suffering mind. The focus of Ellador's study becomes to "understand, if possible, what mysterious ideas and convictions keep you so poor, so dirty, so crowded, so starved, so ill-clothed, so unhealthy, so unhappy, when there is no need of it" (137). Given Ellador's preternatural ability to discern the "ideas and convictions" that motivate Americans, one must assume that the "mystery" here concerns Americans' apparently conscious decision to suffer "when there is no need of it."

While the social worker/reformer remains at the core of Ellador's character—indeed, was Gilman's own vocation—the woman doctor emerges as an equally powerful role. As Frederick Wegener points out, women doctors were persistent and heroic figures in Gilman's writings. She met almost all American women doctors of distinction during her travels through the country; apparently, the pertinacious and competent female physician came to "epitomize, in Gilman's eyes, the larger struggle for professional acceptance and economic parity" (Wegener 50). I would add that their knowledge of the mysterious workings of the human body, coupled with their maternal potential, made them larger than life—

made them into Herland women. In her autobiography, Gilman tells of the attention she received from a couple of Chicago physicians, "Mrs." and "Mr. Doctor" McCracken, who attended not only to Gilman's body but also to her economic needs ("they rescued me from that black house in Little Hell") and her emotional ones ("she well knew what it meant to me, to have a child in my arms again"). Thus Mrs. McCracken earns the title of "wife-and-mother-doctor" (*Living* 190). In labeling her so, Gilman uses the "and" to set apart Mrs. McCracken's role as "wife" from her work as "mother-doctor," the latter attaching the healing powers garnered from her professional training to those emerging from her maternal instincts.

Indeed, women doctors' competency in a variety of matters—physical, spiritual, social, and political—makes them broadly competent; they encompass the potential capabilities of all women. This comprehensiveness is the reason Gilman employs the trope of the woman doctor most consistently in *With Her in Ourland,* making Ellador into a physician/surgeon. The pose of the woman doctor saves Ellador from disabling emotional entanglements, manufacturing the distance she needs in order to remain healthy herself. Yet the recuperative power of the doctoring role is somewhat ironic here, given Gilman's vexed relationship to male doctors' authority.

Gilman consistently excoriated her fictional male doctors for their inability to listen to the stories of their female patients. Martha J. Cutter argues that in her later fiction Gilman creates women doctor-patient relationships whereby "medical information circulates between doctor and patient and between reader and writer, and medical authority is dispersed" ("The Writer as Doctor" 152). *With Her in Ourland* replaces the sick woman with a suffering child and reinforces the primacy of medical authority, connecting the latter to public health work and to Ellador's alien probes. Ellador becomes "a doctor, a hygienist, an investigator" and Van feels certain that that "Herland mind" of Ellador's will find out "what ails us—and how we are to mend it" (*Ourland* 112). As Wegener reminds us, Gilman often presented herself "as a kind of social pathologist treating a badly diseased, even deformed, social organism or body politic" ("What a Comfort a Woman Doctor Is!" 56).

With Her in Ourland deploys this rhetorical strategy for fictional ends, as Van and Ellador agree to treat the nations of Ourland as diagnosable bodies. Ellador decides that Europe was like "'a man with—with delirium tremens. Asia was like something gnarled and twisted with hopeless age. But America is a Splendid Child . . . with . . . ' She covered her face with her hands" (111). Indeed, in making America into a child, Gilman differently disempowers the patient, for not only is it sick; it is also a genderless "it," neither boy nor girl. Thus the child's minor status, its legal dependence and disenfranchisement, become its distinguishing characteristic rather than its gender identity. Given the patient's youth and the strength of Ellador's Herland ethos, doctoring is not attached to paternal but rather to maternal authority in this novel. Ellador responds to America's disease as she would to that of a suffering child; its ills are so horrible that they are initially unspeakable. Eventually, though, Ellador is able to diagnose the problem: though a promising tot, America is now "bloated and weak, with unnatural growth, preyed on by all manner of parasites inside and out, attacked by diseases of all kinds, sneered at, criticized, condemned by the older nations, and yet bravely stumbling on" (118).

What has made the nation "sick" is its unremitting diet of an "ill-assorted and inassimilable mass of human material" (118). In short, a steady diet of immigrants and the persistent presence of unassimilated former slaves have caused the nation's disease. While the "surgical operation" of the Civil War had relieved the "attack of slavery," the "chronic distension" of childish and fecund immigrants persists (122). Thus the final, salient feature of the "Splendid Child's" identity is that it is white, or at least untroubled by the racial mixtures contained in its body prior to the influx of immigrants.

Two of the novel's chapters are titularly concerned with the "diagnosis" of the Splendid Child's disease and, eventually, Ellador begins to proffer cures. She is "as busy, as patient, as inexorably efficient as an eminent surgeon engaged in a first-class operation," Van tells us, as she studies American culture and writes about it (137). Indeed, in consistently metaphorizing the fate of the nation and the whole human race as an uneducated, abandoned, and diseased baby, Gilman associates her concerns with those of fellow reformers like Sanger. Ironically, Gilman initially found egregious Sanger's obsession with birth control and her tendency to link contraception with unfettered sexuality. An essay in Sanger's 1914 magazine, *Woman Rebel*, contends that in order to make herself completely free, woman must "recognize her absolute right to dispose of herself, to give herself, to withhold herself, to procreate, or to suppress the germ of life" (8). Yet both Sanger and Gilman agreed that overpopulation, particularly the unchecked reproduction of the "unfit," would cause the ruin of America; Sanger supported the idea that the "propagation of [America's] degenerate, and imbecile, and criminal should be prevented" (51). Ellador sees the disheartening outcome of such ill-conceived and unwanted reproduction all around her in "stunted, meager starveling children, the millions of poor little sub-ordinary children, children who are mere accidents and by-products of this much-praised 'sex'" (*Ourland* 186). Within Gilman's symbology the government becomes the unfit father of this disgusting progeny—a parent who is "as weak and slow and wavering as a drunken man" and who is, then, unable to train its citizens properly, monitor sexual behaviors, and ensure national health and safety through "responsible" reproductive practices (149). Paternal authority is pathologized here, in need of remedy from the maternal expertise of the woman doctor.

The main reason that Ellador felt obliged to leave Herland is, at heart, the same reason that Margaret Sanger was compelled to distribute her birth-control information despite the risks to her personal safety. Ellador explains, "We have made a nice little safe clean garden place and lived happily in it, but we have done nothing whatever for the rest of the world. We might as well not be there for all the good it does anyone else" (63). Gilman here advocates the dissemination of information crucial to the public health as she understands it. It is not enough merely for the doctor to know how to maintain the public body. Ellador insists that "the doctor . . . has to have his 'chart' to study. But the public ought to know how fever is induced and how it is to be avoided" (79).

Disease is metaphorically likened to war in *With Her in Ourland;* while historical data merely describe the disease, Ellador stipulates a preventative medical approach, whereby knowledge of a disease's etiology will prevent its future outbreak. Ellador insists that the "doctor's chart—his 'history of the case'" is best suited to organizing historical-medical knowledge for the general public, so that past "diseases" (like "tuberculosis or cancer") might be understood from inception through development (80). In this way American history would unfold in a scientific manner—become diagnostic rather than descriptive. The diseases of war and poverty could be eradicated through the dissemination of preventative regimens. Thus the reproduction of medical information would result in the reproduction of healthy, disease-free national bodies.

Linking reproductive information and the reproduction of information, both Gilman and Sanger insist that the highest goal of public-minded health workers is to share their vision with the world. Dissemination was literally and metaphorically at the heart of Sanger's battle with Anthony Comstock, secretary of the New York Society for the Suppression of Vice, whose personal view of decency dictated the inception and implementation of section 211 of the federal statutes (a.k.a. the Comstock laws), which prohibited the mailing of "obscene, lewd, and lascivious" materials (qtd. in Sanger, *Autobiography* 113). After working as an obstetrical nurse in New York, Sanger resolved to find out about all available birth-control methods and to make that information widely available. To this end, Sanger wrote, financed, edited and published the little magazine *Woman Rebel* during the year 1914, intending to disseminate reproductive information to desperate working-class women. Exploiting Comstock's charges of indecency, Sanger often personified *Woman Rebel* in her editorials, rhetorically making the magazine into an audacious and seductive body. And readers responded in kind, one writing of the paper, "It looks good to the eye, feels good under the fingers and, best of all, feels good inside one's head and chest" (*Woman Rebel* 14). This enthusiastic reader's corporeal language suggests that she/he gains sensual pleasure from the woman rebel, noting not only that she is intellectually stimulating (she has "brains") but also physically stimulating (she feels good to the touch, feels good "inside"). More important, the woman rebel has physically penetrated the reader's body and brain, filling the head and chest with new ideas. In this way the paper has done precisely what Comstock and his followers feared: the woman rebel metaphorically inseminates this reader, reproducing her radical ideas.

Though less explicitly erotic, Gilman's *Forerunner* was also interested in exciting the interests of its readers. In the serial's initial "Statement of Purpose," Gilman proclaimed that she, too, intended to "*stimulate* thought; to *arouse* hope, courage and impatience" in her apparently dispassionate readers (qtd. in Ceplair, *Charlotte Perkins Gilman* 195; emphasis added). Indeed, she began publishing the magazine to accommodate her overflowing intellectual energies: "Think I must and write I must, the manuscripts accumulated far faster than I could sell them, some of the best, almost all—and finally I announced: 'If the editors and publishers will not bring out my work, I will!'" (*Living* 304).

With Her in Ourland, which, of course, was serialized in the *Forerunner*, makes Ellador's reformatory zeal explicitly seductive and consequently obfuscates the insinuation of new ideas into the neophyte's consciousness. Ellador and Van's relationship illustrates the amorous dissemination of the Herland ethos. Early on, Van remarks upon the distance between them, writing that Ellador "thought that [he] felt as she did" about the war in Europe, though he confesses that he thought it was "not nearly as badly as she supposed" (*Ourland* 72). However, as the book progresses, Van acknowledges her superior views on all topics and reiterates, "I grew insensibly to adopt her point of view, her scale of measurements, and her eager and limitless nature" (81). He manifests very little resistance to her radical and alien convictions, and is won over by the clean, logical beauty of her intellect and his growing love for her.

There is never any indication that Ellador's views are not correct and true; in this way, Ellador's objective and sterile gaze cleanses the politics of Gilman's personal views. As Val Gough has shown, Gilman links the far-ranging vision garnered through travel to the "transcendence of ideological boundaries" and of personal idiosyncrasies in her utopian fictions ("Twinkling" 136). Free of the "associate ideas and emotions" our brains are so full of, Ellador's views function "like carrying a high-powered light into dark places," leading Van to see things he "never dreamed were there" (*Herland* 159). Through her eyes the familiar becomes unfamiliar, the invisible, visible. Indeed, Gilman implies that it is Van's accession to Ellador's seductive celibacy—her request that they *not* have sexual relations—that clears the clouds from his eyes and allows him to see the world anew. While Sanger's readers garner insight from indulging their sexual energies, Gilman's characters are freed from corporeal desire and personal possessiveness; as Van discovers, "I looked at the world about me, seeing it as I had never seen it before, as it was" (*Herland* 141).

Ironically, while Ellador is literally free from Van's insemination for the majority of the book (they refrain from having sexual intercourse), his mind is penetrated by her vision. Thus, while the bird's-eye view that Ellador cultivates in *With Her in Ourland* might seem to be distinguished from the colonialist and sexually violent work achieved by flight into *Herland*, the two seemingly opposed pursuits are of the same type (Long, "*Herland* and the Gender of Science" 128). Gilman's imagery suggests that Van has been inseminated by Ellador's thought, "as the perception grew within [him]" like an ideological fetus. When he tells Ellador of the new world that has opened before him, the inner vision that he feels stirring inside, Ellador is "dumbly happy—just held [his] hand, her eyes shining" (*Ourland* 167). Together, they have produced Van's new consciousness; his transformation is effected through his willingness to let Ellador penetrate and alter his thoughts. Toward the end of the novel, when Van repeats back the lessons he has learned from Ellador about the limitations of modern women, she praises him: "It's wonderful how clearly you see it" (173).

However, Van and Ellador's ideological reproduction is more parthenogenetic—or, more precisely, parasitic—than bisexual. Van's and Ellador's worldviews have not melded; rather, Van's views have been replaced by Ellador's. Thus, while one may see the book structured as a series of dialogues between Ellador and Van about the cultural crises they encounter, the novel as a whole "actually function[s] as [a] monologic statement" of "truth" (Gough, "Twinkling" 138). There is no sense that Van's ideology has been replaced with an equally idiosyncratic and flawed belief system; both believe in Herland's reality.

The end of the novel suggests that Ellador does not return to Herland untouched by the diseased world she has inhabited. She begs Van to return to Herland with her before "this black stupid confusion—has hurt me any worse. Perhaps it is no harm, that I have suffered so" (*Ourland* 189). However, it is not Ellador's experience of suffering that infects Herland upon her return but rather the colonizing impulses implicit in her work on Van's mind and in the alien imagery Gilman deploys. Indeed, Van had noted in *Herland* that "the untroubled peace, the unmeasured plenty, the steady health, the large good will and smooth management which ordered everything, left nothing to overcome" (*Herland* 99–100). Once the perfect homogeneity of Herland is breached by the entrance of the male explorers and Ellador has been exposed to the heterogeneity of Ourland, Herland's perfect stasis disappears. After Ellador shares her information with the young Herland women upon her return, they begin "planning, as eager missionaries plan, what they could do to spread to all the world their proven gains." They have now been infected with the desire to impose their salvation on the world.

Gilman muddies social responsibility and imperialist force at the end of the Herland saga, remarking, "There began to stir in Herland a new spirit, pushing, seeking, a new sense of responsibility, a larger duty" (*Ourland* 193). Thomas Peyser argues that Gilman's "aim throughout her career was to prevent the incursion of the global upon the local," yet, ironically, Herland *is* the global in *With Her in Ourland*, its duty-bound citizens gearing up at the end of the novel to spread their culture throughout the world (*Utopia and Cosmopolis* 65). Despite her own abhorrence of immigration into America, Gilman symbolically makes women reformers into alien immigrants bent on altering the culture they decide to invade. Indeed, one might argue that this colonizing impulse merely lay dormant in the static land; after all, the desire for social perfection had initially propelled Herland's development, making necessary, for example, the enforced childlessness of those Herland women thought unfit to reproduce. Once something yet again appeared to be "overcome," the lurking imperialistic impulse kicked in to gear. As Kristin Carter-Sanborn explains, Gilman is not able to sever "violence, hierarchy, [and] imperialism" from "peace, egalitarianism, [and] nurture" merely by expunging men from her utopic spaces; indeed, Gilman crafts a "logic of colonialism as anesthesiology: to anesthetize one's own body is self-restraint; to anesthetize the other, colonialism; working together, they constitute feminist middle-class imperialism" (Carter-Sanborn, "Restraining Order" 5, 24). In performing the delicate surgical work of social reformation, Ellador must not only blunt her feelings while "among others" but also induce the others to desensitize and alienate themselves in the name of progress.

HETERODOXY

Gilman's real-life efforts to recruit missionaries for her own social reformations were more difficult than was Ellador's work with Van. In her search for like-minded women, Gilman briefly attended the Heterodoxy Club, which hosted luncheon gatherings for "unorthodox women" and flourished in Greenwich Village from 1912 to the early years of World War II (Schwartz 1). The group's prominent members held widely divergent political views, yet all shared a commitment to women's issues and women's autonomy. The group's founder, Marie Jenney Howe, envisioned their meetings as spaces free from the constraints of polite society, where disagreements could be discussed candidly and beliefs could be challenged and altered. One Heterodoxy member wrote of her tenure in the club, "It has been a glimpse of the women of the future, big spirited intellectually alert, devoid of the old 'femininity' which has been replaced by a wonderful freemasonry of women" (qtd. in Schwartz 1). Though the group's revolving membership tells the lie of this utopian ideal, it seems clear that Heterodoxists, if not achieved, at least imagined a community of strong, individualistic and politically engaged women. Another member wrote:

As I look around and see your faces—
The actors, the editors, the businesswomen, the artists—
The writers, the dramatists, the psychoanalysts, the dancers,
The doctors, the lawyers, the propagandists.
As I look round and see your faces
It really seems quite common to do anything!
Only she who does nothing is unusual.

(qtd. in Schwartz 53)

This catalogue of women's roles inverts the catalogue Gilman presents in *Herland* as Van realizes that he has associated action and profession with men:

When we say *men, man manly manhood,* and all the other masculine derivatives, we have in the background of our minds a huge vague crowded picture of the world and all its activities . . . full of marching columns of men, of changing lines of men, of long processions of men; of men steering their ships into new seas, exploring unknown mountains, breaking horses, herding cattle, ploughing and sowing and reaping, toiling at the forge and furnace, digging in the mine, building roads and bridges and high cathedrals, managing great businesses, teaching in all the colleges, preaching in all the churches; of men everywhere, doing everything—"the world."
(*Herland* 135)

Though Van's description of men's work focuses more on physical labor than on professional employment, his claim that men are "everywhere, doing everything" echoes the Heterodite's sense that women are now equally ubiquitous, commonly doing "anything!"

Yet Gilman struggled with the differences of opinion that inevitably emerged in gatherings of strong-willed women. Her Herlanders might be viewed as members of a "monodoxy": Gilman depicts ambitious, intelligent New Women, and imagines away—or rather breeds out—

troubling dissension. Herlanders are motivated by one mind, one spirit. Though they clearly did not expect uniformity, the Heterodoxists apparently strove for the peaceful and empathetic coexistence of its members. In a 1920 album dedicated to the club and honoring its founder, Marie Jenney Howe, Gilman contributed a poem titled "To Queen Marie":

> Who gathers folk of warring creed
> And holds them all as friends,
> Who ministers to social needs,
> And strives for social ends—
> All praise to her for her deed
> And the great gift she spends.

(qtd. in Schwartz 15)

Gilman approves of Howe's commitment to the social good rather than individual desires and wonders at her seemingly sovereign power to hold this community of women together. Yet the Heterodoxy Club was no Herland; the "folk" were "warring," though Howe's cult of personality created a fragile yoke around them. The group itself acknowledged the contradictions of its social body. In the "preface" to their album, the members consolidated the club into one body, the "hydraheaded Heterodoxy, with its everlasting eating and smoking, its imperviousness to discipline and its strange incapacity for boredom," though beneath its "obstreperous body" is a "warm and friendly and staunch spirit, in which our conglomerate personalities all have a share" (qtd. in Schwartz 103). Though the multifarious body of the club is unified in this last metaphor, it remains diverse and inherently fragmented, a "conglomerate"— revealed as an inherently diseased body through the diagnoses of *With Her in Ourland*—rather than a homogeneous and unitary body.

In fact, Gilman wrote this tribute to Howe after returning to the club in the 1920s. Gilman felt it necessary to resign from Heterodoxy in the mid-teens because she disagreed vehemently with the views of the majority of the women regarding America's role in World War I and beliefs regarding women's sexuality. In her autobiography Gilman briefly mentions her participation in this "small woman's lunch club," which she claims was "composed of various ultra-heretical thinkers, or doers, or those wishing to be so considered, which [she] found interesting for a while" (*Living* 313). Gilman's reference to the club is attenuated here and

her attitude toward its members and their work dismissive. She emphasizes the extremity of their politics, implying that many of the members
were merely poseurs.

Gilman saved her more vituperative comments regarding her fellow
women activists for *With Her in Ourland.* Ellador makes a more pointed
criticism of contemporary feminists, noting of those who work for the
women's movement, "What's worst of all, perhaps, is the strange missing
of purpose in those who are most actively engaged in 'advancing' [the
movement]. They seem like flies behind a window, they bump and
buzz, pushing their heads against whatever is in front of them, and never
seem really to plan a way out" (*Herland* 176). Flies are insignificant
annoyances—and, worse, carriers of disease. Thus it is no surprise that
Ellador's contact with "unnatural" women who do not see the woman's
movement in the same way that she does makes a "sick shudder" run
through her body (177). While Gilman tolerated this bumping and buzz-
ing for a while in her Heterodoxy days, she asserts in her autobiography
that she "wearied of it" when "the heresies seemed to center on sex psychology and pacificism" (*Living* 313).

Though Gilman does not mention Margaret Sanger by name in her
texts, it is fairly clear from the records both left behind that Gilman's
disappointment, in part, stemmed from her disgust with Sanger's widely
held contention that sexual freedom was primary to women's emancipa-
tion in all realms of life. Gilman was familiar with Sanger's lifework, and
Sanger knew of Gilman as well. Indeed, in her autobiography Sanger
singles out Gilman as one of the feminist leaders whom she admired as
"trying to inspire women in this country to have a deeper meaning in
their lives, which signified more than getting the vote" (*Autobiography*
108). Both Gilman and Sanger agreed that feminists who focused on
surface-level "trivialities," such as the issue of women maintaining their
maiden names, would continue to "bump and buzz" because they were
not addressing the root causes of women's problems. Both agreed that
suffrage was not the cure-all for women's social ills. However, Sanger
laments that after addressing the Heterodoxy Club in 1914 she struck "no
responsive chord" from Gilman or her Heterodite cohorts, Marie Howe,
Crystal Eastman, and Henrietta Rodman. "It seemed unbelievable they
could be serious in occupying themselves with what I regard as trivialities when mothers within a stone's throw of their meetings were dying
shocking deaths," Sanger laments (108).

Composed a short two years after Sanger's Heterodoxy presentation, *With Her in Ourland* offers a more candid critique of women like Sanger who advocated birth control, in part, as a means toward sexual freedom. Van reminds Ellador that "some of the 'freest' women are urging more sex freedom. They want to see the women doing as men have done, apparently," and Ellador responds, "They are almost as bad as the antis [those who oppose women's progress]—but not quite. They are merely a consequence of wrong teaching and wrong habits" (187). While Sanger did advocate sexual equality, Gilman argued for the cultivation of women's suprasexuality.

While Sanger pursued birth control because she wanted to maintain the possibility of consequence-free sexual pleasure, Gilman continued to theorize away sexual desire in fiction and, increasingly in later years, life. In her *Forerunner* essay "Birth Control," which appeared in 1915, Gilman details her somewhat ambivalent attitudes toward the birth-control debate. Like Sanger, Gilman thought it "quite right" for doctors and educators to share information regarding the prevention of pregnancy. Also like Sanger, she feared that the birth rates, if left unchecked, would lead to the degeneration of women's physical and mental health and to a bloated population unable to sustain itself. However, Gilman believed that highly evolved Americans would eventually "only crave this indulgence [sexual relations] for a brief annual period," in this way "naturally" lowering the birth rates ("Birth Control" 256). Thus in freeing men and women from sexuality rather than making possible sexual freedom, birth control would become obsolete.

With Her in Ourland undoes the fictional obsolescence of birth control that Herland imagined, bringing pregnancy again to the fore by conveying Ellador to heterosexual Ourland. Yet Ellador religiously practices Gilman's brand of birth control in the novel, advocating abstinence as the sole moral form. Ellador proclaims proudly that if she lives in Ourland she will not have a child: "There is no place in all your world, that I have seen or read of, where I should be willing to raise a child" (188). Indeed, it is Ellador's lack of sympathy for those women who are unwilling or unable to forgo heterosexual relations that proves the insuperable difference between her and other women. For example, Van and Ellador discuss overcrowding after visiting Japan. Van claims that the advances of science allow us increasingly to support all of the people. Ellador asks incredulously, "Why do not the women limit the population, as we did?"

Ellador finds no kinship with any of the women of America either, for none seems to take mothering responsibly. Indeed, Ellador sees women's reproductive irresponsibility as a physical disability, charging, "Those blind mothers! Can't they think what is going to happen to their children?" (137). "It's no use, dear," Ellador tells Van of her reformatory work, "until all the children of the world are at least healthy; at least normal until the average man and woman are free from the taint of sex-disease" (186).

While Sanger agrees that suffering children are to be avoided, she does not attribute their existence to the same sort of "sex-disease"—to the heterosexual relations—that Gilman delineates. Rather, Sanger objects to the linkage of women's sexuality and reproduction. In her 1920 book, *Woman and the New Race,* Sanger, too, links women's reproductive capabilities to the scientific and evolutionary development of the human race. What Sanger calls "free motherhood"—that is, a woman's ability to choose when to have children—ensures that the world would be woman's to "remake, it is hers to build and to recreate" (*New Race* 99). Here Sanger uses language of mechanical and even cosmic proportions to describe the possibilities of women's wombs. And her use of the prefix *re-* (that is, *remake, re-create*) linguistically links those larger pursuits to reproduction. Women's bodies are literally the means of scientific and technological development, and in the rest of the book Sanger details the ways that those bodies must be conformed and fitted to this great human experiment. Though she does not recommend the number of children women should have, Sanger does standardize reproduction, exhorting women to wait until age twenty-two to give birth, to reserve two to three years between pregnancies, and to forgo parenthood if either parent is diseased or if previous children have been afflicted. Within woman is wrapped up "the future of the race—it is hers to make or mar," Sanger argues (93). Like Gilman, she finds the current state of affairs appalling and blames women's uncontrolled productivity, the preeminence of "too prolific mothers," for perpetuating the "tyrannies of the Earth" (4, 3).

Control over their wombs is the key not only to personal freedom but also to the eradication of the world's ills. Sanger contends women could stop famine and overcrowding, end all wars, abolish poverty, and diminish birth defects and the proliferation of the "unfit" (43) simply by controlling and limiting their pregnancies. Indeed, she argues that involuntary motherhood was the chief cause of the "human holocaust" of World War I just ending as she wrote this book.

Though Gilman and Sanger were both discouraged by their inability to find kindred spirits in each other, despite the great similarities in their causes and approaches, the two did remain involved in each other's lives. Indeed, just two years after Sanger's talk at the Heterodoxy Club, Gilman appeared publicly in 1916 at a dinner sponsored by the National Birth Control League to support Sanger as she faced prosecution under the Comstock Laws (Chesler 139). Gilman eventually became a supporter of Sanger's cause, though she never abandoned her belief that universal chastity was a preferable alternative to free love. In her 1935 autobiography she rants still, "Perhaps the most salient change of the present period is the lowering of standards in sex relations, approaching some of the worst periods in ancient history. In my youth there was a fine, earnest movement toward an equal standard of chastity for men and women, an equalizing upward to the level of what women were then. But now the very word 'chastity' seems to have become ridiculous" (*Living* 323). Nearly twenty years after their inception, Van and Ellador remained the ideal of heterosexual love and fidelity for Gilman, their self-imposed chastity more freeing than the so-called free love and promiscuity Gilman lamented.

Gilman and Sanger finally shared the stage at Gilman's last public appearance. At Sanger's January 1934 meeting of the American Conference on Birth Control and National Recovery in Washington, D.C., Gilman offered some closing remarks in a talk on January 17 titled "The World's Mother." In some respects this speech is a return to Ellador's Herland ethos, invoking a society of like-minded mothers who will regain not only "personal freedom" from birth control but will also need to accept "the responsibility which goes with it." Rhetorically wresting the purpose of the birth-control movement from those who advocated free love, Gilman insists the movement is "to give us intelligent conscious motherhood, using judgment to decide when that function shall be exercised" (M. Sanger Papers). Like Sanger, Gilman came to see birth control as necessary to protect the health of the mother and that of the children; to conserve the strength of the father also, that he need not have more to provide for than he is able; to ensure better living conditions for the family; and in a larger social responsibility to so guard our numbers as to end forever that deadly "pressure of population" which is the one perpetual cause of war (M. Sanger Papers).

In her remarks at the conference Sanger, too, emphasized the economic consequences of reproductive technologies; speaking in that time of national Depression, she insisted that birth control "is closely woven in a most vital way with the serious economic problems that confront us in our effort toward national recovery" (M. Sanger Papers). But it is in their efforts to stem the reproduction of "others"—the disabled, the dark-skinned, the uneducated—that Gilman and Sanger were most closely allied. Indeed, Gilman found a way finally to make birth control into the means of theorizing Herland homogeneity within Ourland. Birth control would reinstate the rightful "power of the mother" to "improve the stock," as Gilman had done so successfully in fictional Herland (M. Sanger Papers). And in this way, perhaps, American women would be able to eradicate the burgeoning "others" that made the world an unhealthy heterodoxy. Though seldom able to find common ground, Sanger and Gilman were finally bound by their common, unsettling desire to empower women so that they could breed out the "others" whom Gilman saw as compromising the fate of the human race.

NOTE

I would like to thank Cynthia J. Davis for pointing me to Gilman's last public speech at Sanger's 1934 American Conference on Birth Control and National Recovery, as well as June Johnson at North Central College's Oesterle Library, Madeline Nelson at Northern Illinois University's Founders' Library, and Kathleen Nutter at the Sophia Smith Papers at Smith College for their help in tracking down the documentation from the conference.

12
"All Is Not Sexuality That Looks It"

Charlotte Perkins Gilman and Karen Horney on Freudian Psychoanalysis

Mary M. Moynihan

Charlotte Perkins Gilman (1860–1935) never met Sigmund Freud (1856–1939), but as every Gilman scholar knows, she held nothing but scorn for him, his theories, and the movement he generated. Nor is there any evidence that Gilman ever met or read the works of German psychiatrist Karen Horney, M.D. (1885–1952), who immigrated to the United States in 1932. Today Horney is best known for her writings in the 1920s and early 1930s opposing Freud's ideas on female psychological development (Westkott, *Feminist Legacy of Karen Horney* 53). Each woman wrote from a different perspective and time period, and the specifics of their criticisms share little in common. Gilman's critique rests on her gynaecocentric theory of human evolution; Horney, a pioneer in psychoanalysis, criticized Freud's emphasis on sexuality—his libidinal theory—as the foundation of all human behavior. Yet fundamentally both women recognized the damage of Freud's phallocentric theories on women and humanity, and in spite of their different theoretical orientations, their assessments of Freud converge in a number of places.

Looking at Gilman's appraisal of Freud in comparison with Horney's provides a view of Gilman as both a critic and a product of her times. In addition, Gilman's contempt for Freud was based neither on radical extremism, of which she is often accused, nor on her Victorian horror of sex, as others have asserted. Rather, her appraisal rests on her foresight and realization that Freudian thinking was the most threatening paradigmatic challenge to her gynaecocentric evolutionary theory of the human race. Gilman clearly realized that Freud's theories presented a new rationale to keep women from achieving full humanness.

At first glance, Gilman and Horney represent diametric opposites in terms of their relationship to psychoanalysis. As Karen Horney's biographer, Susan Quinn, says of her subject, "Once Karen had discovered psychoanalysis, it became *the* intellectual and emotional pursuit of her life" (*A Mind of Her Own* 143). Gilman's biographers could easily write, "Once Charlotte discovered psychoanalysis, it became *the* anathema of her life!" Each woman strove in her own way to bring her concerns about Freudianism to the fore. Most of Gilman's work was written prior to the import of Freudian thinking into the United States, and her negative evaluation of Freud focused mostly on her overall concern about the effects of Freud's phallic-centered thinking on women's evolution toward equality and economic independence. Horney, though, began her career as a follower of Freud, just at the time when interest in his work was growing in popularity. Her critique focused particularly on his conceptualization of the instinctual origins of behavior. To Freud, this sex drive, or libido, is the powerful force behind *all* human action. It exists on the unconscious level from birth and shapes all human behavior. Even though most of Horney's early writings were geared primarily to other psychoanalysts, physicians, and academics, her later works, such as *The Neurotic Personality of Our Time* (1937), *Self-Analysis* (1942), and *Are You Considering Psychoanalysis?* (1946), were written for a lay audience. However, *New Ways of Psychoanalysis* (1939) focused on a more educated audience and ultimately led to her being branded as a heretic by orthodox Freudians. Even so, Horney remained a psychoanalyst her entire life and did not abandon the field, in spite of being ousted from the New York Psychoanalytic Society in 1941 because she challenged Freudian orthodoxy.[1]

A look at the way Freud describes women in his works is illuminating and provides a useful reminder of his ideas about women's abilities, experiences, and contributions to culture. Almost everyone is familiar with Freud's theory of penis envy—that upon discovering that her genitals are "inferior," that a woman has a "scar" in place of the penis—a girl becomes envious and desires to have what she visibly lacks. In two essays, "The Dissolution of the Oedipus Complex" (1924) and "Some Psychological Consequences of the Anatomical Distinctions between the Sexes" (1925), Freud expanded upon his concept of "penis envy."[2] He concluded that the desire for the penis, the "masculinity complex," and the desire to bear the father's child remain powerful forces in the adult woman's unconscious. Moreover, because the girl sees herself as already castrated, she does not fear castration and for that reason does not develop the superego in the same way that a boy does. She "transfers" her desire for a penis to a desire to have her father's child, the "penis-child" (312). It is at this point that the mother, once the original object of love, becomes the target of the daughter's jealousy.

In his later essay "Femininity" (1932)—a mostly reiterated version of his two earlier works, "Some Psychological Consequences" (1925) and "Female Sexuality" (1931)—Freud returned to a discussion of the relative weakness of a woman's superego compared to a man's. He maintained that women "show less sense of justice" and are "less ready to submit to the great necessities of life" ("Femininity" 361).[3] He repeated his earlier claims that penis envy causes women's narcissism, and that women "value their charms more highly as a late compensation for their original sexual inferiority" (359–60). He declared that it is because of their narcissism that women have "made few contributions" to the "history of civilization," are "weaker in social interests," and that a woman at thirty years of age "frightens us with her psychical rigidity and unchangeability" (362). Given that Gilman saw women's economic independence and equality with men as the necessary foundation of more humane civilization, it is no wonder that she chafed at Freud's theories. Moreover, Freud was still professing these ideas into the 1930s in spite of criticism from Horney and some of his male colleagues.[4]

Notwithstanding their different perspectives, Gilman's and Horney's examinations of Freud share a number of points in common. As noted above, each woman wrote about the negative impact of Freud's phallic-centered thinking on women. And each recognized the influence of male-dominated cultural and social arrangements on the psyches of women. Both women drew upon their own experiences to challenge the prevailing misogynistic view of women that dominated their times. Considering the impact that Freud's ideas were to have on women, Gilman had good reasons to sound the alarm about a theory she felt used one concept, which Gilman called "sex energy," "to explain whatever you wish to do—invent, discover, decorate, sing, dance, act, paint, manufacture, teach" (*His Religion and Hers* 166). Horney likewise expressed concern with the phallic-centered view, particularly "penis envy" and the "castration complex" used by Freud and his followers. She noted that "interpretations in terms of penis envy bar the way to an understanding of fundamental difficulties such as ambition, and the whole personality structure linked up to them. That such interpretations befog the real issue is my most stringent objection to them, particularly from the thera-peutic angle" (*New Ways* 109–10).

In the foreword to *The Adolescent Diaries of Karen Horney,* Marianne Horney Eckardt writes that her mother recognized the "cultural bias in Freud's male-centered construct of the libido theory" (viii). Marcia Westkott notes that Horney's shift in theoretical emphasis moved from instinct to social relations and was a fundamental rupture with the basis of Freud's theory (62). Born the same year as Gilman's daughter, Horney could represent the next generation of a feminist assessment of Freudian psychoanalysis. Although I am primarily interested in the scholarly bases of their individual critiques of Freud, I have found that the two women, both prolific writers, share many noteworthy biographical similarities. Their biographical comparability also contributes to our understanding of their theoretical concerns with Freudian psychoanalysis.

Karen Danielsen grew up in Germany in an affluent family. The Perkins family lived on far more limited means, and because of the sepa-ration and eventual divorce of her parents, Charlotte often lived close to poverty—moving nineteen times in eighteen years—and oftentimes liv-ing with relatives. But even Karen would feel the pinch of poverty after her mother left her father. Both Charlotte's and Karen's mothers would take in boarders to help them pay rent and other expenses. Charlotte and Karen each had one older brother and each wrote in her diary about the brother being favored by the parents.[5] As girls, both Charlotte and Karen wrote poems. Their diaries told of loves found, then lost; heroes worshipped, then condemned; friends adored, then damned; and moth-ers resented but ultimately supported.

Each woman spent part of her childhood in a father-absent home. Charlotte's father left when she was very young but would periodically pay visits. When she was nine years old, her parents separated perma-nently. Even so, Charlotte greatly admired her father, and as an adoles-cent she wrote to him for advice about readings to help her with her intellectual development. He responded with a list of recommendations, many written by the leading evolutionary thinkers of the day. She de-scribes him as being the less inclined of her parents toward corporal punishment, and she had more contact with him as an adult than Karen would have with her father (though no one would think to describe either woman's relationship with her father as "close").

Karen's parents divorced when she was an adolescent, but her father's occupation as a sea captain meant long absences even before the marital separation. As a young girl, she worshipped him, but during her adolescence she rejected his patriarchal authoritarianism. Unlike Charlotte's father, Karen's was rigid, religiously intolerant, and a tyrant in the home (*The Adolescent* 22). With respect to the influence of their fathers, then, one is inclined to conclude that young Charlotte's feminist ideas, though not actively encouraged by her father, were not stymied by him, whereas Karen Horney's father's despotism led her to rebel against patriarchy. Even so, it would be Gilman's and Horney's mothers who would play more significant roles throughout their daughters' lives.

Each woman's mother experienced extreme emotional turmoil because of her marital situation. Karen's mother, Sonni, was much younger than her husband and lavished physical affection on her children. In contrast, Charlotte's mother, Mary, would not caress her daughter as a child unless she was asleep. Years later Charlotte explained in her autobiography that her mother had taken this extreme measure in order to save her daughter from anguish in the future should she, too, suffer from loss of affection (*Living* 10). Although as adolescents both Charlotte and Karen complained in their diaries about their mothers, each would eventually come to see her mother's situation with greater compassion and understanding. As adults, both Gilman and Horney would live with their mothers and provide for them. Until her death in 1911, Horney's mother lived with her daughter, first in an apartment in Freiburg and later, after Karen married Oskar, with the couple in Berlin. Prior to her death from cancer in 1893, Mary lived with Charlotte, Katharine, and Charlotte's companion, Delle Knapp. Charlotte supported Mary emotionally and financially during that time.

Out of these profoundly personal experiences, both Gilman and Horney addressed the issues of the mother-daughter relationship in more professional venues. Their approaches to the mother-daughter relationship demonstrate their different views and methods of analysis. Gilman's lecture, "A Daughter's Duty," written during her mother's illness, may, according to Gilman biographer Mary Armfield Hill, "be viewed as a persuasive, even acutely insightful piece about daughters' responsibilities to mothers . . . but it can also be viewed as anger unleashed" (Hill, *Making* 195). Nevertheless, the piece is written in classic Gilman style—straightforward and didactic—noting that a daughter's ability to support her mother would be enhanced if the daughter were a wage earner:

> She [the daughter] studies for years, fitting herself for work she loves. Her father dies. The mother claims her daughter's duty—says she cannot spare her, and the girl who might have been earning both fame and fortune, retires into the shelter of the home, to wash dishes . . . and "take care of her mother" at no salary whatever!
>
> A duty is a duty, but there is more than one way of doing it! A girl can take care of her mother as an independent householder and wage earner, providing her with the same delicate generosity let us hope with which the mother once "supported" her; or she can take care of her as a subordinate, a nurse, a companion, upper servant. Why is not the first better? ("A Daughter's Duty," qtd. in Hill *Making* 195–96)

Horney dealt with the same issues and in her typical style. In a diary entry a few days before her mother's death, Horney reflected on the weariness she felt about Sonni's incessant complaints and demands. But in the end she concluded, "I cannot but sympathize with her and her fate, the fate of an aging woman who stands alone in the world without love" (*The Adolescent* 260). After Sonni's death, Horney contemplated the concept of guilt. She wrote about the differences between "an entirely conscious consciousness of guilt" which "would never by itself lead to nervous symptom. . . . [B]ut at bottom have an encouraging and ennobling effect on [one's life]" and "guilt feelings toward repressed wishes [that] have an inimical influence on life, restrictive, making for illness" (264–65).[6] Each woman expressed ambivalent feelings toward her mother. Yet their nurturing and recognition of discrimination against their mothers under patriarchy compelled both to see women's lives not as biologically but culturally determined—with economics predominant for Gilman, social psychology for Horney.

Neither woman would be able to change her mother's feelings of inferiority, but each woman used her mother as the model of what she rejected as culturally produced. No doubt, both women recognized the effect of such feelings on women's self-esteem. All the same, Gilman's nonfiction writings would emphasize a critique of the sexuo-economic arrangements under patriarchy, whereas Horney's would focus on the social psychology of women and, by extension, a critique of Freud's insistence that behavior is instinctive.

It was from their own experiences, and not just from their mothers', that both Gilman and Horney learned hard lessons about gender discrimination. In her diary, each woman expressed concerns about commitment and marriage prior to being wed. Each married at about the same age—Charlotte was twenty-three, Karen twenty-four years—and each would eventually divorce her husband but remain on amicable terms with him. Their reasons for divorce were very different. Charlotte's experiences with depression after the birth of her daughter initially led to a separation from Walter Stetson. And although Karen took lovers during her marriage to Oskar, it was Oskar's financial entanglements during the depression in Germany that ultimately led her to leave him (Quinn, *A Mind of Her Own* 194). Here is another example of both women using their personal experiences—something Freud could not do—as a basis for their later analysis of problems for women in marriage. Among other works, Gilman would write "The Yellow Wall-Paper" (1892), the poem "To the Young Wife" (1893), and a number of other poems published in the third edition of *In This Our World* (1899).[7] Likewise, Horney would address conflicts in marriage a number of times throughout her life. Among her essays on the topic are "On the Psychological Roots of Some Typical Conflicts in Marriage" (1927) and "Problems of Marriage" (1932).[8]

Motherhood as well as marriage would prove formative to each woman's theories of gender. Shortly after her daughter's birth, while in the throes of depression, Gilman wrote, "Even motherhood brought no joy" (*Living* 92). Charlotte nursed Katharine for five months but eventually left Walter and Katharine to visit her longtime friends, the Channings, in Pasadena. She immediately felt better, but on returning she went back into a depression, which led her to seek S. Weir Mitchell's rest cure. From that experience, she began her critique of the treatment of middle-class women by male physicians and her lifelong career of combating theories, such as Freud's, based on a belief that women are anatomically destined to be inferior.

Karen's experiences with childbirth and early motherhood also made her reassess descriptions of motherhood and childbirth as advanced by Freudian psychoanalysis. Karen wrote in her diary: "Nursing is a sort of autoerotic sensual satisfaction" and that in nursing, there is an "intimate union of mother and child that never occurs later" (*The Adolescent* 268). From her personal experiences she would come to question Freud's theory about "penis envy," the "castration complex" and the "penis child." She took these issues up professionally in her 1926 essay, "The Flight from Womanhood: The Masculinity-Complex in Women as Viewed by Men and by Women." She wrote: "At this point I, as a woman, ask in amazement, and what of motherhood? And the blissful consciousness of bearing a new life within oneself? And the ineffable happiness of the increasing expectation of the appearance of this new being? And the joy when it finally makes its appearance and one holds it for the first time in one's arms? And the deep pleasurable feeling of satisfaction in suckling it and the whole period when the infant needs her care?" She goes on to profess that far from being a biological handicap, "the capacity for motherhood" is "a quite indisputable and by no means negligible physiological superiority" (60). She then turns penis envy on its head, so to speak, by noting that men have an envy of motherhood. She asserts, "When one begins, as I did, to analyze men only after a fairly long experience of analyzing women, one receives a most surprising impression of the intensity of this envy of pregnancy, childbirth, and motherhood, as well as of the breasts and of the act of suckling" (60–61). These aspects of motherhood and their importance are themes that both Gilman and Horney would utilize later in their professional writings. Although their theoretical positions would differ—Gilman held to social Darwinism, Horney remained a psychoanalyst—the personal experiences and reflections from their early days of motherhood would inform both women's theories.

Intriguingly, each woman's rejection of a famous male doctor's diagnosis would have a significant and lasting effect on her personal and professional life. In Gilman's case, it was S. Weir Mitchell's prescription that she should "live as domestic a life as possible. Have your child with you all the time. . . . Lie down an hour after each meal. Have but two hours' intellectual life a day. And never touch pen, brush or pencil as long as you live" (*Living* 96). Horney's diagnosis was by Karl Abraham, a well-known colleague of Freud. She wrote that Abraham told her that she had a "wish to throw myself away, prostitute myself—giving myself to any man at random" (*The Adolescent* 242). Abraham's words began to sow the seeds of doubt regarding Freudian analysis that would eventually lead Horney to write "On the Genesis of the Castration Complex in Women," followed by a series of papers, each one more critical of Freud than its predecessor.[9] In each woman's case, the rejection of a male doctor's analysis would lead to a turning point, offering an experience that enabled each to write about women in ways that challenged the status quo.

Both Gilman and Horney came to look to social and cultural factors, not just instincts, to explain women's psychological conditions. Gilman became a celebrated writer and social critic, her numerous writings covering a variety of topics and genres. Lester F. Ward (1841–1913), called the founding father of American sociology (Scott 106), hailed her approach as a "cosmological perspective" (Ward, "Past and Future" 541) because of her vast knowledge of a multiplicity of areas—biology, philosophy, sociology, religion.[10]

Horney, likewise, became a well-known critic of Freud, formulating a new branch of psychoanalysis in which instinct, penis envy, and the Oedipus Complex played little or no part. In "Karen Horney's Flight from Orthodoxy" (1974), Robert Coles eulogizes Karen Horney, calling her a "prophet." He goes on to note, "She . . . dared to look with some distance and detachment at her own profession, and in so doing, anticipated in a limited way a future historical moment" (191). Her challenge to the libidinal theory would cause orthodox Freudians to reject and condemn her. Horney showed increasing interest in anthropology, sociology and religion throughout her life and saw these forces in opposition to Freud's analysis.

Each woman was well known in her time; Gilman was popular with feminists, sociologists, and the general public. Horney's early reputation was more academic and addressed to the psychoanalytic community, but her later works, especially *The Neurotic Personality of Our Time* (1937), brought her work to the general public's attention as well. Yet to varying degrees, both women as well as their works had to be rediscovered by second-wave feminists. Recovery of Gilman's works was much more significant because they had been either ignored or maligned, whereas Horney's legacy, though controversial, lived on at the American Psychoanalytic Institute, renamed the Karen Horney Psychiatric Institute shortly before her death. Be that as it may, Horney's accent on cultural factors seemed to have become somewhat lost to the general public until the resurgence of feminism. Freudian emphasis on penis envy, perpetuated by Helene Deutsch (1884–1982) in *The Psychology of Women,* dominated both popular culture and academic thinking. Second-wave feminists brought Gilman and Horney, along with their distinct critiques of Freud, back into the discourse.[11]

Prior to this rediscovery, at least part of the work of both women would be attributed to men in their intellectual circles. In 1972 Zenia Odes Fliegel examined the history of psychoanalytic writings on femininity and asked why Horney's early works on the topic were "relegated to oblivion" ("Feminine Psychosexual Development" 407). She concluded that Horney's continued "heresies" caused her early ideas to be ignored within psychoanalysis. But more important, Fliegel discovered from her research "the tendency to ascribe to later [male] authors . . . ideas that had originated with [Horney]" (402). This is an all too familiar story of what happens to a woman of ideas: that which is perceived as important in her work is attributed to a man and that which is recognized as directly challenging is conveniently ignored.

This lack of proper recognition also happened with Gilman in comparison with Lester F. Ward, as Judith A. Allen discusses in this volume. He is credited with first developing the gynaecocentric theory with which Gilman is associated. He presented the theory in a lecture in 1888, later published as "Our Better Halves," and Gilman acknowledged her debt to him publicly. Even so, Mary A. Hill notes that in her private letters Charlotte was "considerably more casual about the influence of Ward's theories" (*Making of a Radical Feminist* 266). In a July 1897 letter to future husband Houghton Gilman, Charlotte wrote, "I wrote the Brood Mare long before I read Ward. I've been thinking those things— and much more—for many years" (*Journey from Within* 73). In his Ph.D. dissertation, "Charlotte Perkins Gilman and the Cycle of Feminist Reform," William Doyle claimed that "every word Gilman wrote on the woman question was informed by the sociology of Lester Frank Ward" (175). Even today Gilman's ideas are often seen as reiterations and extensions of Ward's theory rather than original to her.

While Ward may have claimed some of Gilman's glory, no one would ever attribute any of Gilman's ideas to Freud. As noted above, it is widely understood that Gilman held great disdain for his theories and the psychoanalytic movement in general. However, only pieces of criticism and commentary on either subject remain among her published non-fiction or unpublished papers. That is, many of her later writings (1916–35), reviewed later in this essay, contain fragments or short invectives against Freud, Freudians, and psychoanalysis. But the full contents of her lectures about Freud, such as one titled "The Fallacy of Freud" (Lane, *To Herland* 332), are not in existence. For this reason, Gilman biographers and historians have, for the most part, been justifiably cautious in their speculations and are unable to go much beyond cursory analysis of her views on Freud and his legacy.[12]

Most of these commentators recognize that Gilman's criticism of Freud stemmed primarily from her gynaecocentric theory, but they also link her scorn to her having become more "straightlaced" in her later years. Gary Scharnhorst, Polly Wynn Allen, Ann J. Lane, and Larry Ceplair all take this approach to Gilman's objections to Freud. Scharnhorst notes that she "excoriated Freud and the psychoanalysis cult" in *Forerunner* and states that in her later years, Gilman objected more stridently to sexual license (*Charlotte Perkins Gilman* 101). In addition, he points out that she had long expected that, as women improved their status, they would progressively de-emphasize their sexual characteristics. Instead, she noted with alarm that by the 1920s women were more sexually indulgent (112). Lane, too, covers Gilman's views on Freud by writing "in 1921 Gilman lectured on 'The Fallacy of Freud,' which addressed, the brochure stated, 'his evil influence on the life of today.'" Nevertheless, Gilman's opposition to Freud's ideas, Lane speculates, "was likely rooted in a deep fear of the dangers of permitting . . . a male doctor free access to a woman's unconscious." Lane adds, "It is doubtful if Gilman would even have admitted to the existence of 'an unconscious'" (*To Herland and Beyond* 332). Likewise, Ceplair and Allen take up Gilman's objections to Freud. Although these scholars link Gilman's distaste for Freud to her concern for his theories' effect on women, they also link her scorn to her increasing conservatism in her later years (P. Allen, *Building Domestic Liberty* 183n.42).

At least one other critic locates Gilman's contempt for Freud as stemming primarily from her alleged prudery. Jeffrey Berman offers not just a Freudian analysis of "The Yellow Wall-Paper" but of Gilman herself, her autobiography, and her other major nonfiction works as well. His first contention that Gilman's "hatred of Freud . . . and his unholy disciples" was based on her belief that Freudianism was "antithetical to the women's cause and to the imagination itself" ("The Unrestful Cure" 215) seems in line with other critics' claims. However, he continues:

> Gilman also condemned Freud for other, less valid, reasons. She insisted that Freud was responsible for the widespread promiscuity of the age and the lowering of standards in sexual relations. *She was, of course, Victorian in her horror of sex and glorification of chastity.* The deemphasis on chastity, she was convinced, had debased human nature . . . she attacks the "present degree of sex impulse" as pathological, arguing instead for the suppression or redirection of the sexual instinct. In her female utopia, *Herland,* women conceive through parthenogenesis, virgin birth. Men are no longer necessary and procreation is independent of the sex act. (215; emphasis added)[13]

Not coincidentally, in "Toward Monogamy" (1924) Gilman anticipated that her position on "sex impulses" would be viewed with deprecation as Victorian or puritanical and as glorifying chastity. Neither idea fit with the way Gilman lived her life or with her vision of economically independent women. On the contrary, she envisioned a monogamy that was as "free of sex service as from domestic service" (672). She added that she was no more a champion of "celibacy" or "self-denial" than she was of "sublimated sex" (673).

Gilman's disparagement of Freud is related not to her "horror of sex" or "glorification of chastity" but to her realization that Freudian theory, centered on sex as the "mainspring of life," challenged directly her gynaecocentric evolutionary theory. It is upon her theory of human society that she built her entire explanation for the oppression of women in androcentric culture and her theory that women ought to have economic independence in order to develop as full human beings. To Gilman, future equality between the sexes was insured only on the basis of her theory; to deny its validity would be to deny the place of woman in a future culture. Woman's realization that she is "the race-type," the basis of the evolution of humankind, is a necessary ingredient to social progress.

However, like Freud, Gilman also emphasized important biological differences—what she would call "sex distinctions"—between women and men. Unlike Freud, Gilman held the most important sex distinction is women's ability to bear children: motherhood. Had Gilman had more of a sense of humor about Freud's theories, she might have, in a fashion similar to Horney, rejoined Freud and his theory of penis envy with taunts of womb envy. But Gilman's feelings about this issue were far too serious. From her point of view, it is women's duty to improve themselves and then produce children who will also improve the human race so that it may reach its greatest potential. Thus, Gilman would define any theory that deviated from this goal as threatening to women and ultimately to the future of the entire human race. Since it is androcentric, based as it is on the male—the sex type—and his excessive sex indulgence (*Women and Economics* 30), Freudian theory in Gilman's view could only lead to the deterioration of the human race.

Gilman wrote that women have suffered years of "arrested development" (330) because the culture remained androcentric. To Gilman, women were the underdeveloped half of humanity and their contributions had been stymied. It bears repeating that Freud blamed women's narcissism for the fact that women have "made few contributions" to the "history of civilization" ("Femininity" 362)—a point which Gilman would happily have debated with the Viennese doctor. Moreover, since she theorized that woman is the race type, that human society cannot evolve to its highest potential until and unless women are evolving, she would have recognized Freud's theory of penis envy as a monumental threat in this regard. His claim that penis envy is instinctivistic and the cause of woman's weaker superego, along with his belief that narcissism is her destiny, stood as a direct threat to Gilman's gynaecocentric theory that women are the race type.

Gilman had also argued that, through economic independence and the realization of their importance to the evolution of the human race, women would come to take their place with men and androcentric culture would be replaced with a mother-centered one, more in tune with the true evolutionary course of human nature. It was no wonder that Gilman bristled at the sight of young women casting their fate with Freud's phallocentric theory rather than her own. She upbraided Freud and the young women whose behavior she saw as the result of the popularity and persuasion of his theories of over-sexualization. In "Toward Monogamy," Gilman wrote: "Clothed in the solemn, newly invented terms of psychoanalysis, a theory of sex is urged upon us which bases all our activities upon this one function. It is exalted as not only an imperative instinct, but as the imperative instinct. . . . Surely never was a more physical theory disguised in the technical verbiage of 'psychology'" (672).

Similarly, in "The New Generation of Women" she refers to the "solemn philosophical sex-mania of Sigmund Freud, now widely poisoning the world" (735). Although speaking in favor of birth control in "Progress through Birth Control" (1927), she nevertheless used that opportunity to castigate the increasing number of people indulging in sex outside of marriage, claiming that they have been "infected by Freudian and sub-Freudian theories" (628). She no doubt used the verb "infected" purposively, given the effects of venereal diseases particularly on women at the time. Following from her theory that women are the underdeveloped side of humanity, she focuses in "Parasitism and Civilized Vice" (1931) on the negative effects—including prostitution and sexually transmitted diseases—of economically dependent women, including transforming them into sex parasites held down by civilized men (114). She speaks of psychoanalysis this way: "Another obstacle is that resurgence of phallic worship set before us in the solemn phraseology of psychoanalysis. This pitifully narrow and morbid philosophy presumes to discuss sex from observation of humanity only. It is confronted with our excessive development and assumes it to be normal. It ignores the evidence of the entire living world below us, basing its conclusions on the behaviour and desires of an animal which stands alone in nature for misery and disease in sex relation" (123).

Though Gilman despised Freudian psychoanalysis, she was also keenly aware of its pull. She wrote in her autobiography, "One of these men, becoming displeased with my views and their advancement, since I would not come to be 'psyched,' as they call it, had the impudence to write a long psychoanalysis of my case, and send it to me." Before opening the envelope, she gave it to her husband to read; he advised burning it, which she did (314). Her later writings demonstrate that she was consciously aware of why she found Freud and his theories so threatening, and although her theory may have justly gone out of fashion, her warnings about the threat to women of a phallic-based theory proved prophetic.

In the last chapter of her autobiography she reviews and comments upon some of the events and trends she sees in the early part of the twentieth century. She sums up her work this way: "After seven years of the *Forerunner* I had no impulse to write for some time. . . . But there were occasional magazine articles, and . . . another book, *His Religion and Hers*. This seemed to me rather a useful and timely work, treating of matters of both lasting and immediate importance—sex and religion. *Unfortunately my views on the sex question do not appeal at all to the Freudian complex of today . . .*" (327; emphasis added). "Freudian" came to serve as the code word for numerous ills Gilman diagnosed in contemporary society.

Gilman's most fully developed examination of Freudianism as a threat to women and human development appears in *His Religion and Hers* (1923). A focus on that text demonstrates the fuller context for Gilman's antipathy toward Freud. This is her last major work published during her lifetime, and it sets forth an extended criticism of androcentric religion and a vision of incorporating the "essentially motherly attributes" (51) in order to develop a "birth-based religion" (50). Freud, too, was fascinated by religion, so in many ways it is fitting that Gilman's reiterated critique of Freud appears in her book on religion. Nevertheless, she did not want to give him too much attention. Gilman may have had Freud's theory of penis envy in mind as early as 1910 when she stated in *Forerunner* that "*women* are not undeveloped *men* but the feminine half of humanity is undeveloped human" ("Women and the State" 12). However, perhaps from not wanting to give too much credence to his work, she did not provide a detailed critique of Freud but rather chose to concentrate instead on the androcentric culture and on androcentric religion in particular.

Her focus in *His Religion and Hers* is the analytical question: "What might a religion become if based, not on death and a speculative future life, but on birth and our knowledge of human continuity?" Early in the book Gilman decries, "We now see advanced the theory that it is repression which ails us, and that all that is needed to restore us to normality is for women to go as far wrong as men" (65). Later she has a lengthier section naming Freud specifically. She refers to his as a "morbid philosophy" assuming "sex to be the mainspring of life" (165).

Her criticism continues when she goes on to state that the superiority of men over women has no connection to their sex. Rather, she contends that it is due to "their preoccupation with sex, their surrender to its impulses, [which] has been a hindrance and a detriment to human progress" (167). "Human development," she adds, "is largely conscious, increasing as we become able to understand what conditions benefit us and how to apply them more widely, as, for instance, in education" (168). And finally she concludes, "Philosophy, in this man's world, has been heavily modified by sex, and never more so than in the belated revival of phallic worship so solemnly advanced by Freud" (170).

Thus, Gilman again demonstrates her opposition to Freud by identifying him as a major threat to women and to a sociological and rational analysis of the androcentric order. In Gilman's view, following Freud's theories would inhibit the evolutionary movement she predicted. Indeed Freud would take women, and therefore humanity, back to an era of "phallic worship" that would be intolerable. Her opposition to Freud does not rest primarily in her being "straightlaced" (P. Allen, *Building Domestic Liberty* 183) or only being able to see the "horror of sex" (Berman, "The Unrestful Cure" 215). On the contrary, the horror Gilman saw was a theory that devalued women just when she believed they had a chance to restore value and meaning to their lives. Gilman's anger at young women for acting more like men in their sexual behaviors came out of a theory about motherhood. But Gilman's "motherhood" is not based on the nineteenth-century sentimental ideal nor on Freud's neurotic version. To her, the future of the human race relied on women becoming fully human by casting off androcentric culture's prescriptive requirements for women and truly fulfilling their destinies as human beings and as "mothers of the human race."

Gilman's contempt for Freud was also based on her critique of androcentric religion and her vision of how a future woman-centered religion would look. A review of the language Gilman uses to describe all that is Freudian demonstrates the religious nature of her criticism. She refers to Freud as *evil* in the description of her lecture on "The Fallacy of Freud" and to his theory as phallic *worship* (*His Religion and Hers* 170). She sees Freudian thinking as a dangerous throwback to the most oppressive and ancient of patriarchal religions. Gilman's conceptualization of Freudian psychoanalysis as a religion appears to be supported by the language used by members of the psychoanalytic community. Such words as *orthodoxy, cult,* and *disciple* appear frequently. As a case in point, Freudians accused Horney of "heresy." One stalwart Freudian, Roland Dalbiez, titled his 1941 book the *Psychoanalytical Method and the Doctrine of Freud,* as if to raise Freud's theories to the height of religious canonical texts.

The title of Dalbiez's book contrasts with Horney's *New Ways of Psy-*

choanalysis. In that text she acknowledges Freud's contribution to the field, but she also labels many of his views outdated and invalid. She had done the same in many of her other essays, papers, and presentations in the 1930s. Horney had by this time solidified her views on the importance of nonbiological influences on human beings. Thus she disparages the Freudian interpretation, again calling Freud's focus on the libidinal misplaced and his psychology of women erroneous. In her chapter on "Feminine Psychology" in *New Ways,* she notes, "The wish to be a man, as Alfred Adler has pointed out, may be the expression of a wish for all those qualities or privileges which in our culture are regarded as masculine" (108). She furthers her arguments then by noting that the differences between the sexes are culturally based and that lack of recognition of women's achievements is due to the expectations of and discrimination against women in patriarchal societies. On this, Gilman and Horney certainly would have agreed.

Although obviously not opposed to psychoanalysis, Horney joined Gilman in rejecting Freud's focus on sexualization as well as his theory of masculine civilization and its concurrent devaluation of women. In "Flight from Womanhood," Horney states, "It seems to me impossible to judge to how great a degree the unconscious motives for flight from womanhood are reinforced by the actual social subordination of women" (70). Because of Freud's emphasis on "sexualization," Horney also deemed his analysis threatening to humanity in general and women in particular, though she did not share Gilman's fear that the fate of the human race was at stake. According to Freud, all neuroses developed from the infantile sexual drive and to that extent all neurotics were repeatedly attempting to resolve issues arising from the libido. Horney, however, looked at the importance of culture and social influences on both child and adult. From her perspective, new challenges may arise throughout one's life, not just in childhood, and people may suffer from neuroses that are culturally evoked, not simply the result of libidinal or instinctual forces.

Although Horney originally intended only to modify Freud's theories (Paris, *Unknown Karen Horney* 19), from the beginning she was considered to be heretical by orthodox Freudians. She cited the work of German philosopher and sociologist Georg Simmel (1858–1918) to support her critique of Freud's theory. Following Simmel, Horney notes that "our whole civilization is a masculine civilization. . . . [A]ll these are categories which belong as it were in their form and their claims to humanity in general, but in their actual historical configuration they are masculine throughout" ("Flight" 55–56). Horney continued to quote Simmel's observation that "inadequate achievements are contemptuously called 'feminine,' while distinguished achievements on the part of women are called 'masculine' as an expression of praise" (56). She added that "the psychology of women has hitherto been considered only from the point of view of men," and noted "that women have adapted themselves to the wishes of men and felt as if their adaptation were their true nature. That is, they see or saw themselves in the way that their men's wishes demanded of them . . . " (56). And continuing, she asks, "*How far has the evolution of women, as depicted to us today by analysis, been measured by masculine standards and how far therefore does this picture fail to present quite accurately the real nature of women?*" (56–57; emphasis added).

Even in her most negative of appraisals of Freud, however, Horney acknowledges his contributions, something that Gilman never did and would never have done. Whereas Gilman lectured on "The Fallacy of Freud," Horney talked publicly about "The Achievements of Freud" (1935). The titles of these talks clearly contrast their overall evaluations of his achievements. In her talk, Horney contends that one of Freud's "most important" and "imperishable contributions" is that he "made us realize that our actions and feelings can be determined by unconscious motivations" (208). As Lane noted above, this claim that unconscious forces can determine human actions is one of the main ideas for which Gilman rejected Freud in particular and psychoanalysis in general. But even in the piece focusing on Freud's achievements, Horney attacked his death instinct, the subject of his *Civilization and Its Discontents* (1930). She viewed Freud's death instinct as overly pessimistic and "deeply rooted in the mentality of the nineteenth century" ("Achievements" 213).

Gilman and Horney did share certain views: both celebrated women and sought to minimize the differences between men and women. With the exception of reproductive ones, both women downplayed differences between the sexes. Most of Gilman's major nonfiction works take this perspective, and it is certainly illustrated quite clearly in her all-female, yet unmistakably genderless utopian story, *Herland*. Likewise, Horney took up androgyny in "Women's Fear of Action" (*Unknown* 117–23). She states:

> Once and for all, we should stop bothering about what is feminine and what is not. Such concerns only undermine our energies. Standards of masculinity and femininity are artificial standards. All

that we definitely know at present about sex differences is that we do not know what they are. Differences between the two sexes certainly exist, but we shall never be able to discover what they are until we have first developed our potentialities as human beings. Paradoxical as it may sound, we shall find out about these differences only if we forget about them.

In the meantime what we can do is to work together to promote the full development of the human personalities of all for the sake of the general welfare. (123)

Surely Gilman would agree with Horney that "standards of masculinity and femininity are artificial standards," that "differences between the two sexes certainly exist, but we shall never be able to discover what they are until we have first developed our potentialities as human beings," and that there is a need to "work together to promote the full development of the human personalities of all for the sake of the general welfare." Gilman wrote about the same issues in a number of places. One can find her discussions of these topics as early as her 1890 lecture "Human Nature" (*Charlotte Perkins Gilman: A Nonfiction Reader*), in her *Women and Economics* (1898) and *Man-Made World* (1911), and in as late a work as *His Religion and Hers* (1923).

With the resurgence of feminism and a new feminist critique of Freud and androcentric culture, modern scholars are again exploring from a woman-centered perspective the work of Gilman and other nineteenth- and early twentieth-century feminists. Gone are the days when a writer would decree, "Today Mrs. Gilman's reputation has been almost completely eclipsed. The writer has yet to meet a single member of the faculty of a large university who so much as recognizes her name" (W. Doyle, *Charlotte Perkins Gilman* 156). Nor is it likely that someone would deduce that Gilman could be summed up in the phrase "she could see only the horror of sex" (Berman, "The Unrestful Cure" 215). Or that someone would conclude about Horney, "For years I have heard various psychoanalysts dismiss her ideas out of hand, or scorn them as of little value or interest" (Coles, "Karen Horney's Flight" 191).

Gilman and Horney scholars today may express either amusement or outrage at these arrogant conclusions, but these words serve to remind us how almost completely feminist thinking in general and Gilman's and Horney's anti-Freudian writings in particular had been eradicated from

American thought by 1960. Freudian thinking had all but taken over by the end of World War II. In *Modern Woman: The Lost Sex* (1947), one of the most popular and influential advice books of the time, Ferdinand Lundberg and Marynia Farnham, M.D., vilify feminism throughout their volume. Post–World War II newsreels featured Farnham urging women to leave the workplace and return home unless they were ready to face dire consequences.[14] The authors blame mothers for the existence of such men as Adolph Hitler, Benito Mussolini, Al Capone, and Judas Iscariot.

The section of *Modern Woman* titled "The Psychopathology of Feminism" sums up the authors' "Freudian" appraisal of feminism and feminists. Using Mary Wollstonecraft as a case study, they argue that feminist demands for equality rest on unresolved, unconscious Oedipal conflicts. "That Mary Wollstonecraft was an extreme neurotic of a compulsive type there can be no doubt. Out of her illness arose the ideology of feminism" (159–60).

From cover to cover, *Modern Woman* excoriates feminists and their "passive-feminine" male supporters. In appendix 9, "Views of Feminists," the authors set out what they call "concrete evidence about the feminists . . . [to demonstrate that they were] part of a systematic, corrosive ideology" (452). In fact, the authors quote from Gilman in several places as examples of feminists' "Penis Envy," "Masculinity Complex," and, of all things, "Free Love and Promiscuity" (452–56). They also cite Gilman's critique of Freud in their chapter, "A New Evil: Psychoanalysis" (462). They take both Gilman and Lester Ward to task for their "'Feminist' Science" (460–61). Nor does Horney escape their condemnation. They attack her and her emphasis on cultural factors in a lengthy "note" that rambles for several single-spaced pages of text (479–86), whereas they praise Helene Deutsch as a leading female authority on the psychology of women (192, 237).[15]

While Lundberg and Farnham may have tarred Gilman and Horney with the same brush, in this essay I have attempted not only to compare but also to contrast them. Among the differences between them are audience, intent, and method. Gilman wrote political tracts and at every opportunity lectured, wrote, and advised on the benefits of feminist reform of the patriarchy. In her nonfiction treatises she provided structural analyses of the foremost cultural institutions. She gave her major non-fiction works sociologically oriented titles such as *Women and Economics*,

The Home, and *His Religion and Hers.* By contrast, though recognizing the impact of culture, Horney's interests and writings remained focused on helping the individual change herself/himself through professional therapy or self-analysis.

Even this difference highlights one of their major similarities. They were both interested in confronting moral problems and then taking action toward resolving them. Horney states this in her introduction to *New Ways of Psychoanalysis* as well as in her "Can You Take a Stand?" (1939). One can hardly think of much that Gilman wrote that did not focus on questions of morals and ethics, and that did not attempt to provide answers as well.

The purpose of this essay has been to show that Gilman's view of Freud was not based on radical extremism on the one hand or Victorian prudery on the other. Comparing Gilman's and Horney's very different approaches to a critique of Freud connects Gilman with a scholar who, unlike Gilman, did not reject psychoanalysis per se. In their writings about the importance of the impact of culture on our lives, both Gilman and Horney seem to concur that we shape our world *consciously,* to improve our understanding of our past and give meaning to our present and future by doing so. So much for radical extremism.

Moreover, situating Gilman's critique of Freud's emphasis on sexuality alongside Horney's allows us to see that Gilman's antipathy toward Freud had little to do with Gilman having become straightlaced or prudish in her later years. Admittedly, Gilman's works and views are complex and sometimes contradictory, but why is it necessary also to connect her criticism of Freud's emphasis on sexuality to her being "straightlaced"? The implication seems to be that if one is concerned about the effects of a sexual revolution on women, then one must be a prude. Some second-wave feminists were accused of the same thing. Yet, as this essay suggests, Horney shared Gilman's concern with Freud's presumption that the libido is the mainspring for *all* human action. Like Gilman, Horney recognized not the "horror" of sexuality but the horror of the potential effects of Freudian analysis on the lives and fates of men and women alike.

Notes

I dedicate this essay to Cathryn Adamsky, Ph.D., mentor and friend, who called my attention to Karen Horney.

1. Shortly thereafter, Horney and a number of like-minded colleagues set up the rival American Institute for Psychoanalysis.

2. All citations to Freud's essays are from *Freud on Women,* edited by Elisabeth Young-Bruehl (1990). She excerpted the essays from the twenty-four-volume edition of *The Standard Edition of the Complete Psychological Works of Sigmund Freud,* edited by James Strachey.

3. In both reacting to and anticipating criticism from feminists, Freud cautioned, "Here the feminist demand for equal rights for the sexes does not take us far, for the morphological distinction is bound to find expression in psychical development. 'Anatomy is destiny,' to vary a saying of Napoleon's" ("Dissolution" 299).

4. Horney's series of papers in which she criticized Freud now appear in *Feminine Psychology;* others have been translated and published in *The Unknown Karen Horney.*

5. See *The Living of Charlotte Perkins Gilman* 22–23 and *The Adolescent Diaries of Karen Horney* 252.

6. Although these words come from her "private" diary, by 1911 Horney often used her entries to analyze in a professional way her thoughts, feelings, and actions.

7. See Catherine J. Golden's "'Written to Drive Nails With,'" especially her discussion of the section "Woman" from *In This Our World.*

8. Nonetheless, their view of marriage is clearly an issue on which the women differed. Gilman, especially in her later life, wrote in favor of monogamy. As far as we know, she and Houghton had no extramarital affairs during their marriage. Horney seemed to have no similar commitment to monogamy and took lovers throughout her life, regardless of whether she was married or had a long-term partner at the time.

9. These papers compose the collection *Feminine Psychology,* edited and introduced by Horney's student Harold Kelman, in 1967.

10. After making a case for the necessity of, but the attendant difficulty of having, a "cosmological perspective," Ward went on to say, "The only person who to my knowledge has clearly brought out this cosmological perspective is . . . Charlotte Perkins Stetson [Gilman]" ("Past and Future" 541).

11. Horney has not typically been defined as a feminist. Marcia Westkott wrote of Horney's "feminist legacy," not her feminism, for example. Bernard J. Paris notes that Horney's "loss of interest in 'feminine psychology' led some critics to question whether she was ever a true feminist, despite her trenchant critique of the patriarchal ideology of her culture and the phallocentricty of

psychoanalysis" (*The Unknown Karen Horney* 12). He claims that she "opposed a continued emphasis on what is distinctly feminine because she *was* a feminist. . . . She argued [in "Women's Fear of Action"] that an interest in sexual differences 'must be regarded as a danger signal for women, particularly in a patriarchal society where men find it advantageous to prove on biologic premises that women should not take part in shaping the economy and the political order'" (15). That Horney launched these ideas in the 1930s alerts us to how prophetic she was, given that opinions about the delicacy of "woman's nature" were widely argued to keep women out of the labor force both before and after but not during World War I and World War II.

It is also interesting to note that neither Gilman nor Horney called herself a feminist. Gilman's feminist credentials are now taken for granted, and Mari Jo Buhle has provided an explanation of the encoding of the term "humanist" that Gilman said she preferred to the label "feminist." Buhle describes Gilman's preference as part of her Swedish feminist differences with Swedish feminist Ellen Key. In this regard, Gilman's position was defined as one that minimized the difference between the sexes, whereas Key's position focused on their differences. Buhle notes that because of this controversy "scores of writers began to distinguish between being '*human* feminists' and '*female*' feminists. And Gilman understanding the significance of the dispute chose to declare herself a 'humanist'" (Buhle, *Feminism and Its Discontents* 49). See Judith A. Allen's essay, "The Overthrow" of Gynaecocentric Culture: Charlotte Perkins Gilman and Lester Frank Ward," in this volume for more on the Ward-Gilman relationship.

12. One can also find a few unpublished writings by Gilman on Freud in her personal papers in the Schlesinger Library. She made typed notes on Freud's "A General Introduction to Psychoanalysis." In addition, she took several extracts from Freud's writings to incorporate into a lecture titled "Our Transient Sexolatry."

13. Val Gough offers a more plausible explanation for Gilman's use of virgin birth in *Herland*. She argues that Gilman uses parthenogenesis "as a fictional exemplification of the way individual will and environment can change what is considered a biological fact and human nature" ("Lesbians and Virgins" 202). Gough cites Gilman's poem, "Similar Cases," as another example of her commentary on the belief in "immutable human nature" (213). Gough's explanation directs us to Gilman's theoretical stance, rather than, as Berman does, to her supposed hatred of men or fear of sexuality.

14. See Connie Field's 1988 documentary, *The Life and Times of Rosie the*

Riveter, for example, in which Farnham appears in government propaganda castigating women in this way.

15. Today, as scholarship on feminism in general and Gilman and Horney in particular has grown exponentially, it is Freud's reputation that has been shrinking and his conclusions questioned. See John Leland, "The Trouble with Sigmund."

Bibliography

Adams, Hazard. *The Academic Tribes.* New York: Liveright, 1976.

Allen, Judith A. "Reconfiguring Vice: Charlotte Perkins Gilman, Prostitution, and Frontier Sexual Contacts." *Charlotte Perkins Gilman: Optimist Reformer.* Ed. Jill Rudd and Val Gough. Iowa City: U of Iowa P, 1999. 173–99.

Allen, Polly Wynn. *Building Domestic Liberty: Charlotte Perkins Gilman's Architectural Feminism.* Amherst: U of Mass P, 1988.

American Association of University Professors, Yale U Chapter. *Incomes and Living Costs of a University Faculty.* New Haven: Yale UP, 1928. Gilman Papers. Schlesinger Library, Radcliffe Institute, Cambridge, MA.

Ammons, Elizabeth. *Conflicting Stories: American Women Writers at the Turn into the Twentieth Century.* New York: Oxford UP, 1991.

Austin, Mary. "The Castro Baby." 1899. *Western Trails: A Collection of Stories by Mary Austin.* Ed. Melody Graulich. Reno: U of Nevada P, 1987. 223–27.

——. *Earth Horizon.* 1932. With an afterword by Melody Graulich. Albuquerque: U of New Mexico P, 1991.

——. "Greatness in Women." *North American Review* January–June 1923. 197–203.

——. *Land of Little Rain.* Boston: Houghton Mifflin, 1903.

——. *Lost Borders.* New York: Harpers, 1909.

——. *No. 26 Jayne Street.* Boston: Houghton Mifflin, 1920.

——. (Gordon Stairs, pseud.) *Outland.* London: John Murray, 1910.

——. Response to review by Lewis Mumford of *American Rhythm.* Austin Collection, Box 25. Huntington Library, San Marino, CA.

——. *Western Trails: A Collection of Stories by Mary Austin.* Ed. Melody Graulich. Reno: U of Nevada P, 1987.

——. *A Woman of Genius.* Garden City, NY: Doubleday Page, 1912.

——. "Woman Looks at Her World." *Pictorial Review* November 1924. 69.

——. *The Young Woman Citizen.* New York: Woman's, 1918.

Bachofen, Jacob J. *Myth, Religion, and Mother-Right.* London: Routledge and Kegan Paul, 1978.

Barnes, Harry Elmer. "Lester Frank Ward: The Reconstruction of Society By Social Science." *An Introduction to the History of Sociology.* Ed. Harry Elmer Barnes. Chicago: U of Chicago P, 1948.

Barnett, Avrom. *Foundations of Feminism: A Critique.* New York: Robert McBride, 1921.

——. Letter to Charlotte Perkins Gilman. December 28, 1920, and March 6, 1921. Gilman Papers. Schlesinger Library, Radcliffe Institute, Cambridge, MA.

Barry, Jay. *Gentlemen Under the Elms.* Providence: Brown Alumni Monthly, 1982.

Bauer, Dale M. *Edith Wharton's Brave New Politics.* Madison, WI: U of Wisconsin P, 1994.

Baym, Nina. *Woman's Fiction: A Guide to Novels by and about Women in America, 1820–1870,* 2nd ed. Urbana: U of Illinois P, 1993.

Beard, Charles A. "Lester F. Ward." *The New Republic* November 15, 1939: 119.

Beecher, Catharine E. *Letters to the People on Health and Happiness.* 1855. New York: Arno, 1972.

——. *Physiology and Calisthenics for Schools and Families.* New York: Harper, 1856.

——. *A Treatise on Domestic Economy: For the Use of Young Ladies at Home and at School.* Boston: Marsh, Capen, Lyon, and Webb, 1841.

——. *The True Remedy for the Wrongs of Women.* Boston: Phillips, Sampson, 1851. Internet. http://www.assumption.edu/wwhp/Beecher True Remedy.html.

Beecher, Catharine, and Harriet Beecher Stowe. *The American Woman's Home, Or, Principles of Domestic Science.* Hartford: Stowe-Day Foundation, 1994.

Beecher, Charles. *Harriet Beecher Stowe in Europe.* Hartford: Stowe-Day Foundation, 1966.

Beer, Janet. *Kate Chopin, Charlotte Perkins Gilman, and Elizabeth Wharton: Studies in Short Fiction.* New York: Macmillan, 1996.

Berkson, Dorothy. "'So We All Became Mothers': Harriet Beecher Stowe, Charlotte Perkins Gilman, and the New World of Women's Culture." *Feminism, Utopia, and Narrative.* Ed. Libby Falk Jones and Sarah Webster Goodwin. Knoxville: U of Tennessee P, 1990. 100–15.

Berman, Jeffrey. "The Unrestful Cure: Charlotte Perkins Gilman and 'The Yellow Wallpaper.'" *The Captive Imagination: A Casebook on The Yellow Wallpaper.* Ed. Catherine Golden. New York: Feminist, 1992. 211–41.

Bernardin, Susan, Melody Graulich, Lisa MacFarlane, and Nicole Tonkovich. *Trading Gazes: Euro-American Women Photographers and Native North American Indians.* New Brunswick, NJ: Rutgers UP, 2002.

Bierce, Ambrose. "Prattle: A Transient Record of Individual Opinion." *San*

Francisco Examiner. October 4, October 27, November 1, 15, 1891; January 17, May 1, May 22, October 16, December 25, 1892; February 4, June 10, 1894; March 3, April 28, 1895; March 31, October 1, November 12, 1893; September 6, 1896.

Bierce, Ambrose. *The Letters of Ambrose Bierce.* Ed. Bertha Clarke Pope. Vol. 11. New York: Gordian, 1966. 262–91.

"Bierce and Stetson." *Stockton Mail* (California), February 6, 1894: 3.

Blackwell, Alice Stone. "Gems from the Pacific Coast." *Woman's Journal* January 16, 1892. 20.

Blatch, Harriot Stanton. Letters to Lester Frank Ward. June 23 and September 2, 1903. Lester Frank Ward Papers. John Hays Brown Library, Brown U, Providence.

Brown, Gillian. *Domestic Individualism: Imagining Self in Nineteenth-Century America.* Berkeley, CA: U of California P, 1990.

Buhle, Mari Jo. *Feminism and Its Discontents: A Century of Struggle with Psychoanalysis.* Cambridge: Harvard UP, 1998.

Burbick, Joan. *Healing the Republic: The Language of Health and the Culture of Nationalism in Nineteenth-Century America.* New York: Cambridge UP, 1994.

Burnham, John C. *Lester Frank Ward in American Thought.* Washington, D.C.: Public Affairs, 1956.

Burrows, J. W. *Evolution and Society: A Study of Victorian Social Theory.* Cambridge: Cambridge UP, 1966.

Cady, Edwin H. *The Road to Realism: The Early Years (1837–1885) of William Dean Howells.* Syracuse: Syracuse UP, 1956.

Campbell, Donna. *Resisting Regionalism: Gender and Naturalism in American Fiction, 1885–1915.* Athens: Ohio UP, 1997.

Campbell, Oscar James. "The Department of English and Comparative Literature." *A History of the Faculty of Philosophy, Columbia University.* New York: Columbia UP, 1957.

Cape, Emily Palmer. *Lester Frank Ward: A Personal Sketch.* New York: Putnam, 1922.

Carnegie Foundation for the Advancement of Teaching. *The Financial Status of the Professor in America and in Germany.* New York: Putnam, 1908.

Carter-Sanborn, Kristin. "Restraining Order: The Imperialist Anti-Violence of Charlotte Perkins Gilman." *Arizona Quarterly* 56 (summer 2000): 1–36.

Ceplair, Larry, ed. *Charlotte Perkins Gilman: A Nonfiction Reader.* New York: Columbia UP, 1991.

Chamberlin, Katharine Stetson. Letter to Lyman Beecher Stowe. August 30, 1935. Beecher-Stowe Collection, folder 417. Schlesinger Library, Radcliffe Institute, Cambridge, MA.

———. Letter to Willis Kingsley Wing. August 30, 1935. Beecher-Stowe Collection, folder 417. Schlesinger Library, Radcliffe Institute, Cambridge, MA.

Chaney, Lindsay, and Michael Cieply. *The Hearsts: Family and Empire.* New York: Simon and Schuster, 1981.

Channing, Grace Ellery. "Children of the Barren." *Harper's Monthly Magazine* March 1907: 512–19.

———. Letters to Mary J. T. Channing ("Mama"). June 12, 18, 20, 21, 22, 26, July 4, 7, 9, 13, 24, 28, 1888. 83 M201, carton 2. Grace Ellery Channing Stetson Papers. Schlesinger Library, Radcliffe Institute, Cambridge.

———. Letter to William F. Channing ("Papa"). June 7, 1888. 83 M201, carton 2. GECS Papers. Schlesinger, Radcliffe Institute, Cambridge.

"Charlotte Perkins Gilman." *Cleveland Journal.* July 15, 1905: 2. Online. "The Beecher Tradition: Charlotte Perkins Gilman." http://newman.baruch.cuny.edu/digital/2001/beecher/charlotte.htm.

Chesler, Ellen. *Woman of Valor: Margaret Sanger and the Birth Control Movement in America.* New York: Anchor, 1992.

Chopin, Kate. *The Awakening.* 1899. New York: Norton, 1994.

Christie, Jane Johnstone. *Advance of Women From the Earliest Times to the Present.* Philadelphia: Lippincott, 1912.

Chugerman, Samuel. *Lester Ward, The American Aristotle.* Durham: Duke UP, 1939.

Cole, Margaret. *Beatrice Webb.* New York: Harcourt, Brace, 1946.

Coles, Robert. "Karen Horney's Flight from Orthodoxy." *Women and Analysis: Dialogues on Psychoanalytic Views of Femininity.* New York: Grossman, 1974. 187–91.

Connelly, Marguerite. *Success.* Letters to Charlotte Perkins Gilman, May 22, 19, 26, July 29, October 7, 30, 1902; January 27, February 25, March 12, 1903. Gilman Papers. Schlesinger Library, Radcliffe Institute, Cambridge, MA.

Cott, Nancy F. *The Grounding of Modern Feminism.* New Haven: Yale UP, 1987.

Cutter, Martha J. "The Writer as Doctor: New Models of Medical Discourse in Charlotte Perkins Gilman's Later Fiction." *Literature and Medicine* 20 (fall 2001): 151–82.

Dalbiez, Roland. *Psychoanalytic Method and the Doctrine of Freud.* New York: Longmans, Green, 1941.

Darwin, Charles. *The Descent of Man and Selection in Relation to Sex.* New York: Appleton, 1871.

Davidson, Cathy N. *Revolution and the Word: The Rise of the Novel in America.* New York: Oxford UP, 1986.

Davis, Cynthia J. *Bodily and Narrative Forms: The Influence of Medicine on American Literature, 1845–1916.* Stanford: Stanford UP, 2000.

Dawkins, William Boyd. *Cave Hunting: Researches on the Evidence of Caves Respecting the Early Inhabitants of Europe.* London: Macmillan, 1874.

Debbel, John. *The Life and Good Times of William Randolph Hearst.* New York: E. P. Dutton, 1952.

Deegan, Mary Jo. Introduction. *With Her in Ourland: Sequel to Herland.* Ed. Mary Jo Deegan and Michael R. Hill. Westport, CT: Praeger, 1997. 1–57.

Deutsch, Helene. *The Psychology of Women.* New York: Grume and Stratton, 1944–45.

———. "The Significance of Masochism in the Mental Life of Women." *International Journal of Psychoanalysis* 11 (1930): 48–60.

Dicken-Garcia, Hazel. *Journalistic Standards in Nineteenth-Century America.* Madison: U of Wisconsin P, 1989.

Douglas, Ann. *The Feminization of American Culture.* New York: Knopf, 1977.

Doyle, Helen McKnight. *Mary Austin: Woman of Genius.* New York: Gotham, 1939.

Doyle, William T. *Charlotte Perkins Gilman and the Cycle of Feminist Reform.* Diss. Berkeley: U of California P, 1960.

DuCann, C. G. L. *The Loves of George Bernard Shaw.* London: Arthur Barker, 1963.

Eckardt, Marianne Horney. Foreword. *The Adolescent Diaries of Karen Horney.* New York: Basic, 1980. vii–ix.

Egan, Maureen. "Evolutionary Theory in the Social Philosophy of Charlotte Perkins Gilman." *Hypatia* 4 (spring 1989): 102–19.

Ehrenreich, Barbara, and Deirdre English. *For Her Own Good: 150 Years of the Experts' Advice to Women.* New York: Anchor, 1978.

Eldredge, Charles C. *Charles Walter Stetson, Color, and Fantasy.* Lawrence: Spencer Museum of Art, U of Kansas, 1982.

Ervine, St. John. *Bernard Shaw: His Life, Work and Friends.* New York: William Morrow, 1956.

Evans, Deborah. "'Come Out to Colorado with Me—and Grow': *The Crux* and Gilman's New Western Hero(ines)." Paper titled "Many Wests, Many Traditions." The Western Literature Association 32nd Annual Meeting, Albuquerque, NM, October 16, 1997; and the Second International Charlotte Perkins Gilman Conference, Skidmore College, Saratoga Springs, NY, June 8, 1997.

Faber, Esther. Letter to Charlotte Perkins Gilman. September 17, 1908. Gilman Papers. Schlesinger Library, Radcliffe Institute, Cambridge, MA.

Fatout, Paul. *Ambrose Bierce: The Devil's Lexicographer.* Norman: U of Oklahoma P, 1951.

Field, Connie, dir. *The Life and Times of Rosie the Riveter.* Clarity, 1988.

Finlay, Barbara. "Lester Frank Ward as a Sociologist of Gender." *Gender and Society* 13 (April 1999): 251–65.

Fliegel, Xenia Odes. "Feminine Psychosexual Development in Freudian Theory: A Historical Reconstruction." *Psychoanalytical Quarterly* 42 (1973): 385–408.

Freud, Sigmund. *Civilization and Its Discontents.* 1929. New York: Norton, 1989.

———. "The Dissolution of the Oedipus Complex." *Freud on Women.* Ed. Elisabeth Young-Bruehl. New York: Norton, 1990. 294–303.

———. "Female Sexuality." *Freud on Women.* Ed. Elizabeth Young-Bruehl. New York: Norton, 1990. 321–41.

———. "Femininity." 1932. *Freud on Women,* 342–62.

———. "Some Psychical Consequences on the Anatomical Distinctions Between the Sexes." *Freud on Women,* 304–14.

———. *The Standard Edition of the Complete Psychological Works of Sigmund Freud.* 24 vols. London: Hogarth, 1956–66.

———. "The Uncanny." *Literary Theory: An Anthology.* Ed. Julie Rivkin and Michael Ryan. Cornwall: Blackwell, 1997. 154–67.

Gamble, Eliza Burt. *The Evolution of Woman: An Inquiry into the Dogma of Her Inferiority to Man.* New York: Putnam, 1894.

Ganobcsik-Williams, Lisa. "The Intellectualism of Charlotte Perkins Gilman: Evolutionary Perspectives on Race, Ethnicity, and Gender." *Charlotte Perkins Gilman: Optimist Reformer.* Ed. Jill Rudd and Val Gough. Iowa City: U of Iowa P, 1999.

Georgi-Findlay, Brigitte. *The Frontiers of Women's Writing: Women's Narratives and the Rhetoric of Westward Expansion.* Tucson: U of Arizona P, 1996.

Giddings, Franklin H. "Lester Frank Ward." *American Journal of Sociology* 19 (December 1913): 67–68.

Gilbert, Sandra M., and Susan Gubar. "'Fecundate! Discriminate!': Charlotte Perkins Gilman and the Theologizing of Maternity." *Charlotte Perkins Gilman: Optimist Reformer.* Ed. Jill Rudd and Val Gough. Iowa City: U of Iowa P, 1999. 200–16.

———. "Home Rule: The Colonies of the New Woman." *No Man's Land: The Place of the Woman Writer in the Twentieth Century.* Vol. 2: *Sexchanges.* New Haven: Yale UP, 1989. 47–82.

Gill, Valerie. "Catharine Beecher and Charlotte Perkins Gilman: Architects of Female Power." *Journal of American Culture* 21 (1998): 17–24.

Gillette, John M. "Critical Points in Ward's Pure Sociology." *American Journal of Sociology* 20 (January 1914): 31–67.

Gillmore, Inez Haynes. *Angel Island.* 1914. With intro. by Ursula K. LeGuin. New York: Plume, 1988.

———. *The Story of the Women's Party.* New York: Harcourt, 1921.

Gilman, Charlotte Perkins [Stetson]. "As to Purposes." *Charlotte Perkins Gilman: A Nonfiction Reader.* Ed. Larry Ceplair. New York: Columbia UP, 1991. 195.

———. "Birth Control." In Ceplair, *Nonfiction Reader,* 249–55.

———. *The Charlotte Perkins Gilman Reader.* Ed. Ann J. Lane. New York: Pantheon, 1980.

———. *Concerning Children.* Boston: Small, Maynard, 1900.

———. *The Crux.* 1911. Ed. Jennifer S. Tuttle. Newark: U of Delaware P, 2002.

———. "A Daughter's Duty." Unpublished lecture. Schlesinger Library. Quoted in Hill, *Making of a Radical Feminist,* 195–96.

———. *The Diaries of Charlotte Perkins Gilman.* 2 Vols. Ed. Denise D. Knight. Charlottesville: U P of Virginia, 1994.

———. "Dr. Clair's Place." 1915. *The Yellow Wall-Paper and Other Stories.* Ed. Robert Shulman. New York: Oxford UP, 1995. 295–303.

———. "Does a Man Support His Wife?" *Forerunner* September 1911: 140–46.

———. "An Extinct Angel." 1891. In Shulman, *Yellow Wall-Paper,* 48–50.

———. "For Birth Control." *Margaret Sanger Papers Project Newsletter* 15 (spring 1997). Internet. http:www.nyu.edu/projects/sanger/gilman.htm.

———. *Forerunner* November 1909: 32.

———. "From a Hearst Paper." *Forerunner* September 1914: 251.

———. "Fulfilment." 1915. In Shulman, *Yellow Wall-Paper,* 244–52.

——— "Improving on Nature." *"The Yellow Wall-Paper" and Other Stories of Charlotte Perkins Gilman.* Ed. Denise D. Knight. Delaware: U of Delaware P, 1992. 213–17.

———. "Girls of Today." *Suffrage Songs and Verses.* New York: Charlton, 1911. Online. http://digital.library.upenn.edu/women/gilman/suffrage/suffrage.html/.

———. *Herland* [1915]. New York: Pantheon, 1978.

———. *Herland, "The Yellow Wall-Paper" and Selected Writings of Charlotte Perkins Gilman.* Ed. Denise D. Knight. New York: Penguin, 1999.

———. "His Excuse." *Forerunner* April 1916: 85–89.

———. "His Mother." In Knight, *"The Yellow Wall-Paper" and Other Stories,* 73–80.

———. *His Religion and Hers: The Faith of Our Fathers and the Work of Our Mothers.* New York: Century, 1923.

———. *The Home: Its Work and Influence.* New York: McClure, Phillips, 1903.

———. "An Honest Woman." In Lane, *Gilman Reader,* 75–86.

———. "Housewife." *Suffrage Songs and Verses.* New York: Charlton, 1911. Online. http://digital.library.upenn.edu/women/gilman/suffrage/suffrage.html/.

———. "Human Nature." In Ceplair, *Nonfiction Reader,* 44–53.

———. *The Impress* April 1894: 5; July 1894: 3; September 1894: 1. Gilman Papers. Schlesinger Library, Radcliffe Institute, Cambridge, MA.

——. Interview. *Topeka State Journal.* June 15, 1896. Vol. 7

——. "Interviewing." *Forerunner* February 1914: 35–36.

——. *In This Our World.* 3rd. ed. Boston: Small, Maynard, 1898.

——. "Joan's Defender." In Shulman, *Yellow Wall-Paper,* 314–22.

——. "Lester F. Ward Is Dead." *Forerunner* June 1913: 166.

——. Letter to A[my]. W[ellington]. January 8, 1922. Gilman Papers. Schlesinger Library, Radcliffe Institute, Cambridge, MA.

——. Letter to Avrom Barnett. February 26, 1921. Gilman Papers. Schlesinger Library, Radcliffe Institute, Cambridge, MA.

——. Letter to Charles Lummis. April 1, 1898. The Marion Parks Collection at the Braun Research Library, Southwest Museum, Pasadena, CA.

——. Letters to George Houghton Gilman. July 22 and September 18, 1897; July 6, 1898; November 3, 1898; March 2, 1899; December 25, 1899. Gilman Papers. Schlesinger Library, Radcliffe Institute, Cambridge, MA.

——. Letters to Grace Ellery Channing. November 21, 1887; December 3, 1890; Mf-6. Gilman Papers (addendum). Schlesinger Library, Radcliffe Institute, Cambridge, MA.

——. Letters to Lester Frank Ward. January 1, 16, 24, February 10, 21, December 10, 1896; November 22, 1900; January 15, April 18, December 29, 1901; June 13, 30, 1903; January 20, May 8, July 3, 4, August 20, 1904; March 15, 1906; January 2, 31, February 1, April 15, May 20, September 20, 1907; January 26, May 9, July 22, November 6, 1908. Lester Frank Ward Papers. John Hays Brown Library, Brown U, Providence.

——. Letters to Martha Luther Lane. March 13, 1886; January 20, 1890; March 15, 1890. Charlotte Perkins Gilman Letters. Rhode Island Historical Society, Providence, RI.

——. Letters to William Dean Howells. December 10, 1891; March 8, 1898; October 17, 1919. Gilman Papers. Schlesinger Library, Radcliffe Institute, Cambridge, MA.

——. *The Living of Charlotte Perkins Gilman: An Autobiography.* New York: D. Appleton-Century, 1935. Intro. by Ann J. Lane. Madison: U of Wisconsin P, 1991.

——. "Making a Change." In Lane, *Gilman Reader.* 66–74.

——. *The Man-Made World; or, Our Androcentric Culture.* New York: Charlton, 1911.

——. "Martha's Mother." *Herland and Selected Stories by Charlotte Perkins Gilman.* Ed. Barbara Solomon. New York: Signes, 1992. 219–28.

——. "Mr. Howells' Socialism." *American Fabian* February 1898: 5–6.

——. "Mrs. Beazley's Deeds." 1911. In Knight, *"The Yellow Wall-Paper" and Other Stories,* 163–76.

——. "The New Generation of Women." *Current History* August 1923: 731–37.

——. "The New Mothers of a New World." 1913. Ceplair. 247–49.

——. "Newspapers and Democracy." *Forerunner* November 1916: 300–303, 314–18.

——. *"Noblesse Oblige." American Fabian* March 1898: 3. *Woman's Journal* Sept. 1899: 302.

——. "Notes on the Overthrow." March 5, 1908. Gilman Papers. Schlesinger Library, Radcliffe Institute, Cambridge, MA.

——. "One Way Out." *The Impress* December 29, 1894:4–5. Gilman Papers. Schlesinger Library, Radcliffe Institute, Cambridge, MA.

——. "Parasitism and Civilized Vice." *Women's Coming of Age.* Ed. Samuel D. Schmalhausen and V. F. Calverton. New York: Liveright, 1966. 110–26.

——. "Progress through Birth Control." *North American Review* December 1927: 622–29.

——. Review of *A Woman of Genius. Forerunner* October 1912: 279–80.

——. "Sex and Race Progress." *Sex in Civilization.* Ed. Samuel D. Schmalhausen and V. F. Calverton. New York: MacCaulay, 1929. 109–23.

——. "Similar Cases." *Nationalist* April 1890: 165–66.

——. "A Suggestion on the Negro Problem." *American Journal of Sociology* 14 (July 1908): 78–85.

——. "Toward Monogamy." *Nation* (June 11, 1924): 671–73.

——. *Two Storks. Forerunner* February 1910: 12–13.

——. "Vanguard, Rearguard, and Mudguard." *The Century Magazine* July 1922: 348–53.

——. "The Vintage." 1916. In Knight, *"The Yellow Wall-Paper" and Other Stories.*

——. "Wash-Tubs and Woman's Duty." *The Century Magazine* 110 (June 1925): 152–59.

——. "We as Women." *Suffrage Songs and Verses.* New York: Charlton, 1911. Online http://digital.library.upenn.edu/women/gilman/suffrage/suffrage.html/.

——. "The Widow's Might." In Lane, *Gilman Reader,* 98–106.

——. "Woman's Manifest Destiny." *Forerunner* December 1913: 335.

——. *Women and Economics: A Study of the Economic Relation Between Men and Women as a Factor in Social Evolution.* Boston: Small, Maynard, 1898.

——. "Women and the State." *Forerunner* October 1910: 10–14.

——. "The Yellow Reporter." *The Later Poetry of Charlotte Perkins Gilman.* Ed. Denise D. Knight. Newark: U of Delaware P, 1996. 46–48.

——. "The Yellow Wall-Paper." *The New England Magazine* January 1892: 647–56.

——. Unpublished lectures. December 20, 21, 1890. Schlesinger Library, Radcliffe Institute, Cambridge, MA.

Golden, Catherine. *The Captive Imagination: A Casebook on The Yellow Wallpaper.* New York: Feminist, 1992.

———. "'Written to Drive Nails With': Recalling the Early Poetry of Charlotte Perkins Gilman." *Charlotte Perkins Gilman: Optimist Reformer.* Ed. Jill Rudd and Val Gough. Iowa City: U of Iowa P, 1999. 243–66.

Gough, Val. "'In the Twinkling of an Eye': Gilman's Utopian Imagination." *A Very Different Story: Studies on the Fiction of Charlotte Perkins Gilman.* Ed. Val Gough and Jill Rudd. Liverpool: Liverpool UP, 1998. 129–43.

———. "Lesbians and Virgins: The New Motherhood in *Herland.*" *Anticipations: Essays on Early Science Fiction and Its Precursors.* Ed. David Seed. Syracuse: Syracuse UP, 1995. 195–215.

Greeley-Smith, Nixola. "Husbands Do Not Support Wives: Wives Themselves Decide Question." January 7, 1909. Gilman Papers. Schlesinger Library, Radcliffe Institute, Cambridge, MA.

Grote, George. *A History of Greece.* London: J. Murray, 1862.

Gubar, Susan. "*She* in *Herland:* Feminism as Fantasy." *Charlotte Perkins Gilman: The Woman and Her Work.* Ed. Sheryl L. Meyering. Ann Arbor: UMI, 1989. 191–201.

Harper, Ida Husted, ed. *History of Woman Suffrage.* 6 vols. Reproduced electronically. Louisville: Bank of Wisdom, 1999.

Harris, Susan K. *19th-Century American Women's Novels: Interpretive Strategies.* New York: Cambridge UP, 1990.

Harrison, Pat. "Why Psychoanalysis?" *Radcliffe Quarterly* 87 (spring/summer 2002): 10–11.

Hartley, Catherine Gasquoine. *Age of Mother Power: The Position of Women in Primitive Society.* New York: Dodd, Mead, 1913.

———. *The Truth About Women.* London: E. Nash, 1913.

———. *Position of Women in Primitive Society: A Study of The Matriarchy.* London: E. Nash, 1914.

Heatherington, Madelon E. "Romance Without Women: The Sterile Fiction of the American West." *The Georgia Review* 33 (1979): 643–56.

Hedrick, Joan D. *Harriet Beecher Stowe: A Life.* New York: Oxford UP, 1994.

Henderson, Archibald. *George Bernard Shaw: Man of the Century.* New York: Appleton, 1956.

Hill, Mary Armfield. "Charlotte Perkins Gilman and the Journey from Within." *A Very Different Story: Studies on the Fiction of Charlotte Perkins Gilman.* Ed. Val Gough and Jill Rudd. Liverpool: Liverpool UP, 1998. 8–23.

———. *Charlotte Perkins Gilman: The Making of a Radical Feminist, 1860–1896.* Philadelphia: Temple UP, 1980.

———. *Endure: The Diaries of Charles Walter Stetson.* Philadelphia: Temple UP, 1988.

———. *A Journey from Within: The Love Letters of Charlotte Perkins Gilman, 1897–1900.* Lewisburg: Bucknell UP, 1995.

Hoeller, Hildegard. *Edith Wharton's Dialogue with Realism and Sentimental Fiction.* Gainesville: UP of Florida, 2000.

Hofstadter, Richard. *Social Darwinism in American Thought.* Boston: Beacon, 1955.

Holroyd, Michael. *Bernard Shaw: A Biography.* Vol. 1, 1856–1898, *The Search for Love.* New York: Random House: 1988.

Holt, Hamilton. Letter to Gilman. May 31, 1902. Gilman Papers. Schlesinger Library, Radcliffe Institute, Cambridge, MA.

Horney, Karen. "The Achievements of Freud." *The Unknown Karen Horney: Essays on Gender, Culture, and Psychoanalysis.* Ed. and intro. by Bernard J. Paris. New Haven: Yale UP, 2000. 207–15.

———. *The Adolescent Diaries of Karen Horney.* New York: Basic, 1980.

———. "Can You Take a Stand?" In Paris, *The Unknown Karen Horney,* 222–27.

———. "The Flight from Womanhood: The Masculinity Complex in Women as Viewed by Men and Women." *Feminine Psychology.* Ed. and intro. by Harold Kelman. New York: Harper, 1967. 54–70.

———. *The Neurotic Personality of Our Time.* New York: Norton, 1937.

———. *New Ways of Psychoanalysis.* New York: Norton, 1939.

———. "On the Genesis of the Castration Complex in Women." *Feminine Psychology.* Ed. and intro. by Harold Kelman. New York: Harper, 1967. 37–53.

———. "On the Psychological Roots of Some Typical Conflicts in Marriage." In Paris, *The Unknown Karen Horney,* 59–67.

———. "Problems of Marriage." *Feminine Psychology.* Ed. and intro. by Harold Kelman. New York: Harper, 1967. 119–32.

———. *Self-Analysis.* New York: Norton, 1942.

———. "Women's Fear of Action." In Paris, *The Unknown Karen Horney,* 117–23.

———, ed. *Are You Considering Psychoanalysis?* New York: Norton, 1946.

Horsman, Reginald. *Race and Manifest Destiny: The Origins of American Racial Anglo-Saxonism.* Cambridge: Harvard UP, 1981.

Hough, Robert L. *The Quiet Rebel: William Dean Howells as Social Commentator,* 1959. Hamden, CT: Archon, 1968.

Howells, William Dean. "A Reminiscent Introduction." *The Great Modern American Stories.* New York: Boni and Liveright, 1920.

———. *Criticism and Fiction.* New York: Harper's, 1910.

———. "Editor's Easy Chair." *Harper's Monthly* October 1905: 796.

———. "Editor's Study." *Harper's Monthly* April 1891: 804–05.

———. "The New Poetry." *North American Review* May 1899: 589–90.

———. "Recollections of an Atlantic Editorship" (undated). Martin, Gloria M. "Women in the Criticism and Fiction of William Dean Howells." Diss. U of Wisconsin, 1982.

———. *Selected Letters of W. D. Howells.* Ed. George Arms et al. 6 vols. Boston: Twayne, 1980.

———. Letters to Charlotte Perkins Gilman. December 10, 1891; July 11, 1894; June 25, 1897; May 8, 1911. Houghton Library, Harvard U, Cambridge, MA.

Jordan, Elizabeth. Letter to Gilman. December 10, 1908. Gilman Papers. Schlesinger Library, Radcliffe Institute, Cambridge MA.

Kaplan, Amy. "Manifest Domesticity." *No More Separate Spheres! A Next Wave American Studies Reader.* Ed. Cathy N. Davidson and Jessamyn Hatcher. Durham, NC: Duke UP, 2002. 183-207.

Karpinski, Joanne B. "The Economic Conundrum in the Lifewriting of Charlotte Perkins Gilman." *The Mixed Legacy of Charlotte Perkins Gilman.* Ed. Catherine J. Golden and Joanne S. Zangrando. U of Delaware P, 2000. 35–46.

Kaye, Frances W. "The 49th Parallel and the 98th Meridian: Some Lines for Thought." *Mosaic* 14 (1981): 165–75.

Kelley, Mary. *Private Woman, Public Stage: Literary Domesticity in Nineteenth-Century America.* New York: Oxford UP, 1984.

Kessler, Carol Farley. "'Dreaming Always of Lovely Things Beyond': Living toward *Herland,* Experiential Foregrounding." *The Mixed Legacy of Charlotte Perkins Gilman.* Ed. Catherine J. Golden and Joanna Schneider Zangrando. Newark: U of Delaware P, 2000. 89–103.

Keyser, Elizabeth. "Looking Backward: From *Herland* to *Gulliver's Travels.*" *Critical Essays on Charlotte Perkins Gilman.* Ed. Joanne B. Karpinski. New York: G. K. Hall, 1992. 159–72.

Kilmer, Joyce. "War Stops Literature, Says William Dean Howells." *New York Times.* December 16, 1914. Gilman Papers. Schlesinger Library, Cambridge, MA.

Kirkland, Janice, ed. *Forerunner Index.* Tehchapi, CA: Presse Precaire, 2000.

Knight, Denise D. *Charlotte Perkins Gilman: A Study of the Short Fiction.* New York: Twayne, 1997.

———. Introduction. *Herland, 'The Yellow Wall-Paper' and Selected Writings.* New York: Penguin, 1999. ix–xxiv.

Kolodny, Annette. *The Land before Her: Fantasy and Experience of the American Frontiers, 1630–1860.* Chapel Hill: U of North Carolina P, 1984.

———. "Letting Go Our Grand Obsessions: Notes toward a New Literary History of the American Frontiers." *American Literature* 64 (March 1992): 1–18.

Lane, Ann J. Introduction. *Herland: A Lost Feminist Utopian Novel by Charlotte Perkins Gilman.* 1915. New York: Pantheon Books, 1979.

———. "The Fictional World of Charlotte Perkins Gilman." New York: Pantheon, 1980. ix–xlii.

———. *To Herland and Beyond: A Life of Charlotte Perkins Gilman.* New York: Pantheon, 1990.

Lanser, Susan S. "Feminist Criticism, 'The Yellow Wallpaper,' and the Politics of Color in America." *"The Yellow Wallpaper": Charlotte Perkins Gilman.* Ed. Thomas L. Erskine and Connie L. Richards. New Brunswick: Rutgers UP, 1993. 225–56.

LeGuin, Ursula. Introduction. *Angel Island.* 1914. New York: Plume, 1988.

LeLand, John. "The Trouble with Sigmund." *Newsweek* December 18, 1995: 62.

Lemons, J. Stanley. *The Woman Citizen: Social Feminism in the 1920s.* Urbana: U of Illinois P, 1973.

Long, Lisa A. "*Herland* and the Gender of Science." *MLA Approaches to Teaching Gilman's The Yellow Wall-Paper and Herland.* Ed. Denise D. Knight and Cynthia J. Davis. New York: MLA, 2003. 125–32.

Lubbock, John. *Prehistoric Times, as Illustrated by Ancient Remains and the Manners and Customs of Modern Savages.* London: William and Norgate, 1865.

Lundberg, Ferdinand, and Marynia F. Farnham. *Modern Woman: The Lost Sex.* New York: Harper, 1947.

MacKenzie, Norman, and Jeanne MacKenzie. *The Fabians.* New York: Simon and Schuster, 1977.

Madison, Charles Allan. *The Owl among the Colophons: Henry Holt as Publisher and Editor.* New York: Holt, Rinehart, and Winston, 1966.

Martin, Gloria M. "Women in the Criticism and Fiction of William Dean Howells." Diss. U of Wisconsin, 1982.

Mason, Otis Tufton. *Woman's Share in Primitive Culture.* New York: Appleton, 1894.

Matthews, Brander. *The Action and the Word: A Novel of New York.* New York: Harper, 1900.

———. *Americanisms and Briticisms with Other Essays on Other Isms.* New York: Harper, 1892.

———. Brander Matthews Papers. Rare Book and Manuscript Library, Columbia U, New York.

———. Letter to Gilman. October 28, 1892. Folder 137. Gilman Papers. Schlesinger Library, Radcliffe Institute, Cambridge, MA.

———. "More American Stories." *Cosmopolitan* September 1892: 626–30.

———. "The Philosophy of the Short-Story." *Pen and Ink: Papers on Subjects of More or Less Importance.* New York: Longmans, Green, 1888. 70, 93.

Mayreder, Rosa. *Survey of the Woman Problem.* London: William Heinemann, 1913.

McAdoo, Laura Sterrett. Letter to Lester Frank Ward. May 28, 1898. Lester Frank Ward Papers. John Hays Brown Library, Brown University, Providence, RI.

McClay, Wilfred M. "The Socialization of Desire." *Society* 32 (May–June 1995): 65–73.

McLennan, John Ferguson. *Primitive Marriage: An Inquiry into the Origin of the Form of Capture in Marriage Ceremonie*s. Edinburgh: A. & C. Black, 1895.

McMahon, Sean H. *Social Control and Public Intellect: The Legacy of Edward A. Ross.* New Brunswick, NJ: Transaction, 1999.

McWilliams, Carey. *Ambrose Bierce: A Biography.* New York: Archon, 1967.

Mee, Arthur. *Suffolk.* London: Hodder and Stoughton, 1941.

Mitchell, Samuel Chiles. "Some Recollections of Lester F. Ward and James Q. Dealey." *Social Forces* 16 (October 1937): 44–47.

Mitchell, S. Weir, M.D. "Camp Cure." *Nurse and Patient, and Camp Cure.* Philadelphia: Lippincott, 1877.

———. *Wear and Tear, or Hints for the Overworked.* 1887. New York: Arno, 1973.

Morgan, Lewis Henry. *Ancient Society; or, Researches in the Line of Human Progress From Savagery Through Barbarism to Civilization.* Chicago: C. H. Kerr, 1877.

Morris, A. J. A. *C. P. Trevelyan, 1870–1958: Portrait of a Radical.* New York: St. Martin's, 1977.

Muggeridge, Kitty. *Beatrice Webb, a Life: 1858–1943.* Chicago: Academy Chicago, 1983.

Muzzey, Annie L. "The How and The Woman." 1899. *Critical Essays on Charlotte Perkins Gilman.* Ed. Joanne B. Karpinski. New York: G. K. Hall, 1992. 85–89.

Nearing, Scott, and Nellie S. Nearing. *Woman and Social Progress.* New York: Macmillan, 1912.

Norwood, Vera, and Janice Monk, eds. *The Desert Is No Lady: Southwestern Landscapes in Women's Writing and Art.* New Haven: Yale UP, 1987.

O'Connor, Richard. *Ambrose Bierce: A Biography.* Boston: Little, Brown, 1967.

Oliver, Lawrence J., and Gary Scharnhorst. "Charlotte Perkins Gilman v. Ambrose Bierce: The Literary Politics of Gender in Fin-de-Siècle California." *Journal of the West* (July 1993): 52–60.

Olivier, Sydney. *Letters and Selected Writings.* Ed. Margaret Olivier. London: Allen and Unwin, 1948.

Palmeri, Ann. "Charlotte Perkins Gilman: Forerunner of a Feminist Social Science." *Discovering Reality: Feminist Perspectives on Epistemology, Metaphysics, Methodology and Philosophy of Science.* Ed. Sandra Harding and Merrill B. Hintikka. Dordrecht, Netherlands: Reidel, 1983. 97–120.

Paris, Bernard J., ed. *The Unknown Karen Horney: Essays on Gender, Culture and Psychoanalysis.* New Haven: Yale UP, 2000.

Patten, Simon. "The Failure of Biological Sociology." *Annals of the American Academy* 4 (May 1894): 919–47.

Pearson, Hesketh. *G.B.S.: A Full-Length Portrait.* New York: Garden City, 1942.

Perkins, Frederic Beecher. "The Devil-Puzzlers." *The Devil-Puzzlers.* New York: Putnam, 1877. 1–41.

———. Letter to Gilman. October 15, 1878. Gilman Papers. Schlesinger Library, Radcliffe Institute, Cambridge, MA.

Pevsner, Nikolaus. *Suffolk*. London: Penguin, 1961.

Pfeifer, Edward J. "The Genesis of American Neo-Lamarckianism." *Isis* 56 (1965): 156–67.

Porter, Nancy. Afterword. *A Woman of Genius*. By Mary Austin. Old Westbury: Feminist, 1985. 296–321.

Quinn, Susan. *A Mind of Her Own: The Life of Karen Horney*. Reading, MA: Addison-Wesley, 1987.

Rather, Lois. *Bittersweet: Ambrose Bierce and Women*. Oakland, CA: Rather, 1975. 67.

Rawlinson, George. *Five Great Monarchies of the Ancient Eastern World*. London: J. Murray, 1862.

Ross, Edward Alsworth. "Lester Frank Ward." *American Journal of Sociology* 19 (July 1913): 64–67.

———. *Seventy Years of It: An Autobiography*. New York: Appleton-Century, 1936.

Rudnick, Lois. *Utopian Vistas*. Albuquerque: U of New Mexico P, 1996.

Rugoff, Milton Allan. *The Beechers: An American Family in the Nineteenth Century*. New York: Harper and Row, 1981.

Safford, John Lugton. *Pragmatism and the Progressive Movement in the United States: The Origin of the New Social Sciences*. Lanham, MD: UP of America, 1987.

Sanger, Margaret. *Margaret Sanger: An Autobiography*. 1938. Elmsford, NY: Maxwell Reprint, 1970.

———. Margaret Sanger Papers. Sophia Smith Collection. Smith College, Northampton, MA.

———. *Woman and the New Race*. New York: Brentano's, 1920.

———. *The Woman Rebel*. Ed. Alex Baskin. New York: Archives of Social History, 1976.

The Saturday Evening Post. Letter from the editor to Charlotte Perkins Gilman. September 26, 1899. Gilman Papers. Schlesinger Library, Radcliffe Institute, Cambridge, MA.

Scharnhorst, Gary. *Charlotte Perkins Gilman*. Boston: Twayne, 1985.

Scharnhorst, Gary, and Denise D. Knight. "Charlotte Perkins Gilman's Library: A Reconstruction." *Resources for American Literary Studies* 23 (1997): 181–219.

Schwartz, Judith. *Radical Feminists of Heterodoxy: Greenwich Village 1912–1940*. Norwich, VT: New Victoria, 1986.

Scott, Clifford H. *Lester Frank Ward*. Boston: Twayne, 1976.

Seitler, Dana. "Unnatural Selection: Mothers, Eugenic Feminism, and Charlotte Perkins Gilman's Regeneration Narratives." *American Quarterly* 55 (March 2003): 61–88.

Shaw, George Bernard. *Bernard Shaw: Selections of His Wit and Wisdom.* Chicago: Follett, 1965.

——. *Collected Letters 1874–1897,* Ed. Dan Laurence. New York: Viking, 1985.

——. *The Devil's Disciple.* Online. The Project Gutenberg Etext. Produced by Eve Sobol, 2003 [2001]. http://promo.net/pg/.

——. *Diaries, 1885–1897.* Ed. Stanley Weintraub. University Park: Pennsylvania State UP, 1986.

——. *Intelligent Woman's Guide to Socialism and Capitalism.* New York: Garden City, 1928.

——. *On Going to Church.* Boston: John W. Luce, 1905.

——. *The Political Madhouse in America and Nearer Home.* London: Constable, 1953.

——. Preface to the 1908 edition. *Fabian Essays.* 6th ed. London: Allen & Unwin, 1962. 282–92.

Showalter, Elaine, ed. Introduction. *Daughters of Decadence: Women Writers of the Fin-de-Siècle.* New Brunswick, NJ: Rutgers UP, 1993.

Shulman, Robert. Introduction. *The Yellow Wall-Paper and Other Stories.* By Charlotte Perkins Gilman. Ed. Robert Shulman. New York: Oxford UP, 1995. vii–xxxii.

Small, Albion. "Lester Frank Ward." *American Journal of Sociology* 19 (July 1913): 77–78.

Sniegoski, Stephen J. "Lester Frank Ward: The Philosopher of the Welfare State." *Telos* 108 (summer 1996): 47–64.

Snyder, Stephen H. *Lyman Beecher and His Children: The Transformation of a Religious Tradition.* Brooklyn: Carlson, 1991.

Spencer, Anna Garlin. *Women's Share in Social Culture.* New York: Mitchell Kennerley, 1913.

Stanton, Stephen S., ed. *A Casebook on Candida.* New York: Crowell, 1962.

State Historical Society of Wisconsin. Division of Archives and Manuscripts. *Edward A. Ross Papers* [microform].Teaneck, NJ: Chadwyck-Healy, 1985.

Steffens, Lincoln. "Hearst, the Man of Mystery." *The American Magazine* November 1906: n. p.

Stefoff, Rebecca. *Independence and Revolution in Mexico, 1810–1940.* New York: Facts on File, 1993.

Stein, Gertrude. *Everybody's Autobiography.* Berkeley: Exact Change, 1993.

Stern, Bernhard. "Giddings, Ward, and Small: An Interchange of Letters." *Social Forces* 10 (March 1932): 305–18.

——. "Letters of Albion W. Small to Lester F. Ward." *Social Forces* 12 (December 1933): 163–73; *Social Forces* 13 (March 1935): 323–40; *Social Forces* 15 (December 1936): 174–86; and *Social Forces* 15 (March 1937): 305–37.

——. "Letters of Alfred Russell Wallace to Lester F. Ward." *Scientific Monthly* 40 (April 1935): 375–79.

——. "The Ward-Ross Correspondence, 1891–1912." *American Sociological Review* 3, 11, 12, 13, and 14 (June, October, December, and February, 1938–49): 363–401, 595–605, 734–48, 82–94, 88–119.

——. "The Liberal Views of Lester F. Ward." *Scientific Monthly* 61 (August 1950): 102–4.

Stetson, Charles Walter. *Endure: The Diaries of Charles Walter Stetson.* Ed. Mary A. Hill. Philadelphia: Temple UP, 1985.

——. Letters to Mrs. William Channing. May 10, 1892; March 10, 1893. 83-M201, Carton 5. Grace Ellery Channing Stetson Papers. Schlesinger Library, Radcliffe Institute, Cambridge, MA.

——. Letter to Charlotte Perkins Stetson. July 9, 1894. 83-M201, Carton 5. (refiling in process). Grace Ellery Channing Stetson Papers. Schlesinger Library, Radcliffe Institute, Cambridge, MA.

St. John, Christopher. *Ellen Terry and Bernard Shaw: A Correspondence.* New York: Theatre Arts, 1931.

Stineman, Estelle Lanigan. *Mary Austin: The Story of a Maverick.* New Haven: Yale UP, 1989.

Stocking, George Jr., *Race, Culture and Evolution: Essays in the History of Anthropology.* New York: Free, 1968.

Stowe, Lyman Beecher. *Saints, Sinners, and Beechers.* Indianapolis: Bobbs-Merrill, 1934.

Takaki, Ronald. *Strangers from a Different Shore: A History of Asian Americans.* Boston: Little, Brown, 1989.

Terry, Ellen. *Ellen Terry and Bernard Shaw: A Correspondence.* New York: Theatre Arts, 1931.

Tompkins, Jane. *West of Everything: The Inner Life of Westerns.* New York: Oxford UP, 1992.

Trevelyan, Charles Philips. *Letters from North America.* London: Chatto and Windus, 1969.

Tuttle, Jennifer S. "Rewriting the West Cure: Charlotte Perkins Gilman, Owen Wister, and the Sexual Politics of Neurasthenia." *The Mixed Legacy of Charlotte Perkins Gilman.* Ed. Catherine J. Golden and Joanna Schneider Zangrando. Newark: U of Delaware P, 2000. 103–121.

Tylor, Edward B. *Researches into the Early History of Mankind and the Development of Civilization.* Chicago: U of Chicago P, 1865.

United States Bureau of Education. *Salaries in Universities and Colleges in 1920.* Washington, DC: G.P.O., 1920.

Walker, Franklin. *The Seacoast of Bohemia.* Santa Barbara: Peregrine Smith, 1973.

Walsh, Correa Moylan. *Feminism.* New York: Sturgis and Walton, 1917.

Ward, Lester Frank. *Applied Sociology: A Treatise on the Conscious Improvement of Society by Society.* Boston: Ginn, 1906.

———. "A Review of the Theory of the Leisure Class, by Thorstein Veblen." *American Journal of Sociology* 5 (May 1900): 829–37.

———. "Collective Telesis." *American Journal of Sociology* 2 (March 1897): 815.

———. "Cosmic and Organic Evolution." *Popular Science Monthly* 11 (October 1877): 672–82.

———. "Darwin as a Biologist." *Proceedings, Biological Society of Washington, D.C.* 1 (April 1882): 81–86.

———. *Dynamic Sociology.* 2 vols. New York: Appleton, 1883.

———. "Eugenics, Euthenics, and Eudemics." *American Journal of Sociology* 18 (May 1913): 737–54.

———. "Genius and Women's Intuition." *Forum* 9 (June 1890): 401–8.

———. *Glimpses of the Cosmos.* Vol. 1, 1858–71 (1913); vol. 2, 1875–82; vol. 3, 1882–85; vol. 4, 1886–92; vol. 5, 1893–97; and vol. 6, 1897–1912 (1918). New York: Putnam, 1913–18.

———. "The Historical View of Women," *The Independent* 68, no. 3211 (June 16, 1910): 1326–28. Rpt. *Glimpses of the Cosmos.* Vol. 6. New York: Putnam, 1915. 356.

———. Letters to Charlotte Perkins Gilman. December 28, 1895; January 17, 1897; January 3, February 9, 1907; February 11, 1911. Gilman Papers. Schlesinger Library, Radcliffe Institute, Cambridge, MA.

———. Letter to Joanna Odenwald Unger. October 27, 1903. Lester Frank Ward Papers. John Hays Brown Library, Brown U, Providence, RI.

———. "Neo-Darwinism and Neo-Lamarckism." *Proceedings,* Biological Society of Washington, DC. Vol. 6. 1891. 11–71.

———. "On Male Sexual Selection." [*Transactions of the Anthropological Society of Washington.* May 1, 1881. Vol. 1. 37–39]. *Glimpses of the Cosmos,* Vol. 3. New York: Putnam, 1915. 75.

———. "Our Better Halves." *Forum* 6 (November 1888): 266–75.

———. *Outlines of Sociology.* New York: Macmillan, 1898.

———. "The Past and Future of the Sexes." *The Independent* March 1906. 541–47.

———. *The Psychic Factors of Civilization.* Boston: Ginn, 1893.

———. *Pure Sociology: A Treatise on the Origin and Spontaneous Development of Society.* New York: Macmillan, 1903.

———. "Remarks on Spencerian Social Darwinism." *Transactions.* Anthropological Society, Washington, DC. Vol. 2. 1882. 31–33.

———. "Six O' Clock Club Speech." 1888. Lester Frank Ward Papers. John Hays Brown Library, Brown U, Providence, RI.

———. "Social Darwinism." *American Journal of Sociology* 12 (March 1907): 709–10.

———. "The Social Evil." [*The Iconoclast* (September 4, 1871)]. *Glimpses of the Cosmos.* Vol. 1. New York: Putnam, 1913. 238–39.

———. "Weissman's Concessions." *Popular Science Monthly* June 1894. 175–84.

Watson, Barbara Bellow. *A Savian Guide to the Intelligent Woman.* New York: Norton, 1964.

Webb, Beatrice. *The Diary of Bernice Webb, 1892–1905: All the Good Things of Life.* Vol. 2. Eds. Norman MacKenzie and Jeanne MacKenzie. Cambridge: Harvard UP, 1983.

Wegener, Frederick. "'What a Comfort a Woman Doctor Is!' Medical Women in the Life and Writing of Charlotte Perkins Gilman." *Charlotte Perkins Gilman: Optimist Reformer.* Ed. Jill Rudd and Val Gough. Iowa City: U of Iowa P, 1999. 45–73.

Weinbaum, Alys Eve. "Writing Feminist Genealogy: Charlotte Perkins Gilman, Racial Rationalism, and the Reproduction of Maternalist Feminism." *Feminist Studies* 27 (summer 2001): 271–302.

Weinbaum, Batya. *Islands of Women and Amazons: Representations and Realities.* Austin: U of Texas P, 1999.

Weinberg, Julius. *Edward Alsworth Ross and the Sociology of Progressivism.* Madison: State Historical Society of Wisconsin, 1972.

Wellington, Amy. "Charlotte Perkins Gilman." 1930. *Critical Essays on Charlotte Perkins Gilman.* Ed. Joanne B. Karpinski. New York: G. K. Hall, 1992. 67–72.

Westkott, Marcia. *The Feminist Legacy of Karen Horney.* New Haven: Yale UP, 1986.

White, G. Edward. *The Eastern Establishment and the Western Experience: The West of Frederic Remington, Theodore Roosevelt, and Owen Wister.* New Haven: Yale UP, 1968. 197.

Will, Barbara. "The Nervous Origins of the American Western." *American Literature* 70 (June 1998): 293–316.

Williams, Blanche Colton. "Brander Matthews—A Reminiscence." *MS* 1 (July 1929): 1–19.

Wilson, Bee. "Founding Principles." *New Statesman* December 11, 1998. 40–41.

Wilson, Logan. *The Academic Man: A Study in the Sociology of a Profession.* London: Oxford UP, 1942.

The Wisconsin Progressives: The Papers of Richard T. Ely, Edward A. Ross, Charles McCarthy, Charles Van Hise, and John R. Commons. Microfiche. Teaneck, NJ: Chadwyck-Healy, 1985.

Wister, Owen. "The Evolution of the Cowpuncher." 1895. *The Virginian: A Horseman of the Plains.* Ed. Robert Shulman. New York: Oxford UP, 1998.

———. *The Virginian: A Horseman of the Plains.* 1902. Ed. Robert Shulman. New York: Oxford UP, 1998.

"Woman Is Man's Horse, Declares Mrs. Gilman." Gilman Papers. Schlesinger Library, Radcliffe Institute, Cambridge, MA.

Wood, Ann Douglas. "The Literature of Impoverishment: The Women Local Colorists in America, 1865–1914." *Women's Studies* 1 (1972): 4–15.

Wright, Almroth E. *The Unexpurgated Case Against Woman Suffrage.* London: Constable, 1913.

Contributors

Judith A. Allen is professor of gender studies and history, chair of the Department of Gender Studies, and a member of the Board of Governors of the Kinsey Institute for Research in Sex, Gender, and Reproduction, at Indiana University, Bloomington. Her books include *Sex and Secrets: Crimes Involving Australian Women Since 1880* and *Rose Scott: Vision and Revision in Feminism, 1880–1925*. Her latest book is *Gilman's Feminism: Sexuality, History, and Progressivism* (forthcoming). Her current project is a book presently titled *Kinsey's Women: Sexed Bodies, Heterosexualities, and Abortion 1920–1960*.

Cynthia J. Davis is associate professor of English at the University of South Carolina, Columbia. She is the author of *Bodily and Narrative Forms: The Influence of Medicine on American Literature* (2000) and co-author of *Women Writers in the United States: A Timeline of Social, Cultural and Literary History* (1996). Her current project is a biography of Charlotte Perkins Gilman (forthcoming).

Monika Elbert is professor of English at Montclair State University, New Jersey. She has published widely on nineteenth-century American authors, in such journals as *ESQ: A Journal of the American Renaissance*, *New England Quarterly*, and *Legacy*. Her edited collection, *Separate Spheres No More: Gender Convergence in American Literature, 1830–1930*, appeared in 2000.

Melody Graulich is editor of *Western American Literature* and professor of English/American Studies at Utah State University in Logan, UT.

She has published numerous essays and books on Mary Austin. Recent publications include *Trading Gazes: Euro-American Women Photographers and Native North American Indians,* coauthored with Susan Bernardin, Melody Graulich, Lisa MacFarlane, and Nicole Tonkovich; and *Reading The Virginian in the New West: Centennial Essays,* coedited with Stephen Tatum.

Joanne B. Karpinski is the editor of *Critical Essays on Charlotte Perkins Gilman* (1991) and has contributed essays on Gilman to various scholarly anthologies, including the Modern Language Association's *Approaches to Teaching Gilman's 'The Yellow Wall-Paper' and Herland* (2003). She is working on a critical introduction and annotation to Gilman's lectures and preparing to perform as Gilman in the Colorado Humanities Council series that tours libraries in Colorado.

Janice Kirkland earned a Ph.D. from UCLA and has left the California State University faculty to do research. Her publications include an index to Gilman's *Forerunner* (2000).

Denise D. Knight is professor of English at the State University of New York, Cortland, where she specializes in nineteenth-century American literature. She is the author of *Charlotte Perkins Gilman: A Study of the Short Fiction* (1997) and editor of the two-volume edition of *The Diaries of Charlotte Perkins Gilman* (1994), as well as editor of volumes of Gilman's poems and fiction.

Lisa A. Long is assistant professor of English and coordinator of the Gender and Women's Studies Program at North Central College in Naperville, Illinois. She is the author of *Rehabilitating Bodies: Health, History, and the American Civil War* (Pennsylvania, 2003), as well as articles on Charlotte Perkins Gilman, Rebecca Harding Davis, Elizabeth Stuart Phelps, and Charlotte Forten, and is the editor of Paul Laurence Dunbar's 1901 novel, *The Fanatics* (2001). She is currently editing a collection of essays on the subject of white scholars and African American texts and is also working on a book exploring corporeality and scientific authority in the late nineteenth and early twentieth centuries.

Mary M. Moynihan, sociologist, is research associate professor of women's studies at the University of New Hampshire in Durham, where she studies issues relating to violence against women. In addition, she co-coordinates the New Hampshire Women's Oral History Project and has coedited *Images of Women in American Popular Culture* (1985; rev. ed. 1995). She is also the author of "Gilman, Charlotte Perkins" in Yale's forthcoming *Encyclopedia of New England Culture.*

Lawrence J. Oliver is professor of English and associate dean in the College of Liberal Arts at Texas A&M University in College Station. His publications include *Brander Matthews, Theodore Roosevelt, and the Politics of American Literature, 1880–1920* (1992) and an edition of *The Letters of Theodore Roosevelt and Brander Matthews* (1995).

Charlotte Rich is assistant professor of English at Eastern Kentucky University, Richmond. She has published articles on Stephen Crane, Edith Wharton, and María Cristina Mena. She is writing a book about how American women writers of color at the turn of the last century treated the ideals of the New Woman.

Gary Scharnhorst is professor of English at the University of New Mexico in Albuquerque, editor of *American Literary Realism,* and editor in alternating years of the research annual *American Literary Scholarship.* He has published books on Charlotte Perkins Gilman as well as on Bret Harte, Mark Twain, Horatio Alger, Nathaniel Hawthorne, and Henry David Thoreau.

Jennifer S. Tuttle is assistant professor of English at the University of New England in Maine, where she also serves as the Dorothy M. Healy Chair in Literature and Health, and is the faculty director of the Maine Women Writers Collection. She is the editor of a scholarly edition of Gilman's *The Crux* (2002) and has published articles on Gilman, Elizabeth Stuart Phelps, María Amparo Ruiz de Burton, and Owen Wister.

Index